Chaucer

AND THE
TRADITION
OF FAME

Chaucer

AND THE TRADITION

OF FAME: SYMBOLISM IN

THE HOUSE OF FAME

BY B. G. KOONCE

PRINCETON, NEW JERSEY

PRINCETON UNIVERSITY PRESS

MCMLXVI

Publication of this book has been aided
by the Whitney Darrow Publication Reserve Fund
of Princeton University Press and by the
Research Committee of North Carolina State University

Printed in the United States
of America by Princeton University Press

TO THE MEMORY OF
MY MOTHER AND FATHER

. . . whyche werke as me semeth is craftyly made/ and dygne to be wreton & knowen/ For he towchyth in it ryght grete wysedom & subtyll vnderstondyng. . . . For he wrytteth no voyde wordes/ but alle hys mater is ful of hye and quycke sentence.

—WILLIAM CAXTON, EPILOGUE
TO THE *Hous of Fame.*

CONTENTS

CONTENTS

Chaucer

AND THE
TRADITION
OF FAME

INTRODUCTION

TO move from the world of the *Canterbury Tales* to the world of Chaucer's dream-visions requires an orientation of mind not always easy for the modern reader. From the concrete background of an English pilgrimage we enter a realm of conventionalized settings, personified abstractions, and shifting perspectives where many of the familiar narrative techniques do not seem to apply. Perhaps more than Chaucer's other dream-visions, the *House of Fame* presents challenging problems to the present-day reader; for here an apparent disjunctiveness of subject matter and mood is enhanced by an air of deliberate obscurity. As in the other poems in this genre, a semblance of unity is supplied by the dreamer, the fictive projection of the poet whose experience in the temple and desert of Venus and search for "love-tydynges" promised by Jove's eagle motivate the flight to the House of Fame and provide a kind of moving center from which we view the shifting panorama of the three books. In the last analysis, however, neither the precise nature of the dreamer's quest nor the relationship between the various episodes seems wholly clear. Although the theme of fame is introduced in each book and controls the action and subject matter of Book III, the predominant concern with love in Book I and the discursiveness of the eagle's lengthy discourse in Book II obscure any inclusive thematic pattern. This obscurity of Chaucer's central purpose becomes even more pronounced at the end of Book III where the search for tidings, hitherto the focal point of the vision and the most obvious link between the three books, is left unresolved by the surprising comment that these tidings will "not now be told." This puzzling feature of the ending, along with the abrupt conclusion upon the appearance of the unidentified "man of gret auctorite" with whom these tidings are presumably to be associated, is indicative of the problems involved in an attempt to fuse the disparate elements of the poem into a unified structure.

Although the following study of the *House of Fame* claims no final solution to these problems, it does attempt to restore to the reading of the poem a background of medieval meanings, familiar enough to Chaucer's contemporary reader but almost lost to the modern, which will clarify its purpose and provide the basis for a unified interpretation. This attempt involves fundamentally two aspects of the poem: its subject of fame and its allegorical method. Today we are prone to view fame without reference to a single moral or spiritual order; but fame in the Middle Ages was a clearly defined Christian concept, and the desire for fame, whether as poet, saint, or ruler, was a vital problem to be reconciled with the soul's quest for salvation. Underlying the medieval view of fame is a contrast between earthly and heavenly fame, a contrast derived from Scripture and elaborated by St. Augustine and other Scriptural commentators as part of the Christian contrast between two kinds of love, charity and cupidity. The Christian concept of fame is central to the argument of Boethius' *Consolation of Philosophy*, whence it pervades medieval writings; it persists in Renaissance and later treatments of the subject, notably in Milton. But the force of this tradition as a living issue in literature has subsided in proportion to the weakening of the complex theology which gave it birth. Ultimately, against this broader background of medieval Christian doctrine we must view Chaucer's treatment not only of fame but also of love. Far from being two disparate threads unsuccessfully woven into a unified design, love and fame are integral and inseparable aspects of his theme; for without love and its underlying concepts of charity and redemp-

4

tion, the medieval attitude toward fame would have little meaning. In its simplest reduction, the theme of the *House of Fame* is the vanity of worldly fame. But this theme is explored by means of a contrast between earthly and heavenly love and fame which governs the poetic structure and fuses its heterogeneous details into unity. The precise nature of this fusion, however, as well as the peculiar aptness of this structure to a complex investigation of fame, may be overlooked unless we are aware that the poem's fullest meaning appears not on the surface but on the level of allegory.

The specific genre of allegory to which the *House of Fame* belongs—the prophetic dream, or "avisioun," as Chaucer calls it—is one with numerous analogues and antecedents behind which lie a thousand years of authoritative definition of the nature and function of poetic allegory. The failure to relate the poem to this body of traditional poetic theory, as well as the injection into the poem of more modern notions of allegory, has resulted in an inadequate evaluation both of its purpose and meaning and of its literary quality. If the meaning of the *House of Fame* is obscure, it is not because Chaucer is unsure of his purpose or has no control over his art and subject matter but because an intentional obscurity of surface details is a normal device of medieval allegory. As Boccaccio and other medieval authorities on poetry agree, the aims and methods of poetic allegory parallel those of Scripture, where the truths of Christian doctrine are often hidden beneath a veil of symbols which require interpretation.[1] Just as Scripture clothes its wisdom in divinely

---

[1] Boccaccio's views on poetry are developed most fully in the *Genealogia deorum*, Books XIV and XV, which are translated with an introduction and notes by C. G. Osgood in *Boccaccio on Poetry* (Princeton, 1930), reprinted by the Liberal Arts Press (New York, 1956). On the relationship between Scriptural and poetic allegory, see especially XIV, 9, 12, 13. The assumptions underlying medieval literary

ordained "figures," so the poet veils his meanings in "fables" or "fictions."[2] Far from wishing to deprive the reader of truth, Boccaccio insists, the poet conceals his meaning in order to stimulate the intellect and lead it to various interpretations which will make the truth more highly esteemed.[3] But poetry, Boccaccio reminds us, echoing Horace, appeals not only to the intellect but also to the senses; for such is the power of the poet's fables that they delight the unlearned with their pleasing inventions and exercise the minds of the learned with their hidden

---

allegory have been explored with great thoroughness by D. W. Robertson, Jr., who connects Boccaccio's statements with the central tradition of poetic theory stemming from St. Augustine and reaching its most notable expression from the twelfth century onward in the writings of the Christian humanists, for example, John of Salisbury, Bernard Silvestris, Alanus de Insulis, Dante, Petrarch, Boccaccio, and Salutati. Professor Robertson's earlier discussions of the subject are included and expanded in two recent books: *A Preface to Chaucer: Studies in Medieval Perspectives* (Princeton, 1962) and, in collaboration with B. F. Huppé, *Fruyt and Chaf: Studies in Chaucer's Allegories* (Princeton, 1963), both of which relate Chaucer to this tradition.

[2] *Genealogia deorum*, XIV, 13. In XIV, 9, Boccaccio defines *fabula* as "a form of discourse, which, under guise of invention, illustrates or proves an idea; and, as its superficial aspect [*cortex*] is removed, the meaning of the author is clear." The terminology used to distinguish the outer and inner senses of poetry varies. Boccaccio's term *cortex* (XIV, 9) derives from Scriptural commentary, where it is contrasted with the *nucleus* or other designations for the hidden doctrine. Chaucer's "fruyt" and "chaf" (*NPT*, l. 3,443), "corn" and "stree" (*MLT*, 701-702), "whete" and "draf" (Parson's Prol., 35-36) correspond to this distinction. Although "allegory" [*allegoria*] has special connotations in Scriptural commentary, as a rhetorical device it is applied to any text, Scriptural or poetic, in which the surface meaning implies something else. On these and other literary terms, see Robertson, "Some Medieval Literary Terminology," *SP*, XLVIII (1951), 669-92; Robertson, *Preface*, pp. 32, 315-17; and Huppé and Robertson, *Fruyt and Chaf*, chap. I.

[3] *Genealogia deorum*, XIV, 12. Boccaccio's defense of obscurity echoes Augustine's *De civitate Dei*, XI, 19, and *Enarrationes in psalmos* (on Psalms 126 and 146), which are cited along with Petrarch's *Invective contra medicum*, III, and Matt. 7:6: "Give not that which is holy to dogs; neither cast ye your pearls before swine." The Scriptural verse is a standard medieval authority for the use of an obscure veil to protect divine wisdom from the slothful.

meanings. The poet, in short, is an "inventor," one who "brings forth strange and unheard-of creations of the mind" and arranges them in an unusual pattern that serves as a pleasing garment for the truth.[4]

This distinction between the outer and inner modes of poetic allegory—expressed by a poet who influenced Chaucer's poetry—provides a useful and authoritative approach to the *House of Fame*. Outwardly the poem conforms to the principles of allegory in combining heterogeneous elements, both pagan and Christian, into a unique and pleasing design. These elements, predominantly pagan, include Venus, her temple, and the portrayal of the *Aeneid* in Book I, Jupiter and his eagle in Book II, and Fame and her airy abode in Book III. But informing these details, and relating them on the level of allegory, is a background of moralized mythography which has transformed such pagan images into symbols pertaining to Christian doctrine. Thus while Venus and Fame both retain their outward identities as pagan personifications, to Chaucer and other medieval poets they have become convenient symbols for expressing the Christian concepts of love and fame. Mingling with these pagan fictions, moreover, and pointing up their Christian implications, is a pervasive Scriptural imagery whose meanings have been conditioned by a long tradition of Scriptural exegesis. Although one must be cautious in applying Scriptural–exegetical meanings to the imagery of secular poetry, to ignore them is often to overlook a key—sometimes the only one—unlocking the hidden content of poetic sym-

---

[4] *Genealogia deorum*, XIV, 7. A term sometimes applied to the artificial combination of elements in a poet's "invention" is *conjunctura*, the resulting design being a *pictura* or, to use Dante's phrase (*Convivio*, II, 1), a *bella menzogna*, a "beautiful lie" attracting the reader to the allegory underneath. In XIV, 9, 12, Boccaccio appeals to Scriptural allegory as a precedent for the poet's use of lying configurations to veil the truth.

bols.[5] In the *House of Fame* an aura of such meanings surrounds not only the more patent Scriptural (especially Apocalyptic) details of Book III but all of the larger patterns of imagery making up the episodes of the three books: the temple and desert of Venus, the flight with the eagle, the mountain and house of Fame, the whirling house of rumor, and—especially important to an understanding of the poem—the quest for "glad" tidings of a "fer contree" which are the goal of Chaucer's flight to the House of Fame. Along with these other Scriptural patterns, the search for "love-tydynges" is part of a complex allegorical structure which is ultimately designed to reveal the prophetic content of the vision. Although the nature of these tidings is deliberately concealed on the surface, in this Scriptural context their Christian meaning unfolds surely and purposefully and fulfills the deepest implications of Chaucer's theme of fame.

An awareness of Chaucer's Christian subject matter and allegorical technique should bring into clearer perspective a third major aspect of the *House of Fame*: the influence of the *Divine Comedy*. Chaucer's indebtedness to the *Comedy* is evident not only in his threefold structure and use of Dante's invocations but also in similar patterns of im-

---

[5] The importance of Scriptural–exegetical meanings in understanding medieval ecclesiastical art was demonstrated long ago by Emile Mâle, notably in *L'art religieux du XIIIe siècle en France*. More recent attempts to relate this background to the imagery of medieval poetry have been pioneered by Professor Robertson, whose conclusions are most elaborately presented in *A Preface to Chaucer*, where he demonstrates that many of the dominant images and motifs in literature are drawn from a traditional body of moralized pagan mythography and Scriptural–exegetical symbolism often appearing in a more patently Christian context in medieval manuscript illumination, wall painting, sculpture, and other modes of artistic expression. Much of the material in Robertson's *Preface*, especially that relating to Venus and medieval doctrines of love, has an immediate bearing on the *House of Fame* and is referred to in my notes. For a further evaluation of the importance of Scriptural–exegetical meanings in interpreting medieval literature, see

8

agery, as well as verbal echoes, throughout the poem. Any serious use of Dante, however, is apt to be minimized or even dismissed because of obvious differences in subject matter, style, tone, and general artistic complexity. Thus Chaucer's pagan fiction and Dante's predominantly Christian imagery suggest little outward correspondence in meaning or purpose. This difference is enhanced by equally striking differences in style and tone. Although Dante's humor and irony are easily overlooked, his more restrained wit and consciously artistic style contrast noticeably with Chaucer's characteristic humor and colloquial expression.[6] Such differences, considered merely on the surface, have led to the widely held view that Chaucer's imitation of Dante is, at most, a kind of parody. But the *House of Fame*, at least in its ultimate intent, is not a parody of the *Comedy*. While the differences reflect the attitudes, interests, and artistry of two distinctive poets, the similarities reveal a common ground of Christian doctrine which relates the two poems on the level of allegory.[7] An understanding of this common doctrine, however, is hindered both by a purely literal reading of the *House of Fame* and by a modern tendency to reduce the allegory of the *Comedy* to a mere appendage of the surface meaning or to reject it for an aesthetic analy-

---

R. E. Kaske, "Patristic Exegesis in the Criticism of Medieval Literature: The Defense," in *Critical Approaches to Medieval Literature: Selected Papers from the English Institute, 1958-1959* (New York, 1960).

[6] On the range and variety of Dante's humor, see Dorothy L. Sayers, "The Comedy of the *Comedy*," in *Introductory Papers on Dante* (New York, 1954), pp. 151-78.

[7] Discussions of the nature and extent of Chaucer's use of the *Comedy* have accumulated for many years and would be too lengthy to summarize here. For a recent approach to the subject and a selected bibliography, see Mario Praz, *The Flaming Heart* (New York, 1958), pp. 29-86. Regarding the question of parody, I subscribe to Praz's view that Chaucer's use of Dante is basically serious and that he "really meant *The House of Fame* to be a sort of Dantesque journey through the realm of allegory, and tried to assimilate from the *Commedia* what was accessible to his spirit" (p. 52).

9

sis which will appeal to more modern sensibilities. While this approach to Dante's allegory is perhaps in accord with modern predilections and tastes, it does not bring us any closer to the "intended" meaning expounded by Dante and his medieval commentators or to the spirit in which his contemporary reader, including Chaucer, approached the poem. Ultimately, it is in the light of the allegorical meanings and techniques common to both the *Comedy* and the *House of Fame* that we must assess the nature and significance of Chaucer's use of Dante. Once we have done so, it should become apparent that the importance of his imitation lies not in the outward, rhetorical features of the *Comedy* but in those inward patterns of structure and meaning which point to the Christian content of his own vision.[8] Indeed, allowing for the wide differences in the subject matter, scope, and artistry of the two poems, we should become aware that Book I is in a very real sense Chaucer's *Inferno*, Book II his *Purgatorio*, and Book III his *Paradiso*.

In attempting to clarify the Christian subject matter and allegorical method of the *House of Fame*, my two introductory chapters are designed as the background for a more detailed analysis and interpretation of the poem. Since the primary objective is to restore the medieval implications of the symbolism, the analysis is based essentially on materials closest to the tradition in which Chaucer wrote. For this purpose, use is made not only of standard commen-

[8] The conception of the medieval artist as an imitator of the inward rather than the outward aspects of another work of art is substantiated, insofar as it relates to architecture, by R. Krautheimer, "Introduction to an 'Iconography of Mediaeval Architecture,' " *JWCI*, v (1942), 13-14, who demonstrates that medieval notions of similarities between two works of architecture are based not on external form but on inner content. Such an inner similarity between the *Comedy* and the *House of Fame* was no doubt more apparent to Lydgate, who in the Prologue to *The Fall of Princes* presumably refers to Chaucer's poem under the title "Dante in Inglissh."

taries and glosses on Chaucer's most obvious sources—
especially Virgil, Ovid, Scripture, Dante, and Boethius—
but also of numerous moralized mythographies, bestiaries,
lapidaries, encyclopedias, and other repositories of the ideas
and imagery found in the poem. Together, these sources
offer a comprehensive and remarkably consistent body of
traditional Christian symbolism enabling us to penetrate the
surface obscurity of the *House of Fame*. Even so, it is not
always possible to pursue all the latent meanings of symbols in a long allegory in which almost every detail takes
on significance. Conversely, in a study involving the interpretation of symbols, the danger sometimes exists of bur-
dening a symbol with more weight than it should bear or
developing its connotations beyond those intended by the
poet. In view of the spiritual order which is the common
referent of all Christian symbols, this danger to the artistic
integrity of the poem is perhaps less real than the modern
reader might suppose. In any event, wherever different
possibilities of interpretation occur, reliance is placed upon
the immediate context and the controlling concepts of the
allegory to define the limits wherein a symbol may most
meaningfully function.

A combined historical and inductive approach to the
House of Fame has the added advantage of allowing us
to see quite clearly Chaucer's adaptation of traditional poetic theory and subject matter to his own artistic purpose.
Although the elements of his elaborate fiction are drawn
from widely diverse sources, both pagan and Christian, all
have been fused into a unified vision which is Chaucer's
own and which reveals the distinctive facets of his genius.
Much of what is best in his other works is also present here:
the mastery of a complex intellectual and artistic design;
the concrete and harmoniously balanced details of his vivid
pageantry; a richly colloquial style skillfully adapted to
his subject and purpose; and, above all, the incomparable

irony and humor. Since this book is concerned primarily with the meaning underlying the allegory, these qualities, especially the humor, have perhaps not been given all the attention they deserve. Nevertheless, it is hoped that an analysis projected against the intellectual and artistic traditions of the poet's own age will provide a norm revealing that Chaucer is often not only wittier and more ironic than has sometimes been supposed, but also more serious; and that a poem too frequently called digressive, unintegrated, and incomplete is unified both thematically and structurally.

CHAPTER I

THE TRADITION OF FAME

UNLIKE Venus, Fortune, and a few other pagan
deities, Fame occupied a minor position in the
mythography of medieval poets. Although the
pagan bearer of tidings—Virgil's "dea foeda"—was well
known in the Middle Ages, not until her conspicuous role
in the *House of Fame* was she elevated to a position equal
to that of "her suster, dame Fortune." Chaucer's fickle
goddess, wielding her awards of praise, slander, and oblivion, has obvious affinities with her prototype in the *Aeneid*. Also derivative is her elaborate abode, which pre-
serves features both from the *Aeneid* and from Ovid's
more detailed description in the *Metamorphoses*.[1] But in
the *House of Fame* the goddess and her dwelling have
undergone a metamorphosis as complete as anything in
Ovid.

The metamorphosis of Fame involves fundamentally a
medieval attitude toward fame which has transformed the
pagan personification into a symbol utilizable by a Christian
poet. Since fame in the Middle Ages was a clearly defined
Christian concept, the presence of the goddess in the work
of a medieval poet is itself indicative of a distinctive attitude toward the use of pagan material. As Chaucer and
other writers of his age were well aware, the pagan authors, ignorant of Christian doctrine and the providential
order revealed in Scripture, could not relate their ideas
about fame to the divine plan of redemption. Nevertheless,

[1] On the background of Fame and for an estimate of her importance
in medieval writings, see W. O. Sypherd, *Studies in Chaucer's Hous of
Fame* (Chaucer Society, London, 1907), especially p. 105. Although
the pagan personification of rumor appears as early as Homer, Fame's
most elaborate literary development is found in *Aeneid*, IV, 173-88, and
Metamorphoses, XII, 39-63.

13

poets like Virgil and Ovid, by their superior powers of intellect, were able to perceive truths about the nature of fame which approached or even agreed with Christian doctrine and which they sometimes expressed beneath a veil of poetic fiction. The guiding impulse behind the numerous medieval commentaries on pagan authors was to discover and use those truths which were in accord with Christian belief.[2] In this common body of pagan and medieval ideas about fame we find the explanation for the pagan goddess's presence in the work of a Christian poet such as Chaucer. Since Ovid and Virgil clothed their observations about fame in poetic fictions, these fictions provided ready symbols for the medieval poet. At the same time, if the poets drew freely upon pagan ideas and imagery, they made their borrowings subserve an intrinsically Christian purpose. Thus Chaucer's goddess, while retaining her outward identity with the pagan personification of rumor, has become a more complex symbol relating to the Christian doctrine of fame.

Viewed broadly, the process transforming Fame is one which also conditioned the poet's use of other pagan deities, such as Fortune and Venus, both of whom assumed much earlier their distinctive functions as Christian symbols. Although the influence of these deities, especially Fortune, is observable in the later poetizations of Fame, Fame's own metamorphosis is a unique chapter in the medieval

---

[2] The limitation of the pagan view of fame is discussed at length by Augustine, *De civitate Dei*, V, 12-20. At the same time, his statements on the wisdom and utility of pagan writings (for example, *De doctrina Christiana*, II, 40) are authoritative for the later Christian humanists. In the *House of Fame*, Chaucer's view finds notable expression in Book III, where Virgil, Ovid, and other pagans appear among the writers of "hy and gret sentence" whose pillars help to support Fame's castle. For discussions of the medieval approach to the interpretation and use of pagan literature, see E. A. Quain, S.J., "The Mediaeval Accessus ad auctores," *Traditio*, III (1945), 215-64; Jean Leclercq, O.S.B., *The Love of Learning and the Desire for God*, trans. C. Marsh (New York, 1961), chap. VII; D. W. Robertson, Jr., *A Preface to Chaucer*, chap. IV.

poet's use of pagan material. In order to understand more clearly the process transforming Chaucer's goddess and her abode into Christian symbols, we must reconstruct the doctrine of fame which these symbols are designed to convey.

1. The Scriptural Tradition

Underlying the medieval view of fame, as already observed, is a contrast between earthly and heavenly fame, a contrast found in both the Old and the New Testaments and elaborated in the latter and in Scriptural commentary as part of the doctrine of charity and redemption.[3] According to this concept, true fame is heavenly fame, which has its beginning and end in God. God's own fame, or glory, expresses his perfect goodness and is manifested in the praise given him by his creatures.[4] The fame of the Father is shared by the Son, who as deliverer of mankind was "crowned with glory and honor" and gained "a more excellent name" than that of the angels. The Apocalyptic

---

[3] Since the whole of Scripture, according to medieval doctrine, teaches the New Law of charity and redemption, the passages on fame in the Old Testament must be included among those expressive of the Christian concept of fame. On this key principle of Biblical exegesis, see Augustine, *De doctrina Christiana*, III, 10, and Beryl Smalley, *The Study of the Bible in the Middle Ages*, rev. ed. (Oxford, 1952), p. 6.

[4] As defined by Pierre Bersuire (Petrus Berchorius), *gloria* is "a general name signifying most perfectly the fulfillment of all goods [*bonorum omnium complementum*]" (*Opera omnia*, Cologne, 1730-1731, IV, 248, hereafter cited according to this edition). Cf. Etienne Gilson, *The Spirit of Mediaeval Philosophy* (New York, 1940), chap. 7. Since the Scriptural *gloria* may denote attributes referable to God alone, it is a more inclusive and complex term than "fame" (Vulg. *fama*). Like its pagan equivalent, the medieval *fama* may designate not only "rumor," "report," "tidings," "news," etc., but also our modern concept of "renown," "name," "reputation" as manifested in human opinion. Bersuire (*Opera*, IV, 185) summarizes the Biblical meanings of *fama* as *bonum nomen*, *bonus rumor*, and *bona opinio de aliquo*. As a synonym of "fame," the Scriptural *gloria* is applied both to human renown and to the renown of God as reflected in the praise of his creatures, for example, Ecclus. 42:17. The idea of God's fame, or glory, permeates the Psalms.

hymns of praise before God and the Lamb are indicative of the eternal fame they share as Creator and Redeemer of mankind.[5]

In man's pristine state of innocence, no distinction existed between heavenly and earthly fame. As long as Adam lived in harmony with God, his own fame was fame in heaven, his actions and speech a glorification not of himself but of God and the divine image within.[6] But with the Fall human fame acquires new meaning; for Adam's sin, symbolizing the mind's turning away from God to the world, involved an irrational confusion between temporal and eternal glory. Unlike heavenly fame, which lies in the opinion of God, earthly fame comes to mean the opinion of man's fellow creatures, whose judgments may be equally impaired as a result of Adam's sin. As elaborated in Scriptural commentary, Adam's transgression reflects the vainglory of Satan, the prototype of those who seek fame for its own sake. Satan's purpose in tempting Adam was to ruin man's fame in the eyes of God, thereby preventing his participation in the eternal fame forfeited by himself and the other fallen angels. The Christian doctrine of redemption is an answer to Satan's design and an affirmation of God's charity in allowing man through Christ to regain the eternal fame lost by Adam.[7]

Thus Christ and Satan are exemplars of two kinds of fame, one sought for God's glory, the other for its own sake. The contrast is recurrent in the Gospels: "For they

[5] Apoc. 4:9; 5:9-14; 7:9-12; 14:1-5. On Christ's renown as Redeemer, see Heb. 1:1-14; 2:9; 3:3-4; I Cor. 2:8; II Cor. 4:4; Phil. 2:5-11. All Scriptural references are to the Vulgate and the Douay-Rheims translation.

[6] In his unfallen state, man's glory, like that of the angels, was a reflection of and participation in God's glory. Cf. I Cor. 11:7; II Cor. 3:18; Heb. 2:6-7.

[7] According to a common exegetical tradition, vainglory was one of the three temptations involved in Adam's sin, the others being gluttony and avarice. See Gregory, PL, 76, col. 1,136. Satan's temptation of man is said to have sprung from envy, the natural enemy of good fame.

loved the glory of men more than the glory of God";
and again: "How can you believe, who receive glory one
from another, and the glory which is from God alone,
you do not seek?"[8] St. Augustine, commenting on the latter passage, develops this contrast in terms of two cities,
Jerusalem and Babylon, symbols respectively of two kinds
of love, charity and cupidity, or two kinds of fame, one
glorifying God and following the testimony of the conscience, the other glorying in itself and seeking the praise
of men.[9] Man's life since the Fall is portrayed ideally as a
pilgrimage from Babylon to Jerusalem, from the false
glory of the world to the glory of the heavenly city. Fame,
like other temporalia such as honors and riches, is a gift
which God allows man in making his journey. When
sought for its own sake, it leads to idolatry, a glorification
of God's gifts as objects of worship. When based upon
charity and good works, it is a means of glorifying God
and achieving salvation.[10] The way of true fame is exempli-

[8] John 12:43; 5:44. Cf. John 5:41; Gal. 1:10. These and similar
passages make a clear distinction between true and false glory. True
glory is the favorable opinion of God, whose absolute truth and goodness mark the value of all things. Whereas God's glory is what He is
essentially, the glory of men is what they are meant to be, though not
yet perfectly attained (cf. Rom. 3:23; 8:18-21). A late but notable expression of the contrast between human and divine glory is Christ's
reply to Satan in Milton's *Paradise Regained*, III, 60-70, where Job
exemplifies one who was famous "in Heaven, on Earth less known;/
Where glory is false glory, attributed/ To things not glorious, men not
worthy of fame." True glory and renown are received when God,
"looking on the Earth, with approbation marks/ The just man, and
divulges him through Heaven/ To all his Angels, who with true ap-
plause/ Recount his praises. . . ."

[9] *De civitate Dei*, XIV, 28. Augustine's classic definition of the two
loves is in *De doctrina Christiana*, III, 10: "I call 'charity' the motion
of the soul toward the enjoyment of God for His own sake, and the
enjoyment of one's self and of one's neighbor for the sake of God; but
'cupidity' is a motion of the soul toward the enjoyment of one's self,
one's neighbor, or any corporal thing for the sake of something other
than God." This contrast underlies the important discussion of fame in
De civitate Dei, V, 12-20, where Augustine distinguishes true glory
from the false glory of the pagans.

[10] On the false glory associated with idolatry, see Rom. 1:20-25. In

17

fied by Christ's own resistance to Satan's temptation to seek worldly glory and by his words at the end of the Sermon on the Mount: "So let your light shine before men that they may see your good works and glorify your Father who is in heaven."[11]

Although fame acquired through charity and good works may be manifested in human praise, its value is established not by the outward acclaim of men but by an inward relationship between man and God. Therefore, says John of Salisbury, echoing Augustine, if praise is won in the right manner it rests upon a foundation laid by the individual himself.[12] When properly achieved, earthly fame is an

---

De doctrina Christiana, I, 4, Augustine relates the proper use of God's gifts to the Scriptural concept of the pilgrimage, for example, I Pet. 2:11; Heb. 11:13-16.

[11] Matt. 5:16. Cf. 6:1-4. These two passages are key ones in defining the proper Christian attitude toward human praise. In an influential commentary on Christ's Sermon, Augustine carefully explains the implications of those Scriptural passages which may appear to condone the pursuit of praise (trans. Findlay): "the mere fact that a man by means of good works pleases men, does not . . . set it up as an end that he should please men; but let him subordinate this to the praise of God, and for this reason please men, that God may be glorified in him. For this is expedient for them who offer praise, that they should honour, not man, but God" (*De sermone Domini in monte*, I, 7). Cf. II, 2 (on Matt. 6:2-4): "For the praise of men ought not to be sought by him who acts rightly, but ought to follow him who does so, so that they may profit who can also imitate what they praise, not that he whom they praise may think that they are profiting him anything." Augustine refers to Gal. 1:10 ("For do I now persuade men or God? Or do I seek to please men? If I yet pleased men, I should not be the servant of Christ"); Gal. 1:24 ("And they glorified God in me"); Gal. 5:26 ("Let us not be made desirous of vainglory, provoking one another, envying one another"); Gal. 6:4; Matt. 9:8. Cf. Rom. 13:3; 14:18. The commentators express the same attitude toward those Old Testament passages which appear to extol fame for its own sake, for example, Prov. 22:1 ("A good name [*nomen bonum*] is better than great riches; and good favour [*gratia bona*] is above silver and gold"). In *Expositio in Prov.*, PL, 91, col. 1,001, Bede, using Gal. 1:10 as authority, interprets *nomen bonum* as heavenly fame.

[12] *Policraticus*, VIII, 1, 15. Cf. Augustine, *De civitate Dei*, V, 12, and Gal. 6:4: "But let everyone prove his own work, and so he shall have glory in himself only, and not in another."

18

"accident" or "shadow" of virtue (*virtus*). Or, to use a familiar Scriptural figure, it may be compared to a good odor; for, says Pierre Bersuire, just as the rose and certain aromatic trees have an inner fragrance which is outwardly diffused, so those who are good within emit a fame which spreads to the most remote places.[13] In the Old Testament this image is applied to the fame of the many patriarchs, kings, and prophets who are remembered for their wisdom and rectitude.[14] In the New Testament it is linked with Christ's fame while he performed his earthly ministry and with the renown of the saints and apostles who spread his tidings of charity and followed his example in their good works: "For we are the good odour of Christ unto God, in them that are saved and in them that perish. To the one indeed the odour of death unto death; but to

[13] *Opera*, IV, 185. Bersuire defines *bona fama* as *virtutum manifestiva* or a certain spiritual "accident" [*accidens*] emanating and spreading from the virtues [*virtutibus*] of perfect men (IV, 112, 185). Following Augustine, he defines *virtus* as an ordering of the mind [*dispositio*] in which it consents to reason, is in harmony with God, and obeys Him (VI, 225). The pagan writers, for example, Cicero and Virgil, sometimes connect virtue and fame; but Augustine carefully distinguishes true virtue, which is based on the worship of God, from pagan virtue, which "is the slave of human praise" (*De civitate Dei*, V, 19). The association is recurrent among the Christian humanists, such as Petrarch, who compares fame [*gloria*] to the shadow of virtue [*l'ombra della virtù*] (*Secretum*, III). In the *Canterbury Tales*, Chaucer applies this idea to such characters as Constance, Griselda, and Virginia, the last named being praised by all "that loved vertu" and hated only by Envy, "that sory is of oother mennes wele" (Physician's Tale, 111ff.). Cf. the Man of Law's Tale, 150ff., and the Clerk's Tale, 407ff.

[14] For example, Ecclus. 49:1-2: "The memory of Josias is like the composition of a sweet smell." The odor image appears often in the Old Testament, for example, Ecclus. 24:20-28 (on the fame of Wisdom): "I gave a sweet smell like cinnamon and aromatical balm. . . . As the vine I have brought forth a pleasant odour. . . . My memory is unto everlasting generations." For other key passages on fame in this book, see 39:12-20; 41:14-16; 44:1-15. Chapters 44-50 are devoted to the praise of the patriarchs and prophets. According to the commentaries, the fame of Christ is prefigured in the renown of Wisdom and of such men as Joshua (Jos. 6:27), David (I Par. 14:17), and Solomon (II Par. 9:1, 5; III Kings 10:1, 7).

the others the odour of life unto life."[15] Anagogically, the odor of life signifies the blissfulness of eternal fame, not only of those whose virtuous deeds were praised by men but also of those who merited praise on earth but are remembered only by God: "And there are some of whom there is no memorial: who are perished, as if they had never been [born]. . . . But these were men of mercy, whose godly deeds have not failed" (Ecclus. 44:9-10). In the Apocalypse the fragrance of eternal fame is imaged in the prayers presented by one of the angels with incense upon the golden altar before God's throne.[16]

Whereas the odor of life denotes the eternal fame offered by Christ and the life of charity, the odor of death denotes the eternal infamy offered by Satan to those who seek fame through vainglory. Since the desire for praise infects even the virtuous mind, says John of Salisbury, it is sometimes called the "noble" vice. But whoever succumbs to this vainglorious desire, he warns, has already hurled himself over the precipice of sin; for from vainglory stem all those other vices, such as boastfulness and hypocrisy, which accompany the pursuit of praise.[17] Guilty

[15] II Cor. 2:14-16. Cf. Eph. 5:1-2. On the fame associated with Christ's ministry, see Matt. 4:24; 9:26, 31; 14:1; Mark 1:28; Luke 4:14; 5:15; 7:17. In the bestiaries, the sweet odor emitted from the panther's mouth is interpreted as the fame by which Christ attracts men to God. The image of fragrance is applied figuratively to the Blessed Virgin in Cant. 3:6 and appears often in the saints' lives, for example, Chaucer's Second Nun's Tale, Prol., 85ff.

[16] Apoc. 8:3-5. Cf. Ecclus. 35:8-9; Ps. 140:2. Applying the higher levels of Scriptural meaning, Bersuire interprets *odor*, anagogically, as the sweetness and fragrance of heavenly glory; allegorically, as good fame and the redolence of renown; and, tropologically, as the sanctity of virtue (*Opera*, V, 152).

[17] *Policraticus*, VIII, 1. John's analysis of vainglory [*inanis gloria*] is based on Gregory, *Moralia*, XXXIX, 87-89. On the desire for praise as the noble vice [*nobile vitium*], cf. *Policraticus*, VIII, 2, and *Entheticus*, 1. 875, where John refers to it as the last frailty that leaves the exalted mind. This concept—better known in Milton's description of the "last infirmity of noble mind" (*Lycidas*, 1. 71)—appears in Christian writings as early as Augustine, *De civitate Dei*, V, 14; *De sermone Domini in monte*, II (Introduction). Boethius introduces

of this sin are those who "sound a trumpet" before them when they perform their good works. Unlike those who give alms in secret and are praised by God, not men, these seekers of glory, Christ reminds them, receive their reward on earth, not in heaven.[18] But if vainglory is nurtured by worldly praise, remarks Augustine, it is a vice belonging not to praise itself but to the soul seeking renown irrespective of the conscience.[19] Like true glory, vainglory is an inward state of which praise is merely an outward manifestation. But unlike true glory, whose substance (*virtus*) is revealed outwardly as a sweet odor, vainglory emits no fragrance; or if it does, it is the alluring and deceptive odor of false praise by which men are tempted by Satan and led to damnation. Such unmerited praise is typical especially of the fame of hypocrites, who "have the name without the thing, glory without merit, fame without virtue."[20]

Just as there are two kinds of praise, deserved and un-

---

the concept in *De consolatione philosophiae*, II, Pr. 7, 1ff. Like Augustine, Bersuire applies the idea especially to the pagans: "Fame, indeed, is the thing that the noble mind [*cor generosum*] seeks most eagerly; and for that reason the ancients performed all their lofty deeds for the sake of acquiring fame, and they longed for glory and fame as the final reward for their deeds; and this they did because they were ignorant of the true glory of heaven and the true, everlasting reward" (*Opera*, IV, 185). In "Boethius and 'That Last Infirmity of Noble Mind,' " *PQ*, XLII (1963), 176-82, John S. Coolidge cites pagan examples of the concept and traces Milton's statement to Boethius.

[18] Matt. 6:1-2. Augustine, commenting on the succeeding verse ("And when thou dost alms, let not thy left hand know what thy right hand doth"), identifies the left hand [*sinistra*] with the desire for praise and the right hand [*dextera*] with the fulfilling of God's precepts (*De sermone Domini in monte*, II, 2ff.). Following the same interpretation, Bede links giving alms in secret with the good conscience [*bona conscientia*], which is unseen by human eyes and originates in a sound will (*PL*, 92, col. 31). On the trumpet [*tuba*] as a symbol of human praise [*favor humanus*], see *Allegoriae in sacram scripturam*, *PL*, 112, col. 1,069, where the verse from Matthew is cited.

[19] *De civitate Dei*, XII, 8. In V, 12, Augustine quotes Gal. 6:4 and II Cor. 1:12 ("For our glory is this: the testimony of our conscience").

[20] Bersuire, *Opera*, IV, 185.

21

deserved, so there are two kinds of infamy, one which condemns the vicious, another which slanders the virtuous.[21] Indeed, human judgment by its very nature since Adam's sin is fickle and unstable. When based upon reason and charity it dispenses praise or infamy according to merit; otherwise it results in the unbridled tongue which, says St. James, mingles "blessing and cursing," truth and falsehood, and causes evil works to be commended and to prosper and good works to be slandered or forgotten.[22] From man's inveterate confusion since the Fall stem all the lies, jangling, detraction, and other misuses of the tongue making up the empty rumor so often synonymous with fame. But earthly fame, whether praise or slander, truth or falsehood, or both combined, is not lasting. Like grass—to use another Scriptural image—it lacks stable roots and is ultimately a victim of time, which is not only the bestower and the bearer of fame but also its destroyer.[23] For this reason, says Alexander Neckam, recalling Ecclesiastes, those who

[21] Bersuire (*ibid.*, 357-58) distinguishes between two kinds of praise ("one true, another false") and between two kinds of infamy [*infamia*], one just, the other unjust. Whereas the first kind of infamy is bestowed upon the wicked, the second kind is bestowed upon the virtuous, either through malice or through error of judgment. Infamy stemming from malice is most often rooted in envy: "For the wicked, especially the envious, are joyful over the infamy of others and sorrowful over their good fame" (IV, 185). In the bestiaries, this idea is symbolized by the hatred of the dragon (Satan) for the sweet odor of the panther (Christ).

[22] Jas. 3:1-12. Cf. Prov. 8:13. Evils of the tongue are frequently condemned in Scripture, for example, Prov. 6:17; 10:18; 26:28; Pss. 11:3; 38:1-5; 49:18-20; 51:1-6; Ecclus. 28:23-30; Wis. 1:8-11; Jer. 9:4-8.

[23] For the Scriptural basis of the image, see Is. 40:6 ("All flesh is grass, and all the glory thereof as the flower of the field"); Ecclus. 14:18; Jas. 1:10; I Pet. 1:24. On the exegetical tradition of the image and its reflection in medieval secular allegory, see D. A. Pearsall, *The Floure and the Leafe and the Assembly of Ladies* (London, 1962), "Introduction," pp. 29-32. Fame is properly compared to grass, says Benvenuto da Imola, commenting on *Purg.*, XI, 115-17, because just as grass is discolored and desiccated by the advancing heat of summer, so human fame, lacking a stable root, loses its freshness through the effects of time, which bestows, exalts, and destroys the fame of men (*Commentum*, Florence, 1887, III, 318).

wish to be remembered by posterity follow a vain and fleeting shadow.[24] Such fame is but the swelling of the wind—itself similar to smoke, says John of Salisbury; for the higher it ascends, the more quickly it dissipates, and the lower it descends, the denser it becomes—an apt comparison, he concludes, since the desire for praise has its origin in Satan, the prince of all vanity.[25]

2. *The Tradition of Boethius*

Since worldly praise is rooted in the fickle and ephemeral judgments of mankind, the pursuit of fame for its own sake leads inevitably to anxiety and fear. In Scripture this fear of human judgment is contrasted with the fear of God, who at the Last Judgment will distribute eternal fame and infamy according to one's just deserts: "Therefore judge not before the time, until the Lord come, who both will bring to light the hidden things of darkness and will make manifest the counsels of the hearts. And then shall every man have praise from God."[26] Some men, however, fearful of earthly infamy or the loss of renown, fail

---

[24] *De naturis rerum*, II, 155, ed. T. Wright (London, 1863). Cf. Bersuire, *Opera*, IV, 185; Benvenuto da Imola, *Commentum*, III, 318 (on *Purg.*, XI, 91-117). In Wis. 2:4-5, *umbra* designates the transitory nature of fame: "And our name in time shall be forgotten, and no man shall have any remembrance of our works. For our time is as the passing of a shadow."

[25] *Policraticus*, VIII, 5. John cites both Augustine and the pagans as authorities for the comparison. Cf. Boethius, *De consolatione philosophiae*, II, Met. 7; Neckam, *De naturis rerum*, II, 155 ("For what is the puffed up praise of the people but wind?"); Dante, *Purg.*, XI, 100-103. Bersuire (*Opera*, IV, 235) identifies smoke [*fumus*] with *fumus vanae elationis* and, anagogically, with eternal infamy.

[26] I Cor. 4:5. Cf. Prov. 10:7 ("The memory of the just is with praises; and the name of the wicked shall rot"). In Luke 12:4-7, Christ contrasts the fear of human judgment with the fear of God's judgment. On the doctrinal implications of this contrast, see Augustine, *PL*, 36, col. 1,026; Peter Lombard, *PL*, 191, cols. 765-66; Hugh of St. Victor, *PL*, 176, col. 572. The idolatrous aspects of fear are treated in John Ridewall's *Fulgentius metaforalis*, ed. F. Liebeschütz (Leipzig, 1926), pp. 65-71.

to see that God alone is the dispenser of both temporal and eternal fame; or else, not understanding God's ways in temporal affairs, they question his justice and complain of the unequal distribution of fame among the good and the wicked. The classic medieval treatment of this problem, along with the writings of Augustine, is the *Consolation of Philosophy* of Boethius. Itself an essentially Augustinian treatise beneath a carefully controlled fiction, the *Consolation* is an attempt to reconcile the apparently unjust disposition of temporal awards with God's providence.[27] The problem of fame underlies the work, centering upon Boethius, whose fall from prosperity and loss of renown pose the major ideas explored. More particularly, Boethius dramatizes the Christian concept of the exiled pilgrim who has forgotten his heavenly country and is therefore lost in the maze of the world. Lady Philosophy, who comes to comfort him, portrays the divine image of reason which in Boethius has been weakened and which must be restored before the will can be brought into harmony with God.[28] Boethius' lament for his loss of renown prompts Philosophy's appearance and leads her to a solution of the problem of fame that is in accord with the orthodox Christian view.

The problem of fame is introduced in Book I in Boethius' lengthy complaint against Fortune, whom he blames

[27] On the Augustinian content of the *Consolation*, see Etienne Gilson, *History of Christian Philosophy* (New York, 1955), p. 102; Huppé and Robertson, *Fruyt and Chaf: Studies in Chaucer's Allegories* (Princeton, 1963), p. 29; Richard Green, trans., *The Consolation of Philosophy* (The Library of Liberal Arts, New York, 1962), "Introduction," pp. xv-xix. Green (pp. xix-xxiii) and Robertson (*Preface*, pp. 359-60) discuss the fictive covering of the *Consolation*.

[28] Quoting from Trivet's commentary, Robertson observes that the *Consolation* was sometimes regarded in the Middle Ages as a fable consisting of a dialogue between "the spirit suffering from the aggravation of the sensuality, and the reason offering consolation from the vigor of wisdom" (*Preface*, p. 359). In the *Roman de la Rose*, 2,971ff., Reason, one of Philosophy's medieval progeny, is called the image of God (ed. Langlois, Paris, 1914-1924).

for his fall from high place and consequent loss of good name. His erroneous attitude toward fame may be subsumed under three points: he confuses the motives leading men to seek the fame of high place; he views the praise bestowed by mankind as a good in itself; and, of paramount importance, he questions the justice of a divine providence which allows the name of the innocent to suffer and the name of the wicked to prosper. In defense of his own motive in seeking fame, Boethius claims that he was only following Philosophy's dictate that the renown of high place should be sought solely from the desire to rule for the "comune profit." As evidence of his innocence, he cites the many times he risked his high position to uphold the welfare of the people and yet was never drawn from right to wrong. Never did he extol his own name by praising his good deeds, for when a person receives "precious renoun" by boasting of his works, he betrays the dictates of his conscience. Although he has been accused of defiling his conscience, his fame has been due neither to covetousness of high place nor to praise of himself. Yet the reward for his innocence has been "peyne of fals felonye for guerdoun of verrai vertu."[29]

Boethius' feeling of the unjustness of his reward leads to his second major complaint: the people themselves confuse virtue with worldly honor or fame. For most men, he laments, "loken nothyng to the desertes of thynges, but oonly to the aventure of fortune," and they "jugen that oonly swiche thynges ben purveied of God, whiche that temporel welefulnesse commendeth." Or as Chaucer glosses the passage: "Yif a wyght have prosperite, he is a good man and worthy to han that prosperite; and whoso hath adversite, he is a wikkid man, and God hath forsake hym." This confusion of popular opinion leads Boethius to bemoan

---

[29] *Consolation*, I, Pr. 4. All quotations are from Chaucer's translation, ed. F. N. Robinson, *The Works of Geoffrey Chaucer*, 2nd ed. (Boston: Houghton Mifflin, 1957).

the state of his own renown: "Certes it greveth me to thynke ryght now the diverse sentences that the peple seith of me."[30] But his complaint does not end here. Not only does he lament that the innocent suffer while the wicked prosper but he also marvels how God, who oversees all things, can allow "swiche thynges as every felonous man hath conceyved in his thoght ayens innocentz." In short, he asks: "Yif God is, whennes comen wikkide thyngis? And yif God ne is, whennes comen gode thynges?" This complaint culminates in his questioning God's justice in permitting "slydynge Fortune" to control men's affairs while virtue—"cleer and schynynge naturely"—is "hidde in derke derknesses."[31]

Before answering Boethius' particular complaints, Philosophy promises to ease his grief and prepare him for a "more myghty" medicine. But first she diagnoses his malady: he is "sik" with tribulations because he has forgotten the divine country whence he came and therefore has lost the true way and "gon amys."[32] He has complained of Fortune and especially of the injustice of his accusers and the opinion of the multitude; but if he would remember his heavenly country he would know that it is governed neither by emperors nor by the multitude but by one "lord and o kyng, and that is God." Boethius, however, forgetful that God is both the beginning and the end of all things, has entrusted his happiness to the goods of Fortune; and Fortune's gifts, as he has justly observed, are brittle and transitory and are not always distributed according to merit. If he would recall "the kynde, the maneris, and the desserte of thilke Fortune," he would realize that he has neither lost nor can lose "any fair thyng" at her hands. In the first place, his belief that Fortune has turned against

[30] *Ibid.*, 281ff.
[31] *Ibid.*, 192ff.; I, Met. 5.
[32] *Consolation*, I, Pr. 5, 1ff. Cf. I, Pr. 6, 66ff.

him is not true; for in depriving him of the fame of high place she has merely acted according to her nature. Indeed, if Fortune should become stable, she would then cease to be Fortune.[33] Fortune's gifts, moreover, do not belong to man, nor are they conducive to true happiness. If fame and honors are bestowed upon good men—"the whiche thyng is ful selde"—the glory lies not in these things themselves but in the virtue of those who receive them. Therefore the gifts of Fortune by which men "areysen hem as heyghe as the hevene" come not "to vertu for cause of dignyte" but come "to dignyte for cause of vertu."[34]

Philosophy's definition of fame based on virtue brings Boethius' initial confusion into clear focus. In reply to his assertion that on her own authority he never had "covetise" of "mortel thynges" but only wished for virtue's sake to be remembered for his good government, Philosophy concedes that the desire to have fame for the sake of the "comune profit" is a motive that may prompt "hertes as ben worthy and noble of hir nature." Nevertheless, such a desire does not move those hearts "ibrought to the fulle perfeccioun of vertu."[35] If he would consider her teaching carefully, he would see "how litel and how voyde of alle prys is thylke glorye." First of all, astronomy demonstrates that all the environs of the earth "halt but the resoun of a prykke at regard of the gretnesse of hevene." Therefore those who would publish their renown should consider that they are closed within "the leeste prykke of thilke prykke" and that their glory, even within these narrow bounds, may never spread to all mankind.[36] Furthermore, many nations inhabit "thilke lytel habitacle," and because of the diversity

---

[33] *Ibid.*, 17ff; II, Pr. 1.
[34] *Consolation*, II, Pr. 6.
[35] *Ibid.*, Pr. 7, 1ff.
[36] *Ibid.*, 20ff. The image of the pinpoint ("prykke"), used by Chaucer in *HF*, 904-907, derives from Cicero, *De re publica*, VI (the dream of Scipio). Cf. Macrobius, *Commentary*, II, 10.

of languages, customs, and means of communication not only the fame of particular men but also the fame of cities may never reach them. Similarly, the manners and laws among a single group of people may be so divergent that the very thing some men judge "worthy of preysynge" will be judged by others as "worthy of torment." For this reason, if one is spurred on by the desire for fame, he should be satisfied if his name is published among his own neighbors or is constrained within "the boundes of o manere folk." Even so, many a person noble in his time has been forgotten, since even the writings preserving his name are ultimately victims of time. Finally, if one compares earthly renown with the infiniteness of eternity, he will find little cause for rejoicing in the long lasting of his name; for his fame, of as long a duration as he can imagine, will seem not only small but "pleynliche ryght noght." Most men, however, can do nothing without the "audience of the peple" and "idel rumours"; and in their pride and vainglory they forsake conscience and virtue and seek "gerdouns of the smale wordes of straunge folk." But even those who seek glory with virtue find fame of little value when the soul, finally released from the prison of the earth, looks down from heaven and rejoices that it is freed from the longing for earthly things.

After an impassioned reminder that death is contemptuous of all earthly glory and that fame itself is a "second death" when one's name is finally forgotten,[37] Philosophy

[37] *Consolation*, II, Met. 7. Philosophy connects this idea with what becomes the traditional *Ubi sunt* formula: "O! what coveyten proude folk to lyften up hir nekkes on idel in the dedly yok of this world? For although that renoun ysprad, passynge to ferne peples, goth by diverse tonges; and although that greete houses or kynredes shynen with cleere titles of honours; yit natheles deth despiseth al hey glorie of fame, and deth wrappeth togidre the heyghe hevedes and the lowe, and maketh egal and evene the heygheste to the loweste. Where wonen now the bones of trewe Fabricius? What is now Brutus or stierne Caton? The thynne fame yit lastynge of here idel names is marked with a fewe lettres. But although that we han knowen the fayre wordes

concludes the initial stage of her instruction by affirming the value of Fortune's adversities, since good fortune deceives and bad fortune teaches the fragility of earthly goods and sometimes brings its victims back to the path of virtue. Strengthened by the lessons thus far received, Boethius claims to be ready for the sharper remedies promised earlier as the cure for his malady. But first, to prepare him for her stronger medicine and to answer his inquiry as to the nature of true felicity, Philosophy surveys those transitory objects of desire which men confuse with true happiness and mistake for the "sovereyn good"—that state of perfect felicity which she defines as the "congregacioun of alle goodes" and later identifies with God, the source "of al that oughte ben desired." Although the "covetise of verray good" is "naturely iplauntyd in the hertes of men," through error some people confuse the "sovereyn good" with worldly honor, some with riches, some with "voluptuous delyt," and some with "noblesse of renoun," which prompts them to acquire "gloryous name by the artz of werre or of pees." But all of these apparent goods are limited and fail to provide the happiness they seem to promise. As for fame in particular, it is, as Euripides said, "a greet swellere of eres." For many men, undeserving of praise, receive "greet renoun" from the "false opinyoun of the peple," and even when praise is deserved, it means nothing to the wise man, who measures his "good" not by the "rumour of the peple" but by the "sothfastnesse of conscience." And if it seems a "fair thyng" to have "encreced and sprad" one's fame, it follows that it must seem a "foul thyng" not to have done so. But, as she has already proved, there are some "folk" who never hear of a man's

---

of the fames of hem, it is nat yyven to knowen hem that ben dede and consumpt. Liggeth thanne stille, al outrely unknowable, ne fame maketh yow nat knowe. And yif ye wene to lyve the longer for wynd of yowr mortel name whan o cruel day schal ravyssche yow, than is the seconde deth duellynge unto yow."

name, and a person who seems to be "glorious and re-
nomed" will be without glory and renown in another part
of the world. For all these reasons, the esteem or "grace"
of the people is hardly worth considering, because it neither
comes from "wys jugement" nor is destined to last. How
"veyn" and "flyttynge" such praise is and how little it
has to do with merit may be observed in the glory of noble
birth; for if "gentilesse" means only "renoun and cleer-
nesse of lynage," then one's "gentil name" is a "foreyn
thyng," belonging not to the individual who glories in
his lineage, but to others, since "gentilesse" appears to be
"a maner preisynge that cometh of the dessertes of aun-
cestres"; and if "preisynge make gentilesse," only the
ones who are praised are "gentil." Therefore, if one has
no "gentilesse" himself (that is to say, renown that comes
from his own merit), the "gentilesse" of others will not
make him "gentil." If any good is to be found in noble
birth, it is merely in the obligation of "gentil men" not
to abandon the virtues of their forebears. For all mankind
springs from one stock and one Father, who clothed with
bodies the souls "that comen from his heye sete." If one
remembers the noble origin of all men, he will not boast
of his ancestors' glory, since no person is base or "ongentil"
unless he enslaves his heart to vice.[38]

Up to this point, Philosophy has answered two of the
three major problems raised by Boethius' confused attitude toward fame: his misconception of the motives prompting men to seek fame and his trust in worldly renown as
a good in itself. She has yet to resolve his problem of
reconciling God's justice with the apparently unjust distribution of fame and other gifts of Fortune among the
good and the wicked. In order to prove to Boethius that
happiness always comes to the innocent and misfortune to
the wicked, she promises to "fycchen fetheris" in his

[38] *Ibid.*, III, Pr. 6; Met. 6.

thought and show him the way that will bring him "hool and sownd" to his proper "hous" or "contree."[39] In achieving this higher purpose—the "more myghty" medicine to which she refers earlier—Philosophy presents an orthodox Christian solution to the problem of fame.

In reply to Boethius' inquiry as to the reason for the "wrongful" confusion of earthly awards, and particularly his desire to know if this confusion is the result of chance, Philosophy grants that men might think the disposition of earthly awards is confused and "somwhat foolissh" when the reason is unknown. But even though Boethius does not know the cause of "so gret a disposicioun," he should not doubt that God does all things with a purpose and that all the "progressiouns" and motions of mutable nature take their "causes," "ordre," and "formes" from the stability of the divine mind.[40] And the divine mind is to be conceived in two guises: as "purveaunce," which is the divine reason which "disponith" all things; and as "destyne," which is the "unfolding" of God's "purveaunce" in the temporal order. Although the disposition of temporal awards may appear unjust, it is part of the "ryghte ordre of thinges." For nothing proceeding from the divine mind can be evil. Even the adversities suffered by the innocent are part of the providential plan of good. God vexes some people with adversity so that their prosperity will not make them proud; others he allows to suffer so that they may exercise their virtue by patience; and some, who could not be subdued by adversity, have served as examples for others that virtue may not be overcome. On the other hand, the justice of God's providence is also revealed in his awards to the wicked. Thus when sorrows befall "schrewes," everyone knows they were deserved. Also, when the wicked are afflicted, their torment sometimes restrains others from committing felonies and sometimes

[39] *Ibid.*, IV, Pr. 1, 66ff.   [40] *Ibid.*, Pr. 5, 20ff.; Pr. 6, 41ff.

31

amends the wicked. Conversely, the prosperity allowed to the wicked provides an argument to "goode folk" not to trust worldly prosperity. In all these changes of fortune, God brings forth good from evil, although men may not comprehend "alle the subtil ordenaunces and disposiciounis of the devyne entente."[41] Thus, concludes Philosophy, Fortune, whom Boethius has blamed for his loss of fame, is not evil but good; for God, who in his omniscience perceives "alle thinges that ben, or weren, or schollen comen," judges and rewards men according to their merits. For all deeds are performed before the eyes of the judge "that seeth and demeth alle thinges."[42]

3. The Literary Tradition

Along with Scripture and Scriptural commentary, the *Consolation of Philosophy* provides the basic doctrine of the medieval literary treatments of fame. But it remained for the poets to develop a symbolism whereby this doc-

[41] *Ibid.*, Pr. 6, 47ff. In *De civitate Dei*, I, 8, Augustine uses similar reasons to explain why God "maketh his sun to rise upon the good and bad and raineth upon the just and the unjust [Matt. 5:45].

[42] *Consolation*, v, Pr. 2; Met. 2; Pr. 6, 304ff. Although Boethius, as Green observes (p. xv), restricts Philosophy's discourse to the limits of natural reason without direct mention of Christian revelation, the Scriptural implications of the Last Judgment are clear. Cf. Rom. 2:5-8, and Augustine, *De civitate Dei*, I, 8. The Christian import of Philosophy's remarks for Chaucer's contemporaries is evident in Thomas Usk's *The Testament of Love*, for example, I, 8, in which the Boethian ideas on fame (echoing Chaucer's translation) are expanded into the Christian contrast between temporal and eternal fame: "Alas! that mankynde coveyteth in so leude a wyse to be rewarded of any good dede, sithe glorie of fame, in this worlde, is nat but hindringe of glorie in tyme comminge! . . . Trewly, therin thou lesest the guerdon of vertue; and lesest the grettest valour of conscience, and unhap thy renomè everlasting. Therfore boldely renomè of fame of the erthe shulde be hated, and fame after deth shulde be desyred of werkes of vertue. [Trewly, vertue] asketh guerdoning, and the soule causeth al vertue. Than the soule, delivered out of prison of erthe, is most worthy suche guerdon among to have in the everlastinge fame; and nat the body, that causeth al mannes yvels" (*Chaucerian and Other Pieces*, ed. W. W. Skeat, London, 1897, pp. 37-38).

trine might be expressed according to the aims and methods of poetry. Conveniently, the basis for such a symbolism was already available in the pagan writers, particularly Virgil and Ovid, whose personifications of rumor supply the central imagery of Chaucer's dynamic drama of Fame and her awards. Behind Chaucer's unique portrayal of the goddess, however, lie several centuries of attempts to bring such pagan fictions into accord with Christian belief.

Implicit in these attempts, as indicated earlier, is the assumption that the pagan writers were able to perceive truths about the nature of fame which approximated the Christian view. Thus Cicero (as Macrobius' commentary on the dream of Scipio attested for the Middle Ages) could develop a view of fame based upon virtue and a contrast between earthly and heavenly fame which in many particulars would not be out of place in Augustine or Boethius.[43] A similar contrast in the *Aeneid* provides the basis for Chaucer's introduction of his theme in Book I of the *House of Fame*. But if the pagan writers express an attitude toward fame often appearing to be Christian, their view is founded, as Augustine observes, not upon a divine plan of redemption as in Christian doctrine, but upon an eagerness for praise appealing to human rather than to divine judgment.[44] The same distinction applies to Virgil's

---

[43] See, for example, the condemnation of earthly glory in *De re publica*, VI. Cf. Macrobius, *Commentary*, II, 10-11. The continuity of pagan and medieval ideas on fame is discussed by María Rosa Lida De Malkiel in *La Idea de la Fama en la Edad Media Castellana* (Mexico: Fondo de Cultura Económica, 1952), a useful summary of which appears in the review by N. R. Cartier, *Speculum*, XXX (1955), 656-66. One of the ideas developed in her study, part of which is devoted to the Greek and Roman writers on fame, is that alongside the pagan ideal of personal glory there exists an ascetic attitude toward fame, exemplified by Cicero, which looks forward to Macrobius, Augustine, Boethius, and later medieval writers.

[44] *De civitate Dei*, V, 12. Cf. V, 14: "But since those Romans dwelt in an earthly city, and the goal of all their service to it was its safety and a kingdom not in heaven but on earth, . . . what else should they

and Ovid's personifications of fame, which are little more than convenient fictions for portraying the confusion of truth and falsehood typical of popular judgment. To apply medieval terminology, these pagan fictions are limited to a purely verbal allegory; that is to say, unlike Scriptural symbols, wherein the things signified by the words may themselves be symbols of higher spiritual truths, the truths signified by pagan symbols do not go beyond those visible, temporal attributes of fame common to pagan and Christian observation.[45]

This contrast between pagan and Christian symbols may be illustrated by Boccaccio's moralization of Virgil's *Fama* in the *Genealogy of the Gods*. Virgil's description immediately follows the account of the secret bond between Dido and Aeneas:

Forthwith Rumour [Fama] runs through Libya's great cities— Rumour of all evils the most swift. Speed lends her strength, and she wins vigour as she goes; small at first through fear, soon she mounts up to heaven, and walks the ground with head hidden in the clouds. Her, 'tis said, Mother Earth, provoked to anger against the gods, brought forth last, as sister to Coeus and Enceladus, swift of foot and fleet of wing, a monster awful and huge, who for the many feathers in her body has as many watchful eyes below—wondrous to tell—as many tongues, as many sounding mouths, as many pricked-up ears. By night, midway between heaven and earth, she flies through the gloom, screeching, nor droops her eyes in sweet sleep; by day she sits on guard on high roof-top or lofty turrets, and affrights great cities, clinging to the false and wrong, yet heralding truth.[46]

---

love but glory, by which they wished even after death to live in the mouths of those who praised them?" Cf. Bersuire, *Opera*, IV, 185 (n. 17, above).

[45] This distinction, traceable to Augustine (*De doctrina Christiana*, I, 2; II, 1, 24), is discussed by John of Salisbury, *Policraticus*, VII, 12. Cf. Robertson, "Some Medieval Literary Terminology," pp. 677-82.

[46] *Aeneid*, IV, 173-88, trans. H. R. Fairclough, Loeb Classical Library (Cambridge, Massachusetts, 1950).

Following earlier commentators in extolling Virgil as a philosopher whose fiction veils significant truths about fame, Boccaccio begins his explication with a physico-moral interpretation of Fame's origin.[47] The gods, whose anger provokes Earth to bring forth Fame, are the planets to which God has given certain powers to influence men. Although the most benevolent of these planets seem never to act without reason, others (from the viewpoint of mortals) sometimes appear to be angry when they cast down illustrious people whose names men judge worthy of perpetuating. Earth (that is to say, man himself, who springs from the earth) is irritated by the gods and produces Fame because fame is the avenger of death. Thus when men of merit are slain, Fame is always standing by to protect their names from oblivion.

From Fame's origin Boccaccio turns to her more particular attributes. Virgil calls her evil because the honors and dignities that extol men's names are often obtained not by just means but by fraud and violence. But Virgil, Boccaccio interpolates at this point, has here called "fame" what is properly called "infamy"; for when fame is based upon virtue it cannot justly be called evil.[48] With this qualification he proceeds to the details of Fame's appearance. Virgil says that she is small at first through fear because no matter how great are the deeds from which fame springs it seems always to begin with the fear of the listener; for if a rumor is pleasing, he fears it may be false; or if it is

---

[47] *Genealogie deorum gentilium libri*, ed. V. Romano (Bari, 1951), I, 10.

[48] "For if fame (rumor) is set in motion by virtue, then it is not rightfully called evil. Surely, in this instance, the author has improperly used the word 'fame' for 'infamy' [*infamia*], since if we examine the fiction, or rather the reason for the fiction, we observe well enough that infamy, not fame, follows from it" (*ibid.*). Citing the same passage from the *Aeneid*, Isidore distinguishes between the good and bad significations of *fama*: "For fame [*fama*] sometimes pertains to happy things, as in *inlustris fama*, which is praise [*laus*], and sometimes to evil things, as in Virgil: *Fama, malum qua non aliud velocius ullum*" (*Etymologiae*, v, 27, *PL*, 82, col. 213).

displeasing, he fears it may be true. But Fame soon exalts herself to the skies, that is, in the amplification of speech, and after mixing with the lowly she hides her head in the clouds by spreading to kings and other great men. Once started, as Virgil says, nothing is swifter than Fame. Therefore she is said to have many feathers and to be huge and awful like a monster, because rumor, once it begins, can seldom be mastered. She also has many eyes and ears, for without constant vigilance rumor would disappear into nothing. Thus Fame is said to fly even by night, gathering news and carrying it to the most remote places. During the day she sits on guard on turrets and roof-tops, reporting everything she hears as truth, since she does not distinguish between truth and falsehood. For this reason, concludes Boccaccio, Ovid places Fame's dwelling on a high mountaintop at the mid-point of the world where, both day and night, thousands of rumors gather, falsehoods mingle with truth, while Fame herself beholds all things below and searches the world for tidings:

There is a place in the middle of the world, 'twixt land and sea and sky, the meeting-point of the threefold universe. From this place, whatever is, however far away, is seen, and every word penetrates to these hollow ears. Rumour [Fama] dwells here, having chosen her house upon a high mountain-top; and she gave the house countless entrances, a thousand apertures, but with no doors to close them. Night and day the house stands open. It is built all of echoing brass. The whole place is full of noises, repeats all words and doubles what it hears. There is no quiet, no silence anywhere within. And yet there is no loud clamour, but only the subdued murmur of voices, like the murmur of the waves of the sea if you listen afar off, or like the last rumblings of thunder when Jove has made the dark clouds crash together. Crowds fill the hall, shifting throngs come and go, and everywhere wander thousands of rumours, falsehoods mingled with the truth, and confused reports flit about. Some of these fill their idle ears with talk, and others go and tell elsewhere what they have heard; while the story grows in size, and each new teller makes contribution to what he has heard. Here is Credulity, here is heedless Error, unfounded Joy and panic Fear; here sudden Sedition and unauthentic Whisperings. Rumour herself beholds all that is done in heaven, on sea and land, and searches throughout the world for news.[49]

As Boccaccio's moralization makes clear, Virgil's portrayal of Fame is limited to those temporal aspects of fame or rumor which are common to pagan and Christian thought. The same is true of Ovid's description of her abode, which is no more than an elaborate personification of the confusion of rumor and its amplification in speech. Only in one instance—when Virgil calls Fame evil—does Boccaccio betray the concern of the medieval exegete to correct pagan observations in the light of Christian belief; for as Augustine and Boethius affirm, fame, as part of God's temporal order, is not in itself evil: the evil stems from those who acquire or dispense fame falsely or exalt it as an object of idolatry.[50] Ultimately, this more complex Christian attitude toward fame helps to explain the transformation of the pagan Fama in medieval poetry. Whereas the commentators on Virgil and Ovid normally restrict her significance to the limits of verbal allegory, the poets find her a convenient symbol for depicting the nature of fame since the Fall. As one of the gifts bestowed by God upon man while he is making his earthly pilgrimage, she becomes indicative of those temporalia which, if sought for their own sake, can divert one from the path of salvation. Her deification, therefore, typifies the importance of worldly renown as an object of idolatrous worship.[51] At the

---

[49] *Metamorphoses*, XII, 39-63, trans. F. J. Miller, Loeb Classical Library (Cambridge, Massachusetts, 1951).

[50] *De civitate Dei*, XII, 8. Cf. *De consolatione philosophiae*, IV, Pr. 6; Pr. 7.

[51] As Sypherd notes (*Studies*, p. 105), the pagan Fama was not a goddess to be worshiped but, as Virgil calls her, a *dea foeda*. The Christian attitude transforming Fama into a symbol of idolatrous re-

same time, her particular attributes, such as her shifting size, swiftness, and mixture of truth and falsehood, portray the fickle and erroneous judgments proceeding from the sinful hearts of men. In assuming these broader ramifications of the Christian concept of fame, the goddess acquires traits clearly distinguishing her from Virgil's "dea foeda." Although the *House of Fame* is the most elaborate attempt to exploit the potentialities of Fame as a Christian symbol, her metamorphosis from a mere personification of rumor into a symbol of idolatrous renown may be illustrated by two earlier poems: Boccaccio's *Amorosa Visione* and Petrarch's *Trionfi*.

In the *Amorosa Visione* the Christian norm is supplied by patent Scriptural imagery and echoes of Boethius and Dante. A dream-vision, the poem begins with the dreamer, in the role of the distraught lover, falling asleep and dreaming that he is abandoned on a desolate shore. A beautiful lady, reminiscent of Lady Philosophy, appears and offers to lead him to the highest bliss ("somma felicità"). Vowing to forsake vain delights, he accompanies his guide and arrives at the foot of a beautiful castle with two gates. One, on the left, is straight and narrow and leads to a steep stair; the other, on the right, is wide and leads into a luxurious garden. The left gate, suggesting the Scriptural narrow gate, requires that all earthly joys be abandoned before entry. Over the other gate, inscribed in gold, is an invitation to wealth, dignities, and fame— indeed, all the world has to offer.[52] Against this Christian background Boccaccio projects his brief but artistically con-

---

nown is evident in Augustine's contrast between the goddess Felicity, to whom the Romans dedicated a temple, and heavenly felicity, which "is not a goddess but a gift of God" (*De civitate Dei*, v, 16). In iv, 18-25, Augustine applies the same contrast to Fortune and other Roman divinities.

[52] *Amorosa visione*, ed. Vittore Branca (Florence, 1944), I, 28-33; II, 64-69; III, 16-21.

ceived allegory of fame. Tempted by the beauty of the wide gate and dismissing his guide's warning of the difficulty of turning back, the dreamer enters the garden to his right and eventually finds himself in a spacious room where Fame (here called Glory)—along with Learning, Riches, and Love—is portrayed on the walls with scenes of her triumphs. Nothing formed by Nature, he concludes, could be so beautiful as Fame, who sits in majesty on her throne and is adorned imperially with a crown of gold and precious stones. Powerful and magnanimous in mien, she reigns boldly from her ornate chariot of gold, brandishing a sword with which she seems to threaten death and oblivion. In her other hand she holds a golden orb, a symbol of her authority over the world. Identified by a verse written above her—"Io son la Gloria del popol mondano"—she is borne in her chariot by two spirited horses among the countless throngs who follow her.[53]

Like Boccaccio's Glory, Petrarch's Fame is only one of a series of allegorical personages whose triumphs dramatize man's spiritual life on earth. In progressive order Cupid triumphs over the world, Chastity over Cupid, Death over Chastity, Fame over Death, Time over Fame— all caught up at length in a final triumph of Eternity that culminates in a beatific vision of heavenly fame. This Dantesque vision, in retrospect, brings into perspective the Christian conflict underlying not only the allegory of Fame but the whole of the *Trionfi*.

The triumph of Fame begins as the dreamer, after viewing Death's victory over Chastity, sees the triumphant approach of one who draws men from their graves and keeps them alive.[54] This is Fame, a "bella donna" who advances like a star from the East. Accompanying her are all the famous people whose names she has rescued from oblivion.

---

[53] *Ibid.*, VI, 43 ff.
[54] *Trionfi*, ed. C. Calcaterra (Turin, 1927), "Trionfo della Fama," 10-18.

In a place of honor at her right are Julius Caesar and Scipio, who are followed by others who exalted the glory of Rome. Behind the Romans are the famous rulers and warriors of other nations, among them the Trojans' Aeneas and Hector and the Greeks' Achilles ("che di fama ebbe gran fregi") and Alexander the Great, the most renowned of all seekers of fame. Scores of others adorn Fame's triumph, not only kings and warriors but also those renowned for their wisdom. In a place of honor at her left is Plato, who is followed by Aristotle, Pythagoras, Socrates, and Plotinus, as well as by many poets, historians, and orators, all equally famous for their wisdom: Homer, Virgil, Cicero, Livy, Demosthenes—to mention only a few.

Although Fame's triumph concludes with this extended catalogue, the drama of fame is not over. Whereas Fame triumphs over Death in rescuing men from oblivion, Fame herself is conquered by Time, who stops angrily to vow revenge for her unjust usurpation.[55] As Time resumes his swift course, the dreamer for the first time perceives the vanity of putting his trust in anything so ephemeral as fame. All human glory, he concludes, is but snow to the sun before Time, who destroys great names, kingdoms, and every mortal thing in his rapacious flight. But the unthinking masses, accustomed to error, still blindly strive for fame, clinging to the false opinions of their neighbors. Little are they aware that Fame, who conquers Death, is herself in reality but a second death.[56] Asking his heart where he should place his trust, and hearing the reply "In God," he sees before him a new world in which past, present, and future are gathered into one divine center ("punto"), one sovereign good, where yesterday, today, and tomorrow all pass like a shadow before the light of

---

[55] "Trionfo del Tempo," 7ff.

[56] *Ibid.*, 142-45. On fame as a "second death," see *De consolatione philosophiae*, II, Met. 7, and n. 37, above.

Eternity. Thus man's earthly triumphs—culminating in Time's triumph over Fame—all yield, when God permits, to the final triumph of Eternity when those who merited clear renown on earth but whose names were extinguished by Time will achieve a living name in the memory of God. In this new world no mortal secret will be hidden; each conscience will be opened and bared by him who reads all men's hearts. Then those who deserved fame will receive it forever, clothed in the immortal beauty of heavenly fame.[57]

Although Boccaccio's Glory and Petrarch's Fame betray little, if any, indebtedness to Virgil's malicious and unprepossessing goddess, this fact alone is indicative of the new value she has acquired in the Middle Ages. Richly adorned and triumphantly parading their countless worshipers, both display the specious attractiveness leading men to the pursuit of worldly renown. Both, moreover, are projected against a more inclusive background of heavenly love and fame which leaves no doubt as to the vanity of such a pursuit.[58] But these two poets dramatize only one aspect of fame explored by Chaucer in the *House of Fame*. For fame implies not only renown or oblivion but also infamy. Furthermore, it may signify both the end

[57] "Trionfo dell' Eternità," 19ff. For the Scriptural basis of these ideas, see, for example, Ecclus. 44:9; I Cor. 4:1-5.

[58] On the iconographic tradition deriving from Petrarch's Triumph of Fame, see Raimond van Marle, *Iconographie de l'art profane au moyen âge et à la renaissance* (The Hague, 1931-1932), II, 111ff. Because of the widely held view—largely traceable to Burckhardt—that Petrarch and Boccaccio, like Dante, were precursors of the Renaissance revival of the pagan love of personal glory, the Christian attitude of these writers should be emphasized. Although each at times may appear to extol human praise as an end in itself, this praise is clearly one rooted in virtue and, as Augustine affirms of similar passages in Scripture, one redounding to the praise of God (see n. 11, above). For a discussion of the Christian–Augustinian basis of Petrarch's treatment of fame in the *Trionfi*, *Secretum*, and *Africa*, see Aldo S. Bernardo, *Petrarch, Scipio, and the "Africa"* (Baltimore, 1962), especially pp. 64ff. For the same implications of Boccaccio's attitude toward personal fame, see his own statements in *Genealogia deorum*, XV, 13-14.

product of human judgment and the process of rumor indicative of the confusion of human judgment since the Fall. In portraying these more inclusive meanings of the Christian doctrine of fame, Chaucer's goddess retains most of the attributes of Virgil's personification: her swiftness, her shifting size, and her many eyes, ears, and tongues. At the same time, she has acquired other attributes which define more precisely her function as a Christian symbol. Indeed, behind Chaucer's composite portrait of Fame lie several centuries of poetic development of the closely related symbols of Love and Fortune.[59]

Especially associated with Fame is the goddess Fortune, a relationship made clear by Boethius, who includes fame, along with honors and riches, among the gifts bestowed by Fortune. To the medieval poet, just as to Boethius, Fortune is an inclusive symbol (or poetic fiction, as Boccaccio calls her) for the divine disposition of temporalia, as in the *Divine Comedy*, where Dante describes her as God's "ministra e duce" whose seemingly willful actions transcend human understanding.[60] Although Fame and Fortune are always closely linked, Fame's lack of development in earlier literature is sufficiently explained by Fortune's traditional role of distributing temporal prosperity and adversity. Thus like the goddess Love she is sometimes portrayed in her court like a queen, surrounded by attendants and dispensing her awards, including fame and infamy, to her numerous subjects and suppliants.[61] Her

---

[59] On the related and sometimes interchangeable functions of Fortune and Venus and their influence on Chaucer's portrayal of Fame, see Sypherd, *Studies*, pp. 16-17, 112ff.; H. R. Patch, *The Goddess Fortuna* (Cambridge, Massachusetts, 1927), pp. 90, 96, 111ff., 144-45; Paul G. Ruggiers, "The Unity of Chaucer's *House of Fame*," SP, L (1953), 16ff.

[60] *Inf.*, VII, 67-96.

[61] Patch, *The Goddess Fortuna*, p. 60. On Fortune's role as distributor of fame and infamy, see also pp. 63, 89, 111ff., 144-45. Perhaps on the authority of Boethius, who connects "voluptuous delyt" with her gifts, Fortune sometimes assumes a similar control over the fortunes of lov-

idolatrous nature is expressed not only by her deification and haughty display of authority but also by the specious beauty of her sumptuous house or palace. As evidence of her instability, however, one side of her house may be rich and beautiful and the other ugly and squalid. But the fickleness and transitoriness of Fortune's gifts are portrayed above all by her frequently turning wheel, by her personal attributes—her shifting moods and judgments, her two faces (one fair, one foul), her blindfolded eyes, her many eyes, her winged feet—and by the precarious foundation of her abode—a high mountain whose top is buffeted by violent winds and storms and whose steep sides (one luxuriantly beautiful, the other desolate) are slippery and inaccessible or, as in the *Panthère d'Amours*, made of an ephemeral substance such as ice.[62] In addition to these generic attributes, Fortune displays other features appropriate to her particular gifts. Indicative of her power over worldly goods, she is assigned such attendants as Wealth and Honors or the two trumpeters Eur and Maleur, who guard the entrance of her house and publish her decrees of prosperity and adversity.[63] To designate her special authority over fame, Gower gives her two female servants, Renomee and Desfame, who, reminiscent of Virgil's Fama, fly more swiftly than the swallow and carry tidings of her court. For this purpose, like Eur and Maleur, each wears suspended from her neck a large trumpet, one of renown, the other of misery and slander; but in keeping with Fortune's willfulness, these trumpets are often interchanged.[64] Lydgate, undoubtedly under

---

ers, a function normally assigned to Venus and Cupid. Sypherd traces Chaucer's concept of Fame as a divinity on a throne, deciding the fates of her suppliants, to the literary portrayals of Love (*Studies*, pp. 128ff.).

[62] Nicole de Margival, *La Panthère d'Amours*, ed. H. A. Todd (Paris, 1883), 1,958ff. Cf. Sypherd, pp. 114ff., and Patch, pp. 133-34.

[63] Patch, pp. 40-42, 60.

[64] *Mirour de l'Omme*, 22,129ff., ed. G. C. Macaulay, *The Complete Works of John Gower* (Oxford, 1899-1902), Vol. I.

Chaucer's influence, assigns to Fortune not only two trumpets—a golden one of praise and a black one of slander—but also a "hous" called the "Hous of Fame":

Settest up oon in roiall excellence
Withynne myne hous callid the Hous of Fame,—
The goldene trumpet with blastis off good name
Enhaunceth oon to ful hih(e) parties,
Wher Iubiter sit among the heuenli skies.

Anothir trumpet, of sownis ful vengable,
Which bloweth up at feestis funerall,
Nothyng briht(e), but of colour sable,
Fer fro my favour, dedli & mortall,
To plonge pryncis from ther estat roiall,
Whan I am wroth, to make hem loute lowe.
Than of malis I do that trumpet blowe.[65]

Although Fortune in Gower and Lydgate maintains her traditional authority over earthly fame, there is little to distinguish her from Chaucer's fickle goddess. As numerous medieval allegories attest, it is only a slight step from the deification of Fortune to a deification of her gifts—Fame, Honors, and Riches—who take on the generic attributes of Fortune as well as the particular qualities of the gifts themselves.[66] In the *House of Fame* the influence of Fortune appears both in the details of Fame's abode—her airy "hous" or castle, her "feble" mountain of ice, the contrasting permanence and impermanence of the names of "famous folk" on the north and south sides—and in the portrayal of the goddess herself: her sumptuous court; her regal authority; her rich array; her many attendants, worshipers, and suppliants; her fickle decrees; and her trumpets of praise and slander. In combining the

---

[65] *The Fall of Princes*, VI, 108-119.

[66] Patch, pp. 36-37. The specialization of Fortune's and Fame's functions is observable in such personifications as Vaine Gloire, the bastard daughter of Fortune in the *Roman de Fauvel*, Wicked Tongue, Backbiter, and the many other illustrations of the abuses of the tongue which appear in medieval art and literature.

attributes of "her suster, dame Fortune" with those of Virgil's and Ovid's goddess, Fame comes into her own for the first time in medieval literature as a comprehensive symbol of earthly fame. But Chaucer's distinctiveness lies not only in exploiting Fame's potentialities as a Christian symbol but also in making her the focal symbol in a complex allegorical structure designed to explore the fullest doctrinal implications of the contrast between earthly and heavenly fame. This contrast is introduced in Book I, where Fame is projected against a more inclusive allegory centering on Venus, who, like Fortune and Fame, has undergone a process of moralization relating her to the Christian concept of two kinds of love. Together, Fame and Venus are the gathering points for the doctrinal meanings underlying the rich and varied symbolism of the *House of Fame*. In order to gain a clearer perspective of their relationship to one another and to the allegory as a whole, we must examine those features of Chaucer's allegorical structure and poetic method which have conditioned their roles as Christian symbols.

CHAPTER II

THE PROPHETIC TRADITION

1. The Dream Symbolism

THE particular genre of allegory to which the *House of Fame* belongs, the prophetic dream or "avisioun," is defined indirectly in the Proem. On a note of irony foreshadowing his role as the dreamer, Chaucer professes his ignorance of such a learned subject as dreams—

> God turne us every drem to goode!
> For hyt is wonder, be the roode,
> To my wyt, what causeth swevenes
> Eyther on morwes or on evenes;
> And why th'effect folweth of somme,
> And of somme hit shal never come;
> Why that is an avisioun
> And this a revelacioun,
> Why this a drem, why that a sweven,
> And noght to every man lyche even;
> Why this a fantome, why these oracles,
> I not. . . .[1]

Having proclaimed his "ignorance," however, Chaucer at once embarks upon an enumeration of the kinds and causes of dreams which would do justice to the "grete clerkys" to whom he refers us for authority. The relevance of this ironic exposition to the poem as a whole is suggested at the end of the Proem, where Chaucer's opening appeal to God to turn "every drem to goode" is directed to his own dream. But the fullest implications must be sought in the traditional attitudes toward dreams expressed by the "grete clerkys" and implied in Chaucer's discussion. Once these attitudes are understood, we become aware that

[1] All quotations from Chaucer are based on Robinson's second edition (cited above), hereafter referred to as *Works*.

46

Chaucer, beneath his ironic pose, has not only defined the allegorical nature of his dream but also suggested a significant aspect of his theme.

In using a discussion of dreams to establish the allegorical content of his own dream, Chaucer follows the example of the *Roman de la Rose* and ultimately of Macrobius, who at the beginning of the *Commentary on the Dream of Scipio* includes a classification of dreams in order to define the prophetic nature of Scipio's dream.[2] But Chaucer's classification also echoes other "grete clerkys," who follow Scriptural authority in affirming that some dreams are inspired by God and contain a spiritual meaning which must be discovered beneath a veil of symbols. Since this meaning is divinely inspired, only those individuals whose minds are in harmony with God will have the ability to interpret the symbols through which this wisdom is conveyed. Conversely, the intellectual deficiency causing one to misconstrue such dreams may also cause him to attribute spiritual significance to dreams unworthy of interpretation.[3] This distinction between

[2] *Commentary*, I, 3. For a translation of the *Commentary* and the relevant portion of Cicero's *De re publica*, see W. H. Stahl, *Macrobius: Commentary on the Dream of Scipio* (New York, 1952). In the opening lines of the *Roman*, Macrobius is the authority for the statement that dreams are not all trifles but often signify the good or evil that will come to men. On Guillaume's use of a discussion of dreams to establish the allegorical content of his poem, see Charles Dahlberg, "Macrobius and the Unity of the *Roman de la Rose*," *SP*, LVIII (1961), 573ff.

[3] The distinction between true and false dreams is recurrent in Scripture, for example, Ecclus. 34:6-7: "Except it be a vision sent forth from the Most High, set not thy heart upon them. For dreams [*somnia*] have deceived many, and they have failed that put their trust in them." The Scriptural distinction underlies the classifications of dreams by the Biblical commentators, for example, Augustine in *De genesi ad literam*, Gregory in *Moralia in Job*, and by other "grete clerkys," for example, John of Salisbury (*Policraticus*, II, 15), Vincent of Beauvais (*Speculum naturale*, XXVI, 32ff.), Bartholomeus Anglicus (*De proprietatibus rerum*, VI, 24-27), and Robert Holkot (*Liber sapientiae*, Lectio CCII). The standard discussion of Chaucer's use of traditional dream material is in W. C. Curry's *Chaucer and the Mediaeval Sciences*, rev.

dreams of a higher and a lower nature is reflected in the order of Chaucer's catalogue, which follows a traditional classification of dreams according to their origin from inward states of the body or mind or from spiritual forces outside. Dreams originating from inner causes are without prophetic significance and consequently are unworthy of interpretation.[4] The cause may be physical,

> As yf folkys complexions
> Make hem dreme of reflexions. . .

or it may be mental or spiritual, as when

> som man is to curious
> In studye, or melancolyous,
> Or thus, so inly ful of drede,
> That no man may hym bote bede. (29-32)

Dreams resulting from spiritual disharmony occur when the mind, forgetful of God, subjects itself to things of the world or the flesh, or is otherwise guilty of spiritual sloth.[5] The effect of all such disharmony is fear ("drede"), especially when the cause is one's devotion to the unstable gifts

---

ed. (New York, 1960). The application of classical and medieval dream theory to the literary vision has been investigated by Francis X. Newman, "*Somnium*: Medieval Theories of Dreaming and the Form of Vision Poetry" (Princeton dissertation, 1962).

[4] In this category, Macrobius includes the nightmare [*insomnium*] which results from physical or mental distress, such as overindulgence in food and drink or anxiety about the future, and the hallucination [*visum* or *phantasma*] in which the dreamer sees spectres of various sorts. Similar statements appear in John of Salisbury (*Policraticus*, II, 15), who follows the classification of Macrobius; in Honorius of Autun (*De philosophia mundi*, PL, 172, col. 94); and in Bersuire (*Opera*, IV, 77). Curry (pp. 220ff.) identifies the nonprophetic dream as a *somnium naturale*.

[5] In his threefold classification of dreams, Alanus de Insulis, citing Eph. 5:14 ("Rise, thou that sleepest"), identifies his third category with sloth [*pigritia*], through which the dullminded [*stulta*] dream (*PL*, 210, cols. 125-26). Bersuire quotes Scriptural authority for dreams originating from all of the deadly sins (*Opera*, II, 77; VI, 112-13).

48

of Fortune or the equally transitory pleasures of bodily love,[6]

> the cruel lyf unsofte
> Which these ilke lovers leden
> That hopen over-muche or dreden,
> That purely her impressions
> Causen hem to have visions. (36-40)

Not without purpose, Chaucer turns from the inner causes of dreams to those outer forces or "spirites" which "make folk dreme a-nyght." These spirits, the "grete clerkys" agree, may be either good or evil. Thus Augustine warns of the mysterious ways in which evil spirits infesting the air may confuse the minds of sleepers with false visions.[7] Sometimes these outer influences combine with inner causes to produce dreams; for when the mind is disturbed by fear of Fortune or is otherwise oppressed, it becomes easy prey to the illusions or "fantomes" of demons.[8] On the other hand, if the mind is in harmony with God, the spirit is sometimes released from its bodily burden and in dreams, ecstasies, or visions is instructed in truths pertaining to the present or future or one's own moral state. These divinely revealed truths, the "grete clerkys" affirm, appear in two main guises: either directly to the spirit or beneath a veil of "figures" or "enigmas"

---

[6] Macrobius groups erotic dreams, in which the lover dreams of possessing or losing his sweetheart, and dreams of fortune, such as the gain or loss of high position, under the *insomnium*. In *Policraticus*, II, 15, John of Salisbury, following Macrobius, illustrates this type with Dido's dreams of Aeneas [*Aen.*, IV, 9ff.]. The erotic dream appears in medieval love poetry, for example, *Troilus and Criseyde*, V, 246ff. Cf. Robertson, *Preface*, pp. 97-98, 499.

[7] *De civitate Dei*, IX, 18. Cf. *De spiritu et anima*, PL, 40, col. 798; Gregory, *Moralia*, PL, 75, col. 825; John of Salisbury, *Policraticus*, II, 17; Bersuire, *Opera*, VI, 112-13; Prudentius, *Liber Cathemerinon*, VI, 25; and *Roman de la Rose*, 18,499ff., which Chaucer perhaps echoes.

[8] At the end of Book I, this meaning of "fantome" (l. 11) appears in Chaucer's appeal to Christ to protect him from "fantome and illusion" (492-94). Cf. Vincent of Beauvais, *Speculum naturale*, XXVI, 56, and Curry, pp. 209, 214.

49

requiring interpretation. Both find Scriptural authority in the Book of Numbers:

Hear my words: if there be among you a prophet of the Lord, I will appear to him in a vision (*in visione*), or I will speak to him in a dream (*per somnium*). But it is not so with my servant Moses who is most faithful in all my house. For I speak to him mouth to mouth, and plainly; and not by riddles (*aenigmata*) and figures (*figuras*) doth he see the Lord.[9]

Clothed in the obscurity of figures or enigmas were the prophetic dreams and visions of many Scriptural personages, including Daniel, Isaiah, Ezechiel, and, in the New Testament, John the Evangelist, who, says Boccaccio, concealed the deepest mysteries of God in enigmas that at first glance often seem "contrary to the truth."[10] Typically veiled are those dreams sent by God at night when the mind is at rest. Among these were the dreams of Pharaoh,

[9] Num. 12:6-8. Bersuire echoes the Scriptural distinction: "And these [dreams] are sometimes unadorned and plain [*nuda et plana*] and sometimes in figures and riddles [*figuris et aenigmatibus*], as is evident in the many dreams and visions of the prophets, and even in the dream of Scipio" (*Opera*, II, 77). Commenting on I Cor. 13:12, Augustine defines *aenigma* as *obscura allegoria*, implying an allegory in which the *cortex* not only veils the deeper meaning but is itself obscure (*De trinitate*, XV, 9). Cf. Peter Lombard, *PL*, 191, col. 1,662. The enigmatic dream corresponds to Macrobius's *somnium*, which veils the truth in unusual forms and requires an interpretation. The *visio* reveals truths about the future (for example, Scipio's vision of the afterlife), either with or without a veil. The *oraculum* (Chaucer's "oracle," l. 11) is a dream in which a human or divine agent reveals future happenings or what actions one should take or avoid. These three categories are designated as "prophetic," since they all convey divinely inspired truths. Chaucer's "revelacioun" (l. 8) perhaps corresponds to the dream which reveals truth directly to the spirit. His terms "figures" and "avisions" (I. 48) suggest the Scriptural distinction (for example, Num. 12:6-8) between "figurative" and "enigmatic" dreams. In ll. 7, 48, 104, and 513, Chaucer's "avisioun" clearly implies the enigmatic dream. In the *Book of the Duchess*, 284ff., "sweven" is used in this sense, although the term is applied to dreams of various types in Middle English writings. Curry (p. 207) observes that divinely inspired dreams are sometimes designated as *somnia coeleste, divina*, or *doctrina*.

[10] *Genealogia deorum*, XIV, 13. John of Salisbury applies Macrobius's terminology to the Biblical dreams and visions (*Policraticus*, II, 16).

Jacob, Daniel, and Joseph, the latter two being gifted with the power of interpretation.[11] In this category belong the dreams in which God warns men of their sins and directs them to the path of virtue. Such was the dream of Nabuchodonosor, who was warned beneath an enigmatic veil to desist from his pride.[12] Authority for these dreams is also found in the Book of Job:

By a dream in a vision by night, when deep sleep falleth upon men, and they are sleeping in their beds, then he [God] openeth the ears of men, and teaching instructeth them in what they are to learn, that he may withdraw a man from the things he is doing, and may deliver him from pride, rescuing his soul from corruption, and his life from passing to the sword. (33:15-18)

Night, in this instance, comments Gregory in the *Moralia*, signifies the ignorance and concupiscence of the present life. God sends dreams at night because the spirit during sleep is less subject to fleshly and worldly desires and is more easily led to the contemplation of divine truth.[13] These Scriptural connotations of night and sleep are implicit in the opening of many a medieval literary vision.[14] Not inappropriately, therefore, does Chaucer conclude his catalogue with a definition of the prophetic dream or

---

[11] Gen. 28:10-15 (Jacob); Gen. 37:5ff. (Joseph); Gen. 41:1-36 (Pharaoh); Dan. 1:17; 2:19; 7:1-28 (Daniel). Cf. Gen. 40:5-23. On dreams and visions at night, cf. Gen. 20:3 (Abimelech); Gen. 31:24 (Laban); Job 4:13; Matt. 1:20; 2:13; 19 (Joseph); 2:12 (the Magi); Acts 16:9 (St. Paul).

[12] Dan. 4:1-34. Cf. 2:1ff. On the portrayal of Biblical dreams and visions in medieval ecclesiastical art, see Emile Mâle, *Religious Art in France of the Thirteenth Century*, trans. Dora Nussey (New York, 1958), pp. 148, 156.

[13] *PL*, 76, cols. 273ff. In the *Dialogues* (*PL*, 77, cols. 409-12), Gregory classifies the Biblical dreams and visions. On sleep [*dormitio*] as a symbol of contemplation, see *Allegoriae in sacram scripturam*, col. 913.

[14] For their application to Chaucer's dream in the *Book of the Duchess*, see Huppé and Robertson, *Fruyt and Chaf*, pp. 34, 42-43, where they are related to other Scriptural images denoting dreams of contemplation.

"avisioun." In the ironic vein of the rest of the Proem, he leaves it to the "grete clerkys" to decide

> yf the soule, of propre kynde,
> Be so parfit, as men fynde,
> That yt forwot that ys to come,
> And that hyt warneth alle and some
> Of everych of her aventures
> Be avisions, or be figures,
> But that oure flessh ne hath no myght
> To understonde hyt aryght,
> For hyt is warned to derkly. (43-51)

Three basic features of the "avisioun" are noted here. First, it is prophetic ("yt forwot that ys to come"). Secondly, its meaning is embodied in figures that must be interpreted. Finally, the interpretation of these figures is a matter of the spirit or intellect, not of the flesh ("oure flessh ne hath no myght"). Or to follow once more the "grete clerkys," if the intellect is in harmony with God, it will have sufficient understanding to perceive the divine wisdom concealed in the figures. If it has subjected itself to the world or the flesh, and consequently to the illusions of Satan, it may not only attribute spiritual meaning to dreams unworthy of such interpretation but also misconstrue dreams of spiritual content.

Although the "grete clerkys"—John of Salisbury and Pierre Bersuire, for example—include the literary vision, such as Scipio's dream, in the prophetic genre, it is the Scriptural vision to which Boccaccio directly appeals in affirming that poetry and Scripture often agree in their aims and modes of composition.[15] For when actual events

[15] *Genealogia deorum*, XIV, 9, 12, 13. John of Salisbury groups Scipio's dream with the prophetic visions of John, Daniel, and Ezechiel (*Policraticus*, II, 16). Cf. Bersuire, *Opera*, II, 77 (n. 9, above). In the *Epistle to Richard II*, Philippe de Mézière refers to Scipio's dream, along with the dreams of Joseph, Nabuchodonosor, and the Magi, as authority for concealing his meaning beneath an obscure veil (British Museum, MS. Royal 20 B. VI, fol. 3). In Book II, Proem, and the

are not described, neither is concerned with the literal or "superficial" meaning but with what the poet calls "fable" or "fiction" and the theologian calls "figure." According to the degree of similitude on the surface to real events, Boccaccio distinguishes three main categories of poems: those which lack any surface appearance of truth, such as the fables of Aesop; those which seem closer to history than to fiction, as illustrated by Homer's account of Ulysses and the Sirens or Virgil's description of Aeneas tossed by the storm; and those, exemplified by some of Ovid's myths, which at times mingle fiction with truth on the surface and "clothe divine and human matters alike" in fictive personages and events. Although each of these categories has parallels in Scriptural allegory, it is the third category, including the prophetic vision, in which Scripture and poetry "seem as it were to keep step with each other, and that too in respect to the method of their composition."[16] Just as John in the Apocalypse veils the

---

Nun's Priest's Tale, 3,122ff., Chaucer links the "avisiouns" of Scipio and other pagans with those of Isaiah, Daniel, Joseph, Pharaoh, and Nabuchodonosor.

[16] *Genealogia deorum*, XIV, 9. In this category, Boccaccio includes "nearly the whole sacred body of the Old Testament," mentioning specifically the prophetic visions of Isaiah, Ezechiel, Daniel, and John. Cf. XIV, 12, 13. The first category, which Isidore calls *fabula ad mores* (*Etymologiae*, I, 12, 28), is illustrated by the Biblical account of the trees of the forest choosing a king (Judg. 9:8-15). The second category has its Scriptural counterpart in the *exemplum*, or parable, for example, Christ's parables. A fourth category—the "old wives' tales"—is dismissed as unworthy of perusal since it contains no truth at all, either superficial or hidden. Boccaccio's classification, Osgood notes (p. 164), appears to be based on Macrobius (*Commentary*, I, 2), who also dismisses those tales appealing only to the ear. The others he puts into two categories. The first, like Boccaccio's, corresponds to Aesop's fables, in which both setting and plot are fictitious. The second, the *narratio fabulosa*, teaches important truths beneath a fiction. This group is subdivided into two types: either the plot treats matters of a base nature or it presents, under a veil of allegory, more dignified characters and events that reveal holy truths. In this latter category belongs the prophetic vision, such as the dream of Scipio and Plato's vision of Er.

deepest heavenly mysteries in enigmas that sometimes seem contrary to the truth, so the poet often composes visions so obscure that the mind can hardly extract their meaning. But if the prophetic vision is at times more diffi- cult and obscure than other poems, Boccaccio insists, it should not be condemned, for the poet's function is not to expose the hidden truths of his fictions but, whenever mat- ters truly divine are involved, to protect them from the cheapening gaze of the slothful. As Augustine remarks of Scriptural figures, the fictions of poetry are an exercise of the intellect and can be understood if approached by a sound mind.[17]

In these common aims and methods of the Scriptural and poetic visions, we find the artistic propriety of Chau- cer's introductory classification of dreams. It is not for- tuitous, therefore, that he should preface his own dream with a definition of the "avisioun," thereby implying his allegorical intent.[18] His appeal to the Cross to turn "every drem to goode," repeating his opening appeal to God,[19] marks in effect the transference of these meanings to his dream:

[17] *Ibid.*, XIV, 12, 13.

[18] In Book II, Proem, Chaucer explicitly identifies his dream as an "avisyon," associating it with pagan and Scriptural examples. Curry classifies Chaucer's dream as "a pure *somnium coeleste*" (p. 238). Like the dream in the *Roman de la Rose*, it fits Macrobius's definition of the enigmatic dream [*somnium*]. See Dahlberg, pp. 575ff., and n. 9, above. As we later observe in the eagle, who comes from Jupiter and in- structs the dreamer "in mannes vois," Chaucer's "avisioun" also has affinities with the *oraculum*, in which divine truth is revealed by a heavenly or human agent. In the *Parliament of Fowls*, the prophetic nature of the dream is implicit in the role of Africanus and in the pre- liminary summary of Scipio's dream, which foreshadows the allegorical content of the "avisioun." Cf. Huppé and Robertson, *Fruyt and Chaf*, pp. 105ff. In the *Book of the Duchess*, 270ff., Chaucer indicates that his dream is enigmatic and requires interpretation.

[19] As protector against the "fantomes and illusions" of Satan, the Cross is traditionally connected with dreams. In *Liber Cathemerinon*, VI, 125-52, Prudentius warns men to make the sign of the Cross before sleeping if they wish to avoid the "rambling dreams of Satan." Cf. Bersuire, *Opera*, III, 381-82.

For never, sith that I was born,
Ne no man elles me beforn,
Mette, I trowe stedfastly,
So wonderful a drem as I
The tenthe day now of Decembre. (59-63)

In the Invocation that follows, Chaucer further defines his dream in conventional dream imagery, indicating more explicitly that it is an "avisioun" and therefore requires interpretation. His initial "devocion" to Morpheus, the pagan god of dreams, contrasts ironically with the preceding appeal to the Cross. The special force of the irony, however, stems from the meanings which Morpheus and his dreams have acquired in the mythography of the Christian poet. For Morpheus' dreams have little to do with the kind of dream Chaucer is to relate; instead they are "illusions" or "fantasies," dreams of spiritual disharmony besetting the mind in a state of sloth.[20] This meaning is mirrored in his "cave of stoon," an image of the mind devoid of the light of reason.[21] A similar meaning is attributed to the river Lethe, the source of the "strem" on which the cave is located, a symbol of oblivion or the mind's forgetfulness of God.[22] In adding that Lethe

---

[20] In *The Assembly of the Gods* and Nevill's *Castell of Pleasure*, Morpheus appears when the dreamer is in a state of self-admitted sloth. The *Assembly* opens with the dreamer's wondering how he might bring reason and sensuality into accord. Oppressed by sleep, he sees Morpheus, who describes himself as dwelling in a "little corner called Fantasy." On the connection of "phantasies" and Morpheus with worldly solicitude, see Huppé and Robertson, *Fruyt and Chaf*, pp. 40-42, who apply medieval moralizations of Morpheus and his cave (Ovid, *Metamorphoses*, XI, 592ff.) to the story of Ceyx and Alcyone.

[21] Boccaccio, *Genealogia deorum*, I, 31. As a Scriptural image, the cave [*spelunca*] is interpreted tropologically as the mind or conscience [*spelunca conscientiae*], which, says Bersuire, "is clear in the righteous, and stained and darkened in the wicked" (*Opera*, VI, 117). Cf. *Allegoriae in sacram scripturam*, col. 1,051.

[22] Boccaccio, *Genealogia deorum*, I, 17. Cf. *Mythographus Vaticanus Tertius*, in *Scriptores rerum mythicarum Latini tres Romae nuper reperti*, ed. G. H. Bode (Celle, 1834), pp. 190-91 (hereafter cited as *Mythographus Vaticanus III*): "The river Lethe, which is interpreted

is a "flood of helle unswete," Chaucer perhaps reminds us of a connection between Morpheus' dreams and the illusions of Satan, a connotation strengthened by the location of the cave near Cimmeria, the mythical region of darkness where the sun never shines.[23]

The irony of Chaucer's "devocion" to Morpheus is evident in his qualification as to the pagan god's power over his own dream: "If every drem stonde in his myght." But the irony is resolved by his appeal to the Christian God,

> he that mover ys of al
> That is and was and ever shal,

the true author of prophetic dreams.[24] This Apocalyptic echo sets the pattern for the rest of the Invocation.[25] The prayer to God to bring joy to those who hear his poem and "skorne hyt noght"—paralleling John's blessing on those who heed his prophecy—is a reminder that his dream is no illusion of Morpheus but a matter of the intellect and therefore of interpretation. Further suggesting the Apocalypse is the warning to anyone who might "mysdeme" his dream through "presumpcion," "malicious entencion," "envye," "jape," or "vilanye." Just as John promises to

---

as oblivion [*oblivio*], is nothing other than the error of the soul forgetful of the majesty of its prior life, in which state, according to the philosophers, it was located before it was sent forth into the body." See also Macrobius, *Commentary*, I, 10, and *Ovide moralisé*, ed. C. de Boer (Amsterdam, 1915-1938), X, 258-69.

[23] Boccaccio, *Genealogia deorum*, I, 31. During the Middle Ages, Cimmeria was associated with the extreme north, a location identified in Biblical commentary with the dwelling of Satan (cf. chap. V, n. 30, below). In *BD*, 153ff., the darkness of Morpheus' cave is compared to "helle-pit." On this connotation of the cave, see Theodore Spencer, "Chaucer's Hell: A Study in Mediaeval Convention," *Speculum*, II (1927), 180-81. As an image of cupidity, Bersuire interprets *spelunca*, anagogically, as Hell (*Opera*, VI, 17).

[24] Compare Chaucer's similar reservation about Morpheus' power in *BD*, l. 237: "For I ne knew never god but oon."

[25] Cf. Apoc. 4:8. Robinson (*Works*, p. 780) notes reminiscences of Dante, *Par.*, I, 1, and the *Gloria Patri*.

bring down God's punishment with the plagues described
in his vision, so Chaucer prays "Jesus God" to give such
a person every harm that any man has had since the world
began—"dreme he barefot, dreme he shod"—and bring
him to a "conclusion" such as Croesus had from his
"avision" when he "high upon a gebet dyde."[26] The allusion to Croesus' fate is a final reminder that to interpret
a dream of prophetic significance the mind must be in harmony with God. For Croesus, as Chaucer elsewhere tells
us, was one who through pride "mysdemed" a dream
sent by Jupiter and suffered the full penalty.[27]

2. The Symbolic Date

In relation to Chaucer's dream, Croesus' "avision"
takes on more particular interest. For his own dream, we
soon learn, is under the divine auspices of Jupiter, whose
pity and benevolence prompt the eagle's rescue of Chaucer
from the desert of Venus and initiate the quest for tidings
which are the goal of his flight to the House of Fame.
The moralized mythography uniting Jupiter and the
Christian author of dreams becomes apparent in Books I
and II, where Chaucer's experience in the desert, his appeal to Christ for protection, the eagle's timely appearance and explanation of his mission from Jove, the flight
to Fame's mountain and house, and the quest for glad
"love-tydynges" of a "fer contree" form a pattern of
Scriptural imagery which leaves little doubt as to the
Christian implications of the allegory. At the very outset,
however, Chaucer employs a device perhaps designed to
bring these details into a meaningful connection with the
Christian framework of his vision. This device is the date

[26] Cf. Apoc. 1:3; 22:18-20. The admonition is conventional in medieval writings. For another example in dream allegory, see Alanus's
Prologue to the *Anticlaudianus*, PL, 210, cols. 482ff.
[27] "The Monk's Tale," 2,727ff.

assigned to his dream, which took place, he carefully reminds us, on December 10, at night, when he fell asleep

> As he that wery was forgo
> On pilgrymage myles two
> To the corseynt Leonard,
> To make lythe of that was hard. (115-18)

In this conventional dream-vision opening, we may recognize the prototypes in the Old Testament visions where
"night" and "sleep" are indicative of dreams of prophetic
import. The image of the pilgrimage to St. Leonard's
shrine "to make lythe of that was hard," suggesting the
sin-burdened spirit to whom God brings such dreams, reinforces the Scriptural analogy. Although Chaucer obscures
any patent connection between this Christian imagery and
his mysterious date, a connection may be found within the
prophetic tradition, for example in the prophecies of
Ezechiel, in which dates are similarly attached to visions
of prophetic significance and related to important events
in man's spiritual history.[28] A more immediate literary
precedent for Chaucer's date, however, is found in the
prophetic vision whose influence pervades the *House of
Fame*—the *Divine Comedy*, where an idealized Scriptural
date of the events of Easter coincides with Dante's pilgrimage and provides the basis for a symbolic astrological
configuration which mirrors the spiritual meaning of his
journey. But behind Dante's Scriptural-astrological symbolism lies a long tradition in which astrology has been
brought into a close connection with the prophetic vision.
Thus Arnold of Villa Nova, among other Christian
writers, includes the planets, houses, and signs of the
zodiac among those outer influences causing such visions.[29]

[28] For example, Ezech. 1:1-3; 8:1; 20:1; 26:1. Cf. Dan. 10:4;
Zach. 1:1, 7; 7:1. As illustrated below, such dates are sometimes interpreted spiritually and related to the prophetic content of the visions.
[29] *Expositiones visionum quae fiunt in somnia*, in *Opera omnia* (Basel,
1524), I, 4. The passage is quoted and translated by Curry, pp. 211-12.

These visions are called divine, explains Petrus Abanus, because they are brought about by God through the celestial intelligences directing the heavenly bodies and impressing their influences upon the mind in proportion to its aptitude to receive them.[30] As these statements suggest, medieval astrology has been adapted to the Christian concept of a divine order in which the planets in their various configurations are signs or symbols of God's providence— or as Augustine calls them, parables or allegories signifying sacred mysteries pertaining to man's spiritual life.[31] From this viewpoint, the good and evil influences of the planets are to be construed not as causes of good and evil in man but as symbols of his moral state.[32] Before the Fall these influences were expressive of the divine love permeating the whole of creation and reflecting man's spiritual harmony with God.[33] With the Fall, however, this harmony was disrupted and man's relationship with the heavenly bodies assumed new meaning; for the evil un-

[30] Curry, p. 207. Albohazen Haly classifies dreams according to their origin from God, planetary influences, or bodily humors. Dreams of the second class are figurative and of two kinds, true or false, depending on the power, positions, and aspects of the planets at the time of the vision.

[31] *Epistola XV*, *PL*, 33, cols. 210-11. Cf. *De civitate Dei*, v, 1. On symbolic representations of the zodiac and planets in medieval art, see E. W. Tristram, *English Wall Painting of the Fourteenth Century* (London, 1955), p. 6, and Mâle, *Religious Art in France*, pp. 65ff.

[32] The "grete clerkys" insist upon this point, for example, Augustine, *De civitate Dei*, v, 6-7; Neckam, *De naturis rerum*, I, 7: "Although the heavenly bodies bring about certain effects in the world below, they do not impel the free-will to do one thing or another through any necessity." Cf. Dante, *Purg.*, XVI, 55-84. Following Plotinus, Macrobius describes the influences of the planets as symbols or premonitions of good and evil, not their causes (*Commentary*, I, 19). Cf. John of Salisbury, *Policraticus*, II, 19.

[33] In *Convivio* II, 5, 6, 9, Dante describes the planets as having been created to fulfill the end of divine love in the world. This end is achieved by means of divine intelligences (God's ministers or angels) who direct the heavenly bodies and through them impart influences [*effetti*] of love to earthly creatures. Thus God through these influences kindles men's souls to love. In *The Complaint of Mars*, 164ff., Chaucer dramatizes this concept.

59

leashed by Adam's sin now became part of the temporal order and this change was manifested in planetary influences unfelt before the Fall.[34] Thus the benevolence of the Sun and Jupiter is now counteracted by the malevolence of Saturn or Mars. Similarly, the influence of Venus, indicative before the Fall of the bond of natural love directing man's mind to God, now also symbolizes the irrational love turning the mind to physical or worldly delights.[35] These mingled influences also characterize the various signs and houses of the zodiac, whose attributes of good or evil are revealed by means of the planets in their different configurations. In prophetic visions, we are told, these configurations are "figures" by which God impresses truths of doctrine upon the mind. By referring these visions to the particular qualities of the planets and houses whose powers are felt at the time the visions occur, one may interpret the meanings veiled by these figures and be instructed in matters pertaining to the present and future life.[36]

The application of these concepts of medieval astrology to the literary vision is evident in the *Divine Comedy*,

---

[34] As a consequence of "our first parents' transgression," remarks Neckam, "the splendor of all the planets and stars suffered a loss of brightness" (*De naturis rerum*, I, 14). To Adam's sin is also attributed the contrary motions of the planets and the ninth sphere or firmament —the sphere closest to God—a contrast indicative of the contrary motions of the will toward reason or passion: "There are two motions in the soul: one rational [*rationalis*], the other irrational [*irrationalis*]. The rational resembles the motion of the firmament, which goes from east to west; conversely, the irrational resembles the motion of the planets, which move contrary to the firmament" (Arnulf of Orléans, *Allegoriae super Ovidii Metamorphosin*, ed. F. Ghisalberti, in "Arnolfo d'Orléans, un cultore di Ovidio nel secolo XII," *Memorie del R. Istituto Lombardo di scienze e lettere*, XXIV [1932], 181). Cf. Bersuire, *Opera*, II, 110; Lydgate, *Reson and Sensuallyte*, 765ff.

[35] In his Notes on the *Teseida* (ed. A. Roncaglia, Bari, 1941, pp. 413-14, 417), Boccaccio describes the attributes of Venus and Mars which are typical of their planetary influences [*effetti*] since the Fall. According to Bersuire, Saturn's malevolence is indicative of man's fallen nature (*Opera*, II, 111).

[36] Curry, *Chaucer and Mediaeval Sciences*, pp. 207, 212.

where we soon become aware that Dante's vision is attached to a symbolic astrological configuration which points to the spiritual meanings of his pilgrimage. Although Dante does not include an explicit date with his vision, its approximation to an ideal date of the events of Easter is apparent in the basic features of his configuration—the sun's position in Aries at the equinoctial point of Spring and the fullness of the moon—a configuration useful to Dante not as a literal date but as a gathering point for traditional exegetical meanings relating the events of Easter to other important events of Scripture.[37] Thus Dante at the beginning of the *Inferno* associates the sun's position in Aries with the disposition of the zodiac at the time of man's creation—a parallel acquiring special significance in Dante's allegory from the tradition that places the date of Adam's creation on March 25, the date of Christ's death, and his Fall on Friday, the day of the Crucifixion.[38] Behind these parallels between the Old and

[37] For modern calculations supporting an ideal rather than an actual date for Easter in the *Comedy*, see M. A. Orr, *Dante and the Early Astronomers*, rev. ed. (London, 1956), pp. 275ff. As illustrated below, Dante's medieval commentators emphasize the symbolic aspects of his astrological configuration.

[38] On March 25 as the traditional date of the Creation, see Orr, *ibid.*, pp. 129-30, 276. In *De temporum ratione*, LXVI, Bede places the time of the Creation at the vernal equinox, a concept applied to the date of Chauntecleer's "avisioun" (*NPT*, 3,187ff.). Macrobius (*Commentary*, I, 21) links the sun's position in Aries at the vernal equinox with the disposition of the planets at the Creation. In *Inf.*, I, 37-43, the sun's position in Aries is expressive of the divine love [*amor divino*] that first moved the planets. In *Purg.*, I, 21, Venus's appearance in Pisces, her sign at the Creation, coincides with the dawn of Easter Day and the appearance of the four signs symbolizing the Cardinal Virtues, an image of man's unimpaired vision before the Fall. Early calendars place the Creation of Adam, the Crucifixion, the Annunciation, and the Incarnation on March 25. Cf. Augustine, *De civitate Dei*, XVIII, 54, and Mâle, *Religious Art in France*, pp. 186-87. For exegetical material paralleling the day and hour of the Crucifixion with the day and hour of Adam's Fall, see *Glossa ordinaria*, PL, 114, col. 239; Honorius of Autun, *Hexaemeron*, VI, PL, 172, col. 266; Vincent of Beauvais, *Speculum historiale*, I, 56; VII, 45. The same tradition places the Creation and the Fall on the same day.

the New Testaments lies ultimately the Pauline doctrine that interprets the events of the Creation and Fall as prefigurations of the spirit's rebirth through Christ, the New Adam.[39] In the *Comedy* this doctrine is objectified symbolically in a carefully controlled chronological and astrological symbolism relating the stages of Dante's journey to the Crucifixion and Resurrection. Figuratively the beginning of his vision on the night preceding the Crucifixion is a projection of the spiritual state of Dante, who, full of sleep and the Old Adam, enters the "dark wood" of error, an image of the mind turned from the path of reason and virtue ("la diritta via"). The process of spiritual awakening is mirrored in the chronology of Dante's descent to Hell, where the spirit is buried with Christ on Good Friday (symbolic of its death to sin) and rises with him at dawn on Easter Day.[40] Astrologically, this pattern of spiritual renewal is imaged in the central feature of Dante's configuration: the sun's position in Aries. Like the other signs of the zodiac, Aries has acquired special value in medieval astrology as a symbol of man's spiritual life. As the ascendant sign at the time of the Creation and the Resurrection, Aries is called the house of life or birth, and as such it is indicative of man's life before the Fall and of his spiritual regeneration through Christ.[41] These meanings find a related symbol in the sun, "lord and king of the planets," whose light and heat signify the wisdom and charity of Christ, the Sun of Justice, and whose entrance

[39] I Cor. 15:22: "And as in Adam all die, so also in Christ all shall be made alive." Cf. Rom. 5:12-14. On the reflection of this doctrine in ecclesiastical art, see Mâle, *Religious Art in France*, pp. 186ff.

[40] In the medieval liturgy, this meaning underlies the baptism of neophytes on Easter Eve. See Durandus of Mende, *Rationale divinorum officiorum*, VI, 80. For a discussion of the doctrine in relation to Dante's descent, see Charles S. Singleton, *Dante Studies II: Journey to Beatrice* (Cambridge, Massachusetts, 1958), pp. 225ff.

[41] Bersuire, *Opera*, II, 106-107. Cf. n. 44, below. In *Epistola LV*, *PL*, 33, cols. 210-11, Augustine comments on the symbolic aspect of the sun's and moon's position in Aries at the time of Easter.

into the houses of the zodiac designates the divine grace entering the mind and curing it of the ills of cupidity.[42] These benevolent attributes of the sun and Aries bear directly on the events of Easter. For Aries is the mansion of Mars, an image of cupidity and the strife under the Old Law, and his malevolent power in this sign is linked figuratively with the death of Christ.[43] But this unfortunate aspect of Aries is counteracted by the sun, whose exaltation in Aries signifies the spirit's triumph over sin and death through the Resurrection.[44] At the beginning of the *Purgatorio*, Dante's spiritual awakening as he emerges from Hell is imaged in the sun's rising in Aries, in the symbolism of dawn, and in the Purgatorial hymn celebrating the liberation of the Hebrews from their captivity in Egypt—an event which Dante's medieval commentators relate to the astrological configuration of Easter and, following Scriptural commentary, interpret as a prefiguration of the Resurrection and the spirit's release from

[42] Bersuire, *Opera*, IV, 89. Cf. Neckam, *De naturis rerum*, I, 13. In Scriptural commentary, this meaning is applied to Ps. 18:1-7: "The heavens shew forth the glory of God. . . . He hath set his tabernacle in the sun: and he, as a bridegroom coming out of his bride chamber, hath rejoiced as a giant to run the way. His going out is from the end of heaven, and his circuit even to the end thereof: and there is no one that can hide himself from his heat."

[43] Like the other planets, except the sun and the moon, Mars has two signs or "mansions" of which he is "lord": Scorpio, the sign in which it was located at the Creation and has its most powerful influence, and Aries, whose first ten degrees it dominates. Cf. Macrobius, *Commentary*, I, 21. Orr (pp. 272-73) calculates the sun's position at the beginning of Dante's vision as the first face of Aries. Opposing the judicial astrologers, Augustine insists that the influence of Mars is a symbol, not the cause, of evil in man (*De civitate Dei*, V, 1). Following the same tradition, Cornelius Agrippa opposes those astrologers who would attribute to Mars "the occasion and necessary cause of Christ's all-redeeming death" (*The Vanity of Arts and Sciences*, trans. R. L'Estrange, London, 1676, pp. 95ff.).

[44] Just as the sun is exalted in Aries, remarks Bersuire, so Christ the Sun rules and is exalted in its three faces, which are designated as the house of life [*domus vitae*] because they receive and are hospitable to eternal life (*Opera*, II, 105-107). In *Par.*, I, 40-42, and *Canz.*, XV, 41, Dante refers to the sun's special powers in Aries.

the bondage of sin: "When the sun was in Aries the Hebrews were freed from their servitude in Egypt, at which time our poet was freed from the servitude of sin and through the desert of Purgatory arrived at the heavenly Jerusalem."[45]

These exegetical connotations of Dante's Scriptural date add an obviously significant dimension to the spiritual meaning of his pilgrimage. Any equivalent meanings for Chaucer's puzzling date would be difficult to find on the surface. On the level of allegory, however, such an equivalent appears likely when we relate his date to the same source of Scriptural–astrological symbolism. As in the *Comedy* a precedent is found in the Old Testament visions, especially those of Ezechiel, where dates are sometimes attached to the prophecies and associated with other events in Scriptural history. Of particular relevance to Chaucer's flight to Fame's mountain and house is Ezechiel's flight to the mountain and house of God on "the tenth day of the month"—an event paralleled in Scriptural commentary with John's similar flight to the holy mountain and city.[46] In Ezechiel's vision, moreover, the "tenth day of the tenth month"—a Scriptural reckoning of December 10—is connected with one of the most important occurrences in man's spiritual history: the siege and captivity of Jerusalem by Babylon.[47] As we shall observe in Book III, the exegetical meanings of the captivity, the flights of Ezechiel and John, the symbolism of the mountain and house, along with John's conventional symbol, the eagle, combine with a general infusion of Scriptural imagery to call up the Christian implications of Chaucer's flight with Jupiter's eagle. But the common

[45] Benvenuto da Imola, *Commentum*, III, 64. On the sun's position in Aries at the time of the Hebrews' liberation, see Josephus, *Antiquities*, III, 10, which Benvenuto cites. In *Conv.*, II, 1, Dante explains the spiritual meaning of the event. Cf. Bede, *Historia ecclesiastica*, V, 21.

[46] Ezech. 40:1-2. Cf. Apoc. 21:10-11.

[47] Ezech. 24:1-2.

doctrine behind his flight and the Scriptural flights should become evident when we project his date against the background of medieval astrology which gives significance to Dante's date. Although Chaucer does not include an astrological configuration, his use of configurations with dates in other poems, the example of Dante, the traditional connection between the prophetic dream and astrology, and the explicit attribution of his dream to planetary influence in the *Parliament of Fowls*, together provide a strong precedent for such an interpretation.[48]

Of basic astrological importance to Chaucer's dream from Jupiter is that the sun on December 10 is in the sign of Sagittarius, the mansion of Jupiter, and the ninth of the twelve houses of the zodiac. Like the other houses, the ninth is assigned special attributes or "influences" that have acquired value as Christian symbols. As distinguished from the others, the ninth house is the house of faith and religion, and its powers, we are told, are exerted especially in such spiritual matters as prophetic dreams, pilgrimages, and heavenly tidings. Roger Bacon summarizes the chief characteristics of this house:

[48] In *PF*, 113-15, Chaucer attributes his dream to the benevolence of the planet Venus (Cytherea), a detail foreshadowing the allegorical content of his vision. Cf. Huppé and Robertson, *Fruyt and Chaf*, p. 109. In *The Parlement of Foules: An Interpretation* (Oxford, 1957), pp. 56ff., J. A. W. Bennett sees Dante's influence behind Chaucer's welding planetary material to a narrative framework and points out a parallel with *Purg.*, XXVII, 91-99, where Dante attributes to Venus's influence a dream bearing resemblances to Chaucer's. In the *Temple of Glas*, an imitation of the *House of Fame*, Lydgate introduces his vision with astrological data approximating Chaucer's date. An astrological configuration accompanies the date May 3 in *Troilus and Criseyde* and in *NPT* (where it is linked with Chauntecleer's "avisioun") and April 12 in the *Complaint of Mars*. In "Chaucer's Use of Astrology for Poetic Imagery" (Princeton dissertation, 1963), Chauncey Wood offers evidence of Scriptural parallels for these and other dates connected with astrological symbolism in Chaucer's poetry. As illustrated below, it seems likely that the date December 10 evokes both astrological and Scriptural-liturgical contexts. In view of Chaucer's allegorical method, it is assumed that his date, like Dante's, acquires its fullest meaning not as a literal date but as a symbol.

And those who have examined this matter all agree that the ninth house is the house of religion and faith. . . . Hence, as they say, it is the house of pilgrimages and journeys, of faith, deity, and religion, and the house of the worship of God, of wisdom, books, epistles, and of messengers, tidings, and dreams.[49]

The ninth house is properly called the house of pilgrimages and dreams, explains Bersuire, because on pilgrimages one follows the way to the heavenly Jerusalem and in the enigmas of dreams one often gains knowledge of the sins of the present life, the asperities of damnation, and the joys of eternal life.[50] The fortunate aspects of this house derive largely from its connection with Jupiter, the "well-willing planet," whose attributes of love and benevolence identify him symbolically with the Christian deity. Thus Bersuire equates him with Christ, whose goodness "tempered the evil of Saturn, that is, of human nature," when he assumed the flesh of man; and Dante in the *Purgatorio* invokes the "most high Jove" ("sommo Giove") whose wisdom and providence are often hidden from men's understanding.[51] As an astrological symbol, Jupiter is above all significant with respect to the blessings of the next life. For this reason, says Bacon, he is appropriately assigned to the ninth house, because these future blessings are attained not only through faith and worship and the study of divine wisdom but also through the revelations of dreams, ecstasies, and visions in which tid-

---

[49] *Opus majus*, ed. J. H. Bridges (Oxford, 1897), I, 255. Cf. Curry, p. 173, and Bersuire (*Opera*, II, 108), who assigns essentially the same attributes to the ninth house, which is interpreted as *domus ecclesiae et materialis et spiritualis* (IV, 64, 87-90).

[50] *Ibid.*, II, 108. Bersuire cites Dan. 1:17.

[51] *Ibid.*, II, 111; *Purg.*, VI, 118ff. In *Fulgentius metaforalis* (ed. Liebeschütz, pp. 79ff.), John Ridewall interprets Jupiter as divine charity and benevolence. Cf. Bersuire, *Ovidius moralizatus*, ed. F. Ghisalberti, *Studij romanzi*, XXIII (1933), 90. In *Genealogia deorum*, XIV, 13, 14, Boccaccio defends the poet's use of Jupiter as a symbol of the deity.

ings ("rumores") are brought by heavenly messengers concerning the blissful state of salvation.[52]

The benevolent power of the ninth house has immediate bearing on the date of Chaucer's dream; for this power would be felt on December 10, when the sun is in Sagittarius, and especially at night, when Chaucer's dream takes place, since Jupiter then exerts his influence as lord of this house.[53] In the sun, moreover, Jupiter is allied with a planet whose benevolence is felt in any position in the zodiac. As observed earlier, the sun's entrance into the various houses designates the love and grace with which Christ enters the mind and cures it of cupidity; and its passage into the winter solstice in December is a promise of the New Law, since winter and its coldness denote the afflictions under the Old Law and the spiritual frigidity untouched by the Sun of Justice.[54] In this aura of symbolism Chaucer's dream on December 10, as the sun approaches the solstice, takes on further Christian connota-

[52] *Opus majus*, I, 255.

[53] Jupiter shares with the sun and Saturn the lordship of the triplicity of this house, the sun exerting its influence by day and Saturn by both day and night. For a further explanation of these details, see *A Treatise on the Astrolabe*, ed. W. W. Skeat (London, 1872), pp. lxvi ff.

[54] Winter [*hiems*] signifies *infidelitas*, says Honorius of Autun; for just as winter fetters the earth with ice so that nothing grows, so infidelity fetters men's hearts with the coldness of sin so that they do not bear the fruit of faith. This winter lasted until the time of Christ; but when the Sun of Justice appeared, winter passed away, and spring, through the Holy Spirit, unbound the earth with the heat of faith and produced flowers of virtue (*PL*, 172, cols. 391-92). Gregory interprets winter as the present life and the austerity of the Old Law (*PL*, 79, col. 498). Cf. Bede, *PL*, 91, col. 1,110 (on Cant. 2:11); Alanus de Insulis, *PL*, 210, col. 810; *Allegoriae in sacram scripturam*, col. 953. On the basis of John 10:22, these meanings are applied to the feast of the Dedication of the Temple (I Mach. 4:54-59), which is commemorated during the winter to designate the frigidity of the Jews, who did not believe in Christ (*Glossa ordinaria*, *PL*, 114, col. 398). In *Genealogia deorum*, IX, 2, Boccaccio provides an astrological configuration for winter based on the sun's appearance in the ninth house [*Jovis domo*]. In the Franklin's Tale, 1,243ff., a similar configuration for "the colde, frosty seson of Decembre" is the background for the "magyk natureel" which is contrary to "hooly chirches feith."

tions.[55] For in the liturgical year the sun's appearance at the solstice corresponds to Advent, the season celebrating the long-awaited coming of Christ to release mankind from captivity and to heal its spiritual maladies. At the same time, Advent is a season of somberness and remorse, since it anticipates not only Christ's coming at the Nativity and his advent into men's souls but also his second coming at the end of the world.[56] This solemn reminder of the Last Judgment is further symbolized by winter, a foreshadowing of the death awaiting the world and mankind, and by December, a time of penitence, since in this month the Sun of Justice infuses the heart with grace and frees it of the coldness of sloth.[57] These liturgical meanings of

[55] Using a modern computation which places the date of the winter solstice of 1376 on December 11, D. M. Bevington sees a connection between Chaucer's date and the eve of the solstice, the longest night of the year, although he views the association as intentionally comic ("The Obtuse Narrator in Chaucer's *House of Fame*," *Speculum*, XXXVI [1961], 291-92). On the date of the winter solstice, cf. *A Treatise on the Astrolabe*, I, 17; II, 1. In "A Legal Reading of Chaucer's *Hous of Fame*," *University of Toronto Quarterly*, XXIII (1953), 185-92, R. J. Schoeck gives evidence for a relationship between December 10 and the celebration of the Christmas revels at the Inner Temple, a theory considered at the end of the present study. The Scriptural–liturgical connotations of the seasonal openings of medieval dream–visions have been generally overlooked. For their relevance to Chaucer's imagery of spring in *BD* and *PF*, see Huppé and Robertson, *Fruyt and Chaf*, pp. 45-46, 143ff.

[56] Bernard of Clairvaux interprets Christ's Advent as *ad homines, in homines, contra homines* (*PL*, 183, col. 45). Cf. Durandus of Mende, *Rationale divinorum officiorum*, VI, 2. For a convenient discussion of the liturgical meanings of Advent, see J. J. Campbell, *The Advent Lyrics of the Exeter Book* (Princeton, 1959), pp. 3-8. Augustine relates these meanings to the symbolism of the sun and the winter solstice (*Sermo CXCII, PL*, 38, col. 1,013). Just as the sun in its advent to the earth is a remedy and relief for many ills, remarks Bersuire, so "Christ in his Advent restrains and eases the weaknesses of temptation and tribulation" (*Opera*, II, 85). In IV, 89, Bersuire applies this idea to the ninth house in particular.

[57] On winter and its coldness as images of the Last Judgment and the end of the world, see *Allegoriae in sacram scripturam*, cols. 937, 954, and Rabanus Maurus, *De universo, PL*, 111, col. 303. December is called a time of penitence, says Bersuire, because it is a month "when coldness of worship abounds, when Sagittarius, that is, the arrow of con-

Advent and the sun's appearance at the winter solstice lend significance to another astrological feature of Chaucer's date. For on December 10 the sun is in the third face of Sagittarius, a position in which it counteracts the malevolence of Mars and Saturn, especially that of Saturn, who shares with the sun and Jupiter the lordship of Sagittarius and exerts its power both by day and by night.[58] As the oldest and slowest of the planets, Saturn signifies time, particularly before Christ's Advent, and along with Mars he is associated with the adversities under the Old Law. For this reason he is said to wield his evil influence above all in winter; and his attributes of coldness and dryness are indicative of the frigidity and sterility of the spirit and its captivity by sin. The latter meaning is imaged in the prisons and chains in which he ensnares the unwary pilgrim. This power is felt mainly in the ninth house— the house of journeys and pilgrimages—and unless it is counteracted by the benevolent planets the pilgrim will come to grief.[59] Two planets opposing Saturn's power in

---

trition, and the Goat [*Capricornus*], a smelly animal, that is, the stench and abomination of sin and corruption, have power," and "when Christ the Sun of Justice approaches us through grace" (II, 129). Rabanus connects December 10 (the Scriptural "tenth day of the tenth month") with the Last Judgment, a connotation considered later in relation to the Apocalyptic imagery of Book III.

[58] According to Roger Bacon, who follows earlier authority, each face (the ten degrees of the thirty into which the houses are divided) is dominated by a planet whose influence is like a man in an official position of command (*Opus majus*, I, 260-61). Although the assignment varies, the three faces of Sagittarius are commonly assigned to Jupiter, Mars, and the sun, according to which the sun's power would be doubly felt. Firmicus Maternus assigns them to Mercury, the moon, and Saturn, which would put December 10 under Saturn (*Matheseos libri VIII*, eds. W. Kroll and F. Skutsch, Leipzig, 1897-1913, I, 45).

[59] Firmicus, *Matheseos*, II, 139-40. On Saturn's connection with chains and imprisonment, see Boccaccio, *Genealogia deorum*, VIII, 1, and Curry, p. 129. Chaucer employs the idea in the Knight's Tale, 1,084ff., 2,454ff., and the *Legend of Good Women*, 2,596ff. The association of Saturn and Mars with cupidity and the Old Law is imaged in their metals, lead and iron, a traditional moralization underlying the description of Fame's pillars in Book III.

this house are the sun and Jupiter, who temper his harmfulness and turn sadness into joy.[60]

Along with the liturgical implications of Chaucer's date,
these benevolent aspects of the sun and Jupiter in the ninth
house give additional weight to his opening appeals to
God and the Cross to turn his dream "to goode." More
importantly, the astrological connotations of December 10
suggest a unifying point of reference for the major details of his vision framework. The most obvious contact
with this astrological background is the dream from Jupiter, whose influence in the ninth house is called up by the
dream itself and by the glad "love-tydynges" of a "fer
contree" with which he is to reward Chaucer through his
flight with the eagle. Although Chaucer conceals the
meaning of these tidings on the surface, Jupiter's identity
with the Christian deity and his function of revealing
heavenly tidings again evoke the contexts of Scripture and
the liturgy in which such tidings are indicative of Advent
and the tidings of salvation and future judgment which
Christ brings to mankind. As we later see, these Christian
connotations of Jupiter's tidings are implicit both in the
Scriptural image of the "fer contree" (*terra longinqua*)
and in the spiritual state of Chaucer the dreamer, whose
need for consolation and glad tidings elicits Jove's
"routhe" and prompts the appearance of the eagle. At the
very beginning, however, the Scriptural pattern underlying Chaucer's need and quest for tidings becomes explicit
in his comparing himself to a pilgrim traveling wearily to
St. Leonard's shrine, an image of the sin-burdened spirit
to whom God brings relief through dreams and tidings.
The motif of captivity, symbolized by the influence of
Saturn and the liturgical meanings of winter, December,
and the sun's appearance during Advent, is here particu-

---

[60] Alanus, *Anticlaudianus*, II, 3; IV, 7. Cf. Honorius of Autun, *De
philosophia mundi*, PL, 172, col. 63. Firmicus (II, 139-40) discusses
the felicity resulting from the sun's position in the ninth house.

larized in St. Leonard, the patron saint of prisoners, whose power to liberate sinners of all sorts from their chains is a recurrent symbol in medieval literature of the spirit's release from the prison of the world or flesh. In this role Leonard is the proper object of appeal by those who are caught in the chains of any temporalia, such as carnal love, fame, or riches, which divert the pilgrim from his heavenly goal. Thus Lydgate, in "A Prayer to St. Leonard," petitions the saint to remember all those who are "in cheynes bounde" or "exsiled from their contree" and to bring reason to those who are "pensiff" and "distraut in thouht."[61] Leonard, moreover, is a symbol of good fame— the fame that draws men by its sweet odor to the praise of God. The martyrologists make the most of this point in etymologizing his name: "Leonard is as much to say as the odour of the people. And it is said of *leos*, that is, people, and of *nardus*, that is, a herb sweet smelling, for by the odour of good fame he drew the people to him, and by the odour of good renomee."[62]

In St. Leonard the Christian concepts of love and fame find an inclusive symbol. As an exemplar of heavenly love or fame, Leonard designates both the goal of man's earthly pilgrimage and the way to that goal for those who wearily travel to his shrine to ease their spiritual burdens ("to make lythe of that was hard"). In portraying himself as one who can scarcely travel the necessary "myles two," Chaucer repeats the ironic note of the Proem and Invocation.[63] At the same time, he reveals his essential role in

---

[61] *The Minor Poems*, ed. H. N. MacCracken (Oxford, 1934), Vol. I.

[62] *The Golden Legend*, trans. William Caxton, The Temple Classics (London, 1900), VI, 132.

[63] For evidence of a personal allusion behind the humor, see H. M. Smyser, "Chaucer's Two-Mile Pilgrimage," *MLN*, LVI (1941), 205-207, who observes that a convent of St. Leonard's was located about two miles from Chaucer's dwelling in London. However, the phrase "myles two" also suggests Matt. 5:41 ("And whosoever will force thee one mile, go with him other two"), where, according to the *Glossa*

the *House of Fame*. As the image of the pilgrimage implies, Chaucer is more than a mechanical device or a portrayal of the poet himself. Like the dreamer in the *Roman
de la Rose*, *Piers Plowman*, *Pearl*, *Amorosa Visione*, and
numerous other medieval dream poems, he is representa-
tive of every man who must travel the weary road between Babylon and Jerusalem. In this symbolic role he is
typically characterized at the outset as one who has lost
sight of his spiritual goal by putting his trust in worldly
things. Consequently, like Boethius, he feels the weight
of his earthly chains. As the eagle diagnoses his malady,
he is full of "hevynesse" and is "disesperat of alle blys"
because Fortune has disturbed his "hertys reste." More
particularly, as the poet of love, he has become so involved in the praise of Venus and Cupid and their servants
that he is caught temporarily in their chains. Chaucer,
therefore, must be freed from his chains and, like
Boethius, reminded of the heavenly "contree" which is
the source and end of all true love and fame. This process
of spiritual education underlies the central action of the
House of Fame and motivates the quest for "love-tydynges" of a "fer contree." This symbolic pattern also connects the allegory once again with the prophetic vision
which exerted the greatest formative influence on the
poem: the *Divine Comedy*. In the vision framework, in
the device of dating their visions, and in the central concept of the pilgrimage, we may observe a common source
in the prophetic tradition. But these outward features of
the vision genre merely point toward more important
parallels in structure and meaning on the level of allegory.
In order to view these parallels more closely, we must
examine those aspects of the *Comedy* which relate the
methods and subject matter of the two poets.

---

ordinaria, it is an image of the spirit's release from bodily captivity
(*PL*, 114, col. 97).

3. "Dante in Inglissh"

That the deepest meaning of the *Comedy* appears not on the surface but on the level of allegory is attested both by Dante's medieval commentators and by his own statement in the *Letter* to Can Grande della Scala that the meaning of his poem has not just one sense but several senses. Whereas one sense is "that which is conveyed by the letter" and is called "literal," the other is "that which is conveyed by what the letter signifies" and is called "allegorical or mystical." On the basis of this familiar medieval distinction between the literal and allegorical meanings of poetry, Dante allies his method more specifically with that of Scripture, observing that the spiritual meanings—allegorical, moral, and anagogical—may be designated generically as "allegorical" since they all differ from the "literal or historical." With this clarification of his method, Dante proceeds to distinguish between his subject "as literally understood" and his subject "as allegorically intended." In its literal sense only, his subject is "the state of souls after death," since the progress of the whole work "hinges on it and about it." In its allegorical sense, his subject is "man," who "by good or evil deserts" and the "exercise of his freedom of choice" becomes "liable to rewarding or punishing justice."[64]

Whereas Dante in the *Letter* applies the meanings and terminology of Scriptural allegory to the subject of the *Comedy*, in the *Convivio* (II, 1) he distinguishes between Scriptural and poetic allegory, noting that while the poets —Ovid, for example, in the story of Orpheus—observe a similar distinction between their literal and allegorical meanings, the theologians take the allegorical sense "otherwise than the poets do." Although Dante does not elaborate upon this difference, it would appear to imply a con-

[64] *The Latin Works of Dante Alighieri*, The Temple Classics (London, 1904), pp. 347-48.

ventional distinction between allegory as a rhetorical designation for the nonliteral meanings of both poetry and
Scripture and its more specialized usage as an exegetical
term for one of the three higher levels of Scriptural
meaning.[65] At the same time, Dante's examples from Ovid
and Scripture suggest a further distinction between poetic
allegory and much of Scriptural allegory on the basis of
the relationship between their literal and allegorical meanings. Whereas the allegorical meanings of poetry (as in
the story of Orpheus) are contained in a "fiction" or
"fable"—or in Dante's phrase, a "bella menzogna"—
whose literal sense has significance only as a *pictura* attracting the reader to the allegory underneath, the allegorical
meanings of Scripture are often contained in figures whose
literal sense is significant both as a veil for the allegory
and as a portrayal of actual events. To use Dante's example from Scripture, the meaning of Israel's exodus from
Egypt is embodied in a *cortex* not only "true in its spiritual intention"—that is to say, "when the soul goeth forth
out of sin, it is made holy and free in its power"—but also
"manifestly true according to the letter." This passage, in
short, "even in the literal sense, by the very things it signifies, signifies again some portion of the supernal things of
eternal glory."[66]

[65] It is as a rhetorical trope, rather than as an exegetical term, that
Boccaccio, Petrarch, and other medieval humanists parallel poetic and
Scriptural allegory, since both veil the deeper meaning in a figurative
cortex. In *De doctrina Christiana*, III, 29, and *De trinitate*, XV, 9, Augustine applies the rhetorical usage to Scripture. Dante uses the term in
both senses in the *Letter*. His reduction of the meanings of the *Comedy*
to two levels, allegorical and literal (or historical), reflects the rhetorical sense. In its exegetical sense, *allegoria* designates the foreshadowing of the truths of the New Testament in the Old. As distinguished
from the tropological and anagogical levels, it denotes those truths pertaining to Christ and the Church.

[66] On this distinction between poetic and Scriptural allegory, see
Robertson, "Some Medieval Literary Terminology," p. 683. In *Introductory Papers on Dante*, p. 103, Sayers observes that Dante's term
historia, applied in the *Letter* to the "literal" meaning, denotes both a

Although this distinction between the literal meanings in Scriptural and poetic allegory applies to Dante's examples in the *Convivio*, it does not apply to all Scriptural allegory nor does it apply to the genre of allegory employed in the *Comedy*. For in at least three categories— the prophetic vision, the moral fable, and the parable— Scripture parallels poetry in embodying its allegorical meaning in a "fiction" whose literal sense has no importance as a portrayal of actual events. As we have seen, it is to these three genres, and to the prophetic vision in particular, that Boccaccio appeals in demonstrating the similar aims and methods of Scriptural and poetic allegory; for when historical events are not described, neither is concerned with the literal meaning but with the allegory underneath. Whereas the fable "lacks all appearance of truth" on the surface, and the parable "is more like history than fiction," the prophetic vision, like much of Old Testament allegory, conceals "divine and human matters alike" beneath a veil that resembles both truth and fiction. This affinity between the prophetic visions of Scripture and poetry perhaps explains in some degree the seeming discrepancy between Dante's remarks on allegory in the *Convivio*, where he distinguishes between poetic and Scriptural allegory, and those in the *Letter*, where he illustrates his poetic method in the *Comedy* by applying the exegetical levels of Scriptural allegory to the exodus from Egypt.[67] For in adopting the form and techniques of the

portrayal of actual ("historical") events and (in its other original Latin sense) a "story" or fiction.

[67] For varying modern views of Dante's remarks on allegory in the *Convivio* and the *Letter*, see C. S. Singleton, *Dante Studies I: Commedia—Elements of Structure* (Cambridge, Massachusetts, 1954), pp. 84-98, and the articles by Singleton and R. H. Green in *Comparative Literature*, IX (1957), 118-35. Robertson (*Preface*, pp. 348-51) emphasizes the agreement of Dante's method in the *Comedy* with traditional poetic theory. Cf. Huppé and Robertson, *Fruyt and Chaf*, pp. 15-16.

prophetic vision, Dante does not equate his poem with Scripture itself—a divinely written revelation of God's wisdom and providence—nor does he employ a method contrary to the practice of the poets. Rather he follows both Scriptural and poetic precedent in clothing his allegory in a *cortex* resembling both truth and fiction but lacking significance as a representation of real events.[68] Furthermore, in applying the higher exegetical meanings —allegorical, moral, and anagogical—to the subject matter of the *Comedy*, Dante does not remove his poem from the realm of poetic allegory as understood by the Middle Ages. As many medieval poems illustrate, just as Scripture in the fable, parable, and vision employs fictions comparable to those of the poet, so the poet in his fictions often employs figures deriving from Scripture and referring, as Dante says, to "the supernal things of eternal glory." Only in the allegory of the pagan poets, as in Ovid's story of Orpheus or Virgil's account of Fame, are the symbols limited to a purely verbal allegory.[69]

[68] The medieval commentators on the *Comedy*, for example, Boccaccio, Benvenuto da Imola, and Francesco da Buti, discuss the nature of the *fizioni poetiche* in which Dante veils his allegorical meaning. For a convenient anthology of early commentaries, see *La Divina Commedia nella figurazione artistica e nel secolare commento*, ed. G. Biagi (Turin, 1924-1939). Although Dante does not employ the conventional machinery of the dream at the beginning of the *Comedy*, the poem was traditionally regarded as a dream–vision comparable to the Scriptural visions; and Dante, like Ezechiel, John, and other prophets, appears in illustrations depicting him as beholding his vision while asleep. In *Dante and His Comedy* (New York, 1963) p. 4, Allan H. Gilbert suggests that Chaucer probably regarded Dante's vision as a fictive dream comparable to his own.

[69] In "Alan of Lille's *De Planctu Naturae*," *Speculum*, XXXI (1956), 656, R. H. Green expresses the view that Dante's "allegory of the poets" was applied in one way to the allegory of pagan poetry and in another to the fabulous allegory of medieval poets. In the latter, the "sacramental aspect of the *visibilia* of nature" enabled the Christian poet "to exploit the allegories of Scripture even when the 'things' of his discourse are placed in a context which is fictional." Again a model is found in the Scriptural visions, where, to quote Augustine, "things are said which signify nothing [spiritually], but are, as it were, the frame to which those things which do signify are attached" (*De civitate*

The conformity of the allegorical method of the *Comedy* to traditional poetic theory and practice is observable not only in the vision framework but also in the diverse elements making up the complex surface pattern of the three books. The fictive quality of the poem's literal sense is perhaps most obvious in the elaborate mythographical and fabulous imagery which provides the machinery for much of the action, especially in the *Inferno*. But it is also discernible in the more patent Christian imagery, including the three controlling concepts of the poem: Hell, Purgatory, and Paradise. In their literal sense, as we are told in the *Letter,* these concepts signify "the state of souls after death." But this literal meaning, as Dante's portrayal makes clear, acquires importance not as an actual representation of the places, personages, and events described but as a poetic projection of the doctrine underlying these concepts. For example, in locating Hell at the center of the earth, Purgatory on an island in the Southern Hemisphere, and Heaven above the fixed stars, Dante is not representing a cosmographic scheme true either to him or to his age but an abstract moral pattern by which he externalizes the spiritual drama of man both in its temporal and eternal aspects. To pursue the meanings of Dante's twofold subject, Hell, in its literal sense, is the place and condition of the damned who are suffering eternal torments for their choice of cupidity on earth. Allegorically, it is an image of man in a state of sin in the present life. Similarly, Purgatory, as in Catholic theology, is the place and condition of the redeemed souls who are being purged of their sins and prepared for their ascent to God in Paradise. Allegorically, it portrays the condition of penitence whereby the soul purges its guilt in this life.

Dei, XVI, 2). On the use of Scriptural figures in the fictive coverings of medieval poetry, see Robertson, *Preface*, pp. 349-51, and "Some Medieval Literary Terminology," pp. 681-83.

Finally, Paradise is the place or condition of the beatified souls in Heaven. In the allegory, it is an image of the soul in a state of grace or contemplation, enjoying the foretaste of the bliss of Heaven, its true home and city.[70] Around these multiple meanings of the *Comedy* all the details, both fictive and historical, function as aspects or images of the inner drama of the spirit. On all levels, moreover, these details are subsumed under the more inclusive fiction which provides the central action of the poem: the journey of Dante the poet.

As a modern commentator on the *Comedy* reminds us, the "literal" Dante—that is, the Dante in the "story" (*historia*)—is "always himself—the Florentine poet, philosopher, and politician, and the man who loved Beatrice."[71] But like the many other historical personages in the poem, Dante is clearly not "historical" in the sense of much of Scriptural allegory in which the personages described are involved in actions "manifestly true according to the letter." As the nature of his journey indicates, the real Dante is part of a fictive action which is true only in reference to the Scriptural concept of the pilgrimage of the spirit.[72] Outwardly this concept is projected in the *Inferno, Purgatorio,* and *Paradiso*—inclusive symbols around which

[70] Francesco da Buti summarizes the literal and allegorical meanings of Dante's subject: "The literal sense concerns Hell, Purgatory, and Paradise, into which places he feigns that he was led by different persons, as is evident in the poem; and this I treat literally, whenever I can, according to the Catholic faith, although it is mixed with poetic fictions [*fizioni poetiche*]. And the allegory or moral truth concerns the state of persons in the world in three different conditions: in sin, in penitence, and in contemplation" (*Commento*, Pisa, 1858-1862, I, 23-24).

[71] Dorothy Sayers, trans., *The Divine Comedy: Hell*, Penguin Classics (Baltimore, 1959), p. 67.

[72] The doctrinal ramifications of the pilgrimage are the main subject of Singleton's *Journey to Beatrice*, in which the central theme of the allegory is stated as the "conversion of the soul from the grief and misery of sin to the state of grace" (p. 6). The present summary is limited to those aspects of Dante's pilgrimage which relate most directly to Chaucer's fiction.

gather all the doctrinal ramifications of the poem but which bear particularly on Dante's journey. To follow the medieval commentators on the *Comedy,* the poet's visits to Hell, Purgatory, and Paradise mark the progressive stages by which the spirit, turned toward sin and therefore from God, undergoes a process of self-knowledge and purification and is freed of its guilt and brought to the contemplation of eternal glory and bliss. At the beginning of the *Inferno* Dante's spiritual state is mirrored in the dark wood, symbolic of the error deflecting the mind from the path of reason and virtue, and in the imagery of "night" and "sleep," indicative of spiritual ignorance and sloth.[73] As a phase of Dante's education, the descent to Hell is the initial stage which the spirit must undergo before it can be purged of sin and directed to the higher truths of salvation. More particularly, it is a descent not of evil but of virtue—the descent whereby the mind, considering its own vices and the fragility of worldly things, directs its thoughts to the Creator.[74] This process, preliminary to actual purgation, is embodied outwardly in the divine guidance and instruction of Virgil, a symbol of the natural light of reason (*ratio*) which disciplines the passions and informs and directs the will.[75] Chronologically,

[73] Francesco da Buti, I, 24-25; Benvenuto da Imola, I, 74-75. Dante puts the time of his entrance into Hell at night, comments Benvenuto, because just as night is a time of darkness, blindness, and sin, so Hell is a place of mental darkness, ignorance, and pain.

[74] The virtuous or moral descent—by which "someone descends intellectually to a consideration of worldly things [*terrenorum*]" so that by perceiving their nature he will despise them—is one of four meanings applied by Pietro Alighieri to the descent to Hell. The others are the way of nature—the spirit's descent at birth into the fallen condition of the world; the way of vice—the descent of those who put their trust in earthly things; and the way of artifice—a descent by necromancy (*Commentarium,* Florence, 1845, pp. 11-17).

[75] Francesco da Buti (II, 202) interprets Virgil as "the reason [*ragione*] accompanying and guiding the sensuality [*sensualità*]." Cf. Benvenuto, III, 23: "Virgil designates the reason, which guides, rules, and disciplines passion." More particularly, he is *ratio naturalis* (III, 90), that is, the natural reason unillumined by grace. On this limita-

as we have seen, Dante's descent to Hell on Good Friday and emergence at dawn on Easter Day parallel the Crucifixion and Resurrection, images of the soul's death to sin and of the awakening that leads to purgation. The process of purgation is symbolized by the *Purgatorio*, indicative, tropologically, of the soul's penitence and purification in this life. As an image of Dante's own purgation, this process is mirrored in the continued guidance of Virgil and in the arduous ascent of the Mountain of Purgatory, where the spirit, still full of sleep and the Old Adam, is illumined by divine grace (symbolized by the eagle appearing to Dante in a dream and bearing him to the gate of Purgatory) and enters the final stages of purification which prepare it for the contemplation of the mysteries of Paradise.[76] This final stage—foreshadowed in the invocation to Apollo, a symbol of heavenly wisdom (*sapientia*)—is fulfilled in the Earthly Paradise, where the guidance of Virgil (the light of natural reason) yields to that of Beatrice (the light of faith or divine revelation), by whose instruction the spirit ascends in contemplation through the heavenly spheres to the Empyrean and in a final mystic vision (typified by St. Bernard) views the glory of eternal light and love.[77]

Dante's spiritual journey brings the allegory of the

---

tion of Virgil, see Singleton, *Journey to Beatrice*, pp. 31ff. Cf. n. 77, below.

[76] "By this eagle, beneath the fictive veil, the author means the prevenient grace of God" (*Commento alla Divina Commedia D'Anonimo Fiorentino*, Bologna, 1868, II, 152). Jacopo della Lana interprets the eagle as the intellect (*Commento*, Bologna, 1866, II, 103). According to Francesco da Buti (II, 200), he is the mind infused with the love of the Holy Spirit. Cf. Benvenuto, III, 248.

[77] Benvenuto interprets Paradise morally as the spirit's ascent to heaven through contemplation (I, 296ff.). On the closely related meanings of Beatrice as "faith," "grace," "wisdom," "revelation," and "theology," see Singleton, *Journey to Beatrice*, pp. 23ff. He connects her with Virgil and Bernard as one of the three gradations of light illuminating the mind in its ascent to God.

Comedy into its closest contact with the allegory of the *House of Fame*. In Chaucer's fiction the pattern of the pilgrimage is reflected not only in the central image of the poet's journey and quest for tidings but also in more concrete parallels in structure and imagery relating the actions of the two poems. Structurally the most conspicuous parallel is the division into three books, a parallel reinforced by Chaucer's use of two of Dante's invocations and by a network of details equating the stages of the poets' journeys. Among the more obvious images suggesting the *Comedy* are the desert of Venus in Book I, the flight with Jupiter's eagle in Book II, and the mountain of Fame in Book III, paralleling the "gran diserto" of Hell, the flight with the golden eagle of Purgatory, and the purgatorial mountain whose ascent leads to the beatific vision of Paradise. While these parallels leave little doubt as to Chaucer's deliberate imitation of Dante's pilgrimage, Dante's Scriptural–exegetical symbolism and Chaucer's pagan fiction reveal little outward correspondence in either purpose or meaning. Viewed allegorically, however, these similarities reflect a common body of Christian doctrine connecting Chaucer's imagery with the spiritual meanings of Dante's pilgrimage.

Most clearly relating the doctrine of the two poems is the background of moralized pagan mythography which supplies the major elements of Chaucer's fiction and much of the allegorical machinery of the *Inferno*, where pagan imagery of the underworld is utilized in the topographical features of Hell and in such figures as Charon, Cerberus, Minos, Plutus, and the Furies—all of whom have been metamorphosed into symbols in a Christian allegory of sin and damnation.[78] The process transforming these pagan

[78] Referring to the Furies and Medusa in particular, Dante warns those who have sound intellects to "mark the doctrine that is hidden beneath the veil of the mysterious verses" (*Inf.*, IX, 61-63). While all of these images, like the goddess Fame, retain their pagan affinities on

images into Christian symbols has already been observed in Chaucer's central fiction, the goddess Fame, whose metamorphosis from a personification of rumor into a providential agent of earthly fame and infamy perhaps owes at least a hint to Minos, Dante's infernal judge.[79] Similar metamorphoses appear in the roles of Chaucer's other pagan deities, such as Jupiter, Morpheus, and, as we later see, Venus, who, along with Fame, is a controlling symbol for the doctrinal ramifications of the Christian concepts of love and fame. At the same time, in order to evoke the Christian implications of these pagan fictions, Chaucer has employed other symbols which bring his poetic technique into a closer correspondence to Dante's Scriptural–exegetical method; for just as Dante has woven pagan images into his predominantly Christian *cortex*, so Chaucer has included details in his pagan *cortex* which have significant referents in Scripture and have assumed the function of Scriptural figures. To illustrate with two of the major symbols in Book III, both the mountain and the house of Fame, while retaining their pagan identities on the surface, have Scriptural prototypes relating them to the Christian contrast between earthly and heavenly fame. Thus the Scriptural house (*domus*), in reference to cupidity, may signify the world and its *temporalia*—an appropriate connotation, we later observe, for Fame's unstable "hous" and awards. As a contrasting symbol, however, the house may also signify the house of God, either the Church militant or the heavenly Paradise, the source and end of true fame. Similarly, the Scriptural mountain

the surface, they function as aspects of sin or remorse or as providential agents of punishment. Thus Cerberus may signify gluttony, Medusa the hardness of impenitence, the Furies remorse, Minos the self-accusing conscience, etc. Dante's early commentators provide a wealth of mythographical material which points to a common tradition behind the pagan fictions of the *Comedy* and the *House of Fame*.

[79] Cf. chap. v, n. 105, below.

(*mons*) is a conventional symbol of vainglory or cupidity, the unstable foundation of all earthly striving after fame or other worldly goods. But it may also designate, as in the Apocalypse, the foundation of God's house, the stable basis of eternal fame. As these ambivalent meanings indicate, the house and mountain, like many other Scriptural symbols, are referable to both good and evil and acquire more precise significations on the higher levels of Scriptural exegesis, that is to say, in reference to the Church or the world (allegorical), the individual spirit (tropological), or the afterlife and eternity (anagogical).[80] Comparable meanings inform Chaucer's other key symbols, such as the temple and desert in Book I and the eagle in Book II. Ultimately, this strong infusion of Scriptural–exegetical meanings, many of them traditional in medieval art and literature, enables Chaucer to explore the deepest implications of the contrast between earthly and heavenly fame. Since he is concerned primarily with the problem of fame as it relates to the temporal order, the house and mountain function more obviously as symbols of worldly fame. Simultaneously, by a process of Scriptural inversion, these symbols also evoke their spiritual opposites, the heavenly house and mountain. This ambivalence of Chau-

---

[80] In *De doctrina Christiana*, III, 25, Augustine discusses the contrasting significations of Scriptural symbols. Although he does not use the later medieval terminology for the higher Scriptural levels, his exegetical approach and his emphasis on a knowledge of Scriptural "signs" and their contrasting implications are an important impetus behind the many Scriptural encyclopedias (for example, *Allegoriae in sacram scripturam*, Rabanus's *De universo*, Alanus's *Distinctiones*) and other influential repositories of the conventional meanings assigned to the visible signs of God's creation. These meanings appear in such important sources of poetic imagery as the bestiaries and lapidaries and are often reflected in the mythographies and other moralizations of pagan writings, some of which, like the *Ovide moralisé*, Bersuire's *Ovidius moralizatus*, and Ridewall's *Fulgentius metaforalis*, overtly apply Scriptural–exegetical meanings to the fictions of the poets. All of the major symbols in the *House of Fame* are found in moralized contexts elsewhere in medieval literature and art, and some, like the mountain and house, have a long exegetical tradition behind them.

cer's major symbols brings his Christian subject matter into a more definable relationship with Dante's subject matter and method. Although the *Comedy*, strictly speaking, is not a poem about fame, it is fundamentally concerned with the problem of justice or rewards for good and evil which is central to the Christian problem of fame.[81] Allowing for the wide differences in the scope and complexity with which the two poets explore their themes, the essential difference in their methods is the level on which their Scriptural symbols most immediately operate. In the *Comedy*, as Dante tells us, the literal subject, the state of souls after death, is merely a means of revealing the good and evil on earth by which men subject themselves to eternal fame or infamy. Dante, in other words, explores his theme from the viewpoint of a vision of the next life. Chaucer, on the other hand, explores his theme from the viewpoint of the present life. More concisely, whereas Dante reveals the temporal through the eternal, Chaucer reveals the eternal through the temporal.[82]

In the final analysis, Chaucer's desire to evoke the anagogical aspects of his theme perhaps best explains his use of the *Comedy*. Dante's poem provides, as it were, an extra dimension, though not an indispensable one, reinforcing the prophetic content of his own vision. At the same time, as in the *Comedy*, this higher meaning acquires a more immediate function in relation to the cen-

[81] On the importance of the idea of fame in the *Comedy*, see Gilbert, *Dante and His Comedy*, pp. 132-37. In its eternal aspect, the Christian view of fame is implicit in the contrasting infamy and glory of the souls in Hell and Paradise. In its temporal aspect, it finds expression in the remarks of Oderisi in *Purg.*, XI, 91-117, and in the concern for worldly praise and infamy of some of the spirits in Hell, for example, *Inf.*, XIII, 76-78; XVI, 82-85; XXVII, 61-66; XXIX, 103-105.

[82] Singleton applies the term "evocation" to Dante's technique of implying the allegorical through the literal meanings of his symbols (*Journey to Beatrice*, p. 8). A term equally appropriate to Chaucer's method is "symbolic reversal" or "inversion," since such symbols as the mountain and house "evoke" not only their allegorical equivalents but also their spiritual opposites.

tral allegory of the pilgrimage. That is, in both poems the prophetic content becomes an integral part of the experience of the poet, whose need for spiritual instruction initiates a pattern of education leading to a higher stage of understanding. In the *Comedy* this process is symbolized by the concepts of Hell, Purgatory, and Paradise, whose moral meanings mark the progressive stages of Dante's spiritual journey. Although Chaucer's pilgrimage is projected in symbols less patently Christian, the stages follow a similar pattern, with Dante's three books contributing a convenient frame of reference for the spiritual meanings of his journey.[83] While more detailed parallels with the *Comedy* will be considered in the following chapters, a brief description of the main stages of Chaucer's pilgrimage should reveal the most important points of contact with Dante's allegory.

In Book I Chaucer's equivalent of Dante's experience in the "gran diserto" and sterile waste of Hell is his own experience in the temple and desert of Venus. The context of the *Inferno* is called up not only by the desert but also by a version of the *Aeneid* in which Aeneas' journey, sojourn with Dido, rescue by Mercury from the desert of Libya, and descent to Hell are linked by a rich network of symbolic associations with Dante's and Chaucer's pilgrimages. These related meanings find inclusive symbols in the temple and desert, whose Scriptural–exegetical connotations connect the allegory of Book I most closely with the doctrine of the *Inferno*. Outwardly this connection is reflected in Chaucer's attitude in the desert, where his fear

---

[83] Although the threefold division of the *House of Fame* is clearly modeled on that of the *Comedy*, the use of numerical symbolism as a structural device appears elsewhere in medieval allegory. In *The Testament of Love*, Thomas Usk employs a threefold structure comparable to Dante's in allegorizing his Boethian account of the mind's progress from error to an understanding of heavenly felicity. As in the *Comedy*, Book I is equated with the state of error or torment in Hell without grace, Book II with the state of grace and purification from sin, and Book III with the state of eternal bliss and glory (III, I).

and confusion and his rescue by the eagle parallel Dante's spiritual state in the "gran diserto" and his rescue by Virgil. In Book II this parallel continues in the flight with the eagle, whose affinity with the eagle of the *Purgatorio* is conspicuous in the details describing his appearance and descent and whose role as divine guide and instructor, especially his promise of "glad" tidings of a "fer contree," suggests Virgil's heavenly mission. Dante's purgation, imaged in the guidance of Virgil and the ascent of the mountain of Purgatory, has its counterpart in Chaucer's flight with the eagle and arduous ascent of Fame's mountain. In Book III, if anywhere, the allegory would seem to take on the nature of parody; for here we have no Earthly Paradise or vision of heavenly glory but a vision of earthly glory and its origin in the confused and unstable judgments of mankind. But the warning to look for an equivalent anagogical meaning in Fame's sumptuous abode is implicit in Chaucer's use of Dante's invocation to Apollo, along with the reminder of his "o sentence," and in the profusion of symbolism from the Apocalypse and the Old Testament visions relating his flight to the flights of Ezechiel and John. In this richly figurative context, Book III reveals itself as Chaucer's own *Paradiso*, albeit a false, worldly "paradise" whose transiency and deceptive beauty are betrayed by the very imagery with which it is described. As we have seen, it is the typical ambivalence of his major symbols that enables Chaucer to express the eternal norms behind this mutable paradise of Fame and her temporal decrees. While retaining their functions as symbols of worldly fame, the mountain and house point toward their spiritual opposites, the holy mountain and house, the source of eternal fame and the goal of man's earthly pilgrimage. This higher meaning is inherent both in the descriptive details of Book III and in the central quest for tidings of a "fer contree." Despite their obscurity on the surface, these tidings fulfill a pro-phetic content as profound and purposeful as that of the *Paradiso*.

While the *Divine Comedy* perhaps contributes the most important elements to the central action and structure of the *House of Fame*, within this Dantean framework ap-pear other influences which have conditioned the Christian ideas and symbolism of the poem. The most significant of these influences is the *Consolation of Philosophy*, a fic-tive vision whose form, imagery, and ideas place it in the allegorical tradition behind Chaucer's and Dante's poems.[84] The imagery and subject matter of the *Consolation* per-meate the *House of Fame*, especially Books II and III. In Book II Philosophy's instruction of Boethius is implicit in the function of the eagle, in the content of his discourse, and in the flight itself, a parallel called up explicitly by Chaucer's comparing his ascent to Boethius' flight with the feathers of Philosophy. In Book III the Boethian attitude toward fame underlies the central theme and is a primary inspiration behind the drama of Fame and her awards, which in large part is a fictive elaboration of Philosophy's exposition of the nature of Fortune and her gifts as it ap-plies to fame. Along with the basic patterns of Scriptural ideas and imagery, Dante and Boethius supply the major elements, structural and thematic, directing us to the Christian "sentence" beneath the pagan fictions of the allegory. Like all other derivative features, however, these elements have been adapted to a unique intellectual and artistic design and to a style and tone distinctively Chaucerian. The dominant note of the poem is one of irony, a medieval rhetorical device subtly applied by Chaucer to his own role in the allegory. There are, we might say, two Chaucers apparent. One is Chaucer the

---

[84] On the vision form of the *Consolation* and its importance in the tradition of literary allegory, see Green's "Introduction," *The Consola-tion of Philosophy*, pp. xxi-xxiii.

poet, properly concerned with the truthful interpretation of his "avisioun"; the other is Chaucer the dreamer, the fictive portrayal of the poet who is designed to aid the allegory. One is the master ironist, fully aware of the implications of his allegory; the other, more often than not, is the butt of the irony. As in the *Comedy*, this self-directed irony is characteristic of the poet's role as the pilgrim, whose frequent confusion of spiritual values betrays his need for instruction. On the surface, the prevalent note of irony accounts for much of the humor, as well as some of the obscurity, of the *House of Fame*. On the level of "sentence," it provides a unity of tone which subserves and enhances the intellectual content of the prophetic vision.

CHAPTER III

THE HOUSE OF FAME—HELL

BESIDES establishing the role of Chaucer, whose pilgrimage evokes a wide range of symbolic associations with the *Inferno*, Book I of the *House of Fame* introduces the contrast between earthly and heavenly fame to be explored more fully in Book III. This contrast, however, is projected against a more inclusive allegory of love which has its unifying symbol in Venus, who is described at the beginning of the dream and whose role is conspicuously emphasized in the events of the *Aeneid* portrayed on a wall in her temple. The relevance of these details to the central theme of fame is evident in Chaucer's elaboration of the episode of Aeneas and Dido, whom he uses to illustrate contrasting attitudes toward love and fame. But the deepest implications of the allegory must be sought in the Christian meanings underlying the portrayal of Venus and her temple in medieval poetry and mythography.

A typical moralization of Venus is found in Boccaccio's Notes on the *Teseida*:

Venus is two-fold; by the first can be and should be understood every honest and legitimate desire, such as to desire a wife in order to have children, and desires similar to this; and this Venus is not meant here. The second Venus is she through whom all lasciviousness is desired, and who is commonly called the goddess of love (*dea d'amore*); and she it is whose temple and other qualities belonging to it are described here by the author, as appears in the text.[1]

In contrasting two Venuses, one "honest and legitimate," the other unlawful and lascivious, Boccaccio follows a

---

[1] *Teseida*, ed. Roncaglia, p. 417 (on *Tes.*, VII, 50-66). The translation follows D. S. Brewer, *Chaucer* (New York, 1953), p. 82.

tradition ultimately traceable to the pagan philosophers and poets. But in medieval poetry and mythography this contrast has been brought into accord with the Christian concept of two kinds of love, charity and cupidity.[2] The first Venus, as Boccaccio indicates, is associated with the love expressed in marriage, which God ordained in Paradise for the purpose of increasing and multiplying. More broadly, this is the divine love which, says Boethius, not only "halt togidres peples joyned with an holy boond," "knytteth sacrement of mariages of chaste loves," and "enditeth lawes to trewe felawes" but also "governeth erthe and see"—in short, binds all creation into harmony with God.[3] Thus Bernard Silvestris, similarly contrasting the two Venuses, identifies the "legitimate" Venus with "mundana musica" or "mundi concordia," that is, the natural law or "justice" pervading the elements, the stars, and every temporal and animate thing.[4] In Christian theology this bond of love is defined as the motion causing all of God's creatures to act according to their natures,

[2] On the background and significance of the two Venuses, see D. W. Robertson, Jr., "The Subject of the *De Amore* of Andreas Capellanus," *MP*, L (1953), 147ff., and *Preface*, especially pp. 125-26, 370-74. Cf. Brewer, *Chaucer*, pp. 63ff.; Green, "Alan of Lille's *De Planctu Naturae*," pp. 667ff. The contrast between the two Venuses is recurrent in medieval mythographies and moralizations of pagan authors, for example, Ovid and Virgil. Influential statements appear in the glosses of Remigius of Auxerre, John the Scot, and Alexander Neckam on Martianus Capella's *The Marriage of Philology and Mercury*. Cf. Bernard Silvestris, *Commentum super sex libros Eneidos Virgilii*, ed. G. Riedel (Greifswald, 1924), pp. 9, 64; *Mythographus Vaticanus III*, ed. Bode, p. 262; and Ridewall, *Fulgentius metaforalis*, ed. Liebeschütz, p. 45. For a late but relevant account of the Christian significance of the two Venuses, see Burton's *Anatomy of Melancholy*, Part. 3, Sect. 1, Memb. 1, Subs. 2, where they are equated with Augustine's definitions of charity and cupidity and the two cities, Jerusalem and Babylon.

[3] *De consolatione philosophiae*, II, Met. 8. John the Scot defines this love [*amor*] as a chain or bond [*vinculum*] linking all created things in amity and concord (*De divisione naturae*, I, 74, *PL*, 122, col. 519).

[4] *Commentum*, p. 9. On the related meanings of "love," "music," and "justice" as Christian concepts of the divine order, see Robertson, *Preface*, pp. 122-29.

such as to reproduce their species. In man this love is fulfilled by means of reason, the divine image or faculty
placing him above brute creation and directing the will,
as Boccaccio says, to marriage and other "honest and legitimate" desires. As such, Venus signifies the natural and virtuous behavior of man when he exercises his rational
nature.[5] As long as reason dominates the will, he maintains
a harmonious bond with God; but when reason is subjected to the will and passions, this natural order is broken.

The disruption of the divine bond of love through sin
is symbolized by the second Venus, who, as Boccaccio explains, is commonly called "the goddess of love." Her
carnal rather than spiritual nature is suggested by the various names ascribed to her, such as "lechery," "lasciviousness," "voluptuousness," "carnal delight," "concupiscence
of the flesh," and "mother of all fornication." Although
these names identify Venus more obviously with sexual
love, her carnality expresses the uncontrolled appetite
from which all of the vices proceed. In the *De planctu
naturae* of Alanus de Insulis, she is equated with original
sin and the irrational love corrupting the natural goodness
of God's creation. In this broader sense she may also symbolize the inordinate love of any temporal good, especially
physical delight, for its own sake. Like Fortune and Fame,
therefore, she typifies the idolatry by which men substitute
God's gifts for God himself as objects of worship.[6] To-

---

[5] In *Annotationes in Marcianum*, VIII, 8, John the Scot interprets the
good Venus as *bonas ac naturales humanae animae virtutes*.

[6] According to John the Scot, the shameful Venus designates *gen-
eralis et specialis libido* and original sin (*ibid.*). Green applies the
generalized meaning of *libido* to the sexual terms describing Venus in
De planctu naturae, where she symbolizes the uncontrolled sensuality
by which men deviate from the law of Nature and the good Venus
("Alan of Lille's *De Planctu Naturae*," pp. 667ff.). In "The Subject
of the *De Amore*," p. 150, Robertson observes that the term *fornicatio*,
applied to Venus by Bernard (*Commentum*, p. 9), is a generic name for
any deliberate departure from God's law or any act against created
nature. In this broader sense, Venus is indicative of idolatry, which in
Scripture is often designated as *fornicatio* (cf. Rabanus Maurus, *PL*,

gether the two Venuses signify the two kinds of love, charity and cupidity, which have governed man's actions since the Fall. Whereas man before the Fall was governed by the first Venus, in his unredeemed state he is governed by the second. Under God's plan of redemption man's proper end is to restore his original nature under the law of the spiritual Venus. Not to do so is to perpetuate his subjection to the carnal bond of the other.[7]

Although Chaucer makes no attempt to distinguish between the two Venuses, his portrayal of the goddess is composed of a cluster of details traditionally identified with the carnal Venus:

> . . . for in portreyture,
> I sawgh anoon-ryght hir figure
> Naked fletynge in a see.
> And also on hir hed, pardee,
> Hir rose garlond whit and red,
> And hir comb to kembe hyr hed,
> Hir dowves, and daun Cupido,
> Hir blynde sone, and Vulcano,
> That in his face was ful broun. (131-39)

As in the *Parliament of Fowls,* where Chaucer is more clearly indebted to Boccaccio's description of Venus and her temple, the predominance of sensual details betrays the goddess's nature. Thus her floating naked in the sea brings to mind the ubiquitous medieval account of her libidinous origin from Saturn, whose genitals were cut off and cast into the sea by Jove.[8] Bernard Silvestris, fol-

---

107, col. 811). On the wrongful Venus as a symbol of Nature's corruption through man's sin, see also Robertson, *Preface*, pp. 199-202, and Huppé and Robertson, *Fruyt and Chaf*, pp. 120ff.

[7] Robertson, "The Subject of the *De Amore*," pp. 148-50.

[8] Most of the details of Venus's "portreyture" are traceable to Fulgentius (*Mitologiae*, II, 1), who interprets Saturn's castration as an allegory of lust arising from excess (*Opera*, ed. R. Helm, Leipzig, 1898, pp. 39-40). Robertson discusses the iconographic tradition behind the portrayal of Venus in the Knight's Tale (*Preface*, pp. 372-73). Cf. Brewer, *Chaucer*, pp. 71-72.

lowing Scriptural commentary, interprets the sea as the perturbations of the flesh. Venus "fleteth in a se," explains Lydgate, since it mirrors the adversities of love and "his stormy law."[9] More particularly, we are told, Venus is described as naked because acts of lechery are difficult to conceal and "denude" the lover of reason and counsel.[10] Similar meanings inform Venus's "rose garlond whit and red." Unlike the white and red garland signifying chaste love and martyrdom, this garland has its prototype in the Book of Wisdom, where it is a symbol of lechery (*luxuria*) and its ephemeral delights.[11] Just as the roses of this garland are red and prick with their thorns, comments Fulgentius, so lechery blushes with shame and pricks with the stings of sin.[12] Venus's lechery is also symbolized by her doves, birds said to be especially disposed to "acts of Venus." When accompanying the true Venus, Bernard affirms, they are indicative of chastity. In this instance, however, they are to be construed as libido, as in the *Roman de la Rose*, where they lead Venus's chariot in her battle against Chastity.[13] Although Chaucer departs from

[9] *The Troy Book*, II, 2,543ff. Cf. Bernard, *Commentum*, pp. 10, 45. Venus is depicted as floating in the sea, explains Boccaccio, to show that the life of lovers is mixed with bitterness and is driven by various tempests to frequent shipwrecks (*Genealogia deorum*, III, 23).

[10] *Mythographus Vaticanus III*, pp. 228-29.

[11] Wis. 2:8-9: "Let us crown ourselves with roses, before they be withered: let no meadow escape our riot." In *Allegoriae in sacram scripturam*, col. 1,040, this garland is interpreted as the delights of the present life [*delectationes vitae presentis*]. Cf. Robertson, "The Doctrine of Charity in Mediaeval Literary Gardens," *Speculum*, XXVI (1951), 29, and *Preface*, p. 192, where the Scriptural passage is applied to the garland of the lover in the *Roman de la Rose*. The garland of Venus has an early literary ancestor in the garlands of Venustas, the follower of Luxuria in *Psychomachia*, 440-42. On the contrasting rose garland of martyrdom, see *PL*, 109, cols. 930, 1,115, and Chaucer's Second Nun's Tale, 220-24.

[12] *Mitologiae*, ed. Helm, p. 40. Just as the rose gives us pleasure for a short interval and then withers, says Boccaccio, so lust [*libido*] is a brief delight and causes long penitence (*Genealogia deorum*, III, 23). Cf. *Mythographus Vaticanus III*, p. 250.

[13] Lines 15,779ff. (ed. Langlois). Citing the "fables of the poets,"

the more conventional portrait by having Venus hold a comb rather than a conch shell, her comb also depicts her sensuality, as does her hair, both suggesting Guillaume's sensual portrait of Idleness, the porter of the gate leading into the garden of love in the *Roman*.[14] Finally, Venus betrays her nature by the company she keeps. When she appears as the wife of Vulcan and the mother of Cupid, warns Bernard, we should know her as "voluptatem carnis."[15] The juxtaposition of Cupid and Vulcan, moreover, brings to mind Ovid's account of Venus's adultery with Mars, by whom she begot Cupid. Vulcan, who is informed of the adultery by Apollo, is said to signify the fire of lascivious desire and hence is called the husband of Venus.[16] Whereas Venus is interpreted as carnal de-

---

Bersuire interprets the doves [*columbae*] drawing Venus's chariot as the lecherous [*luxuriosi*] "who, engaging in libidinous acts, serve the shameful Venus" (*Opera*, II, 181). Cf. Fulgentius, *Mitologiae*, p. 40; Boccaccio, *Genealogia deorum*, III, 23. On the contrasting doves of the chaste Venus, see Bernard, *Commentum*, pp. 64, 106-107.

[14] "Ydelnesse" is described as having a comb "for to kembe and tresse" herself (Mid. Eng. trans., 595ff.). In *Remedia amoris*, 135ff., Ovid associates Venus with idleness [*Venus otia amat*]. In Claudian's *Epithalamium de nuptiis Honorii Augustii*, I, 249-50, one of the three Graces parts Venus's hair with a comb. See John M. Steadman, "Venus' *Citole* in Chaucer's *Knight's Tale* and Berchorius," *Speculum*, XXXIV (1959), 620-24, who discusses both the comb and the "citole," the latter being held by Venus in the Knight's Tale, l. 1,959, and also connoting carnal love. Cf. Betty N. Quinn, "Venus, Chaucer, and Peter Bersuire," *Speculum*, XXXVIII (1963), 479-80, who finds a basis for Venus's comb in an edition of Bersuire's *Ovidius moralizatus*. In the *Parliament of Fowls*, 267ff., the "untressed" hair of Venus emphasizes her sensuality and suggests the portrayals of Luxuria, who in medieval art holds both a mirror and a comb. See Mâle, *Religious Art in France*, p. 119, and Robertson, *Preface*, pp. 92, 190-91, 198. In *English Wall Painting of the Fourteenth Century*, pp. 102-103, Tristram illustrates the connection of the comb and mirror with Pride.

[15] *Commentum*, p. 10.

[16] *Mythographus Vaticanus III*, p. 244. The Mars and Venus story (Ovid, *Met.*, IV, 167-89) is typically moralized as an example of virtue overcome by lust. Boccaccio interprets Apollo (the sun), who discovers Venus's adultery, as *sapientia* (*Genealogia deorum*, IX, 3). For other moralizations, see Fulgentius, *Mitologiae*, pp. 47-48; *Mythographus Vaticanus III*, p. 262; and Giovanni del Virgilio, *Allegorie*

light, Cupid denotes the passion predisposing the mind to such delight when reason becomes subject to the will.[17]

These carnal meanings of Chaucer's Venus find a fit symbol in her temple or "chirche." Although the temple, like Venus, retains its pagan identity, as a symbol it is an additional point of reference for the contrast between carnal and spiritual love. Again the meanings underlying Chaucer's fiction are clarified by Boccaccio, who describes the features of the temple which make it appropriate to the goddess of love. These features include not only its copper substance, whose properties Boccaccio equates with the qualities of carnal love, but also its location—a pleasant garden spot on Mount Cithaeron, near Thebes, whose climate, neither too hot nor too cold, is conducive to lechery and whose inhabitants offer numerous sacrifices in honor of Venus.[18] On the walls of the temple in the Knight's Tale, these details are repeated in the portrayal of "al the mount of Citheroun" where "Venus hath hir principal dwellynge," along with "al the gardyn and the lustynesse." But these idolatrous connotations of Venus and her temple are more concretely developed in the *Parliament of Fowls,* where the temple and its environs are part of a larger allegorical setting designed to convey the con-

---

librorum Ovidii Metamorphoseos, ed. F. Ghisalberti, *Il Giornale Dantesco,* XXXIV (1933), 253.

[17] Boccaccio, *Genealogia deorum,* III, 22. Cf. III, 23-24; IX, 3. Fulgentius (*Mitologiae,* p. 69) interprets Cupid as wrongful desire [*cupiditas*]. In *Mythographus Vaticanus III,* pp. 261-62, he is said to be the son of Venus because love is born of the desire for carnal pleasure. For the particular attributes linking Cupid with Venus in traditional iconography, see E. Panofsky, *Studies in Iconology* (New York, 1939), chap. IV; Robertson, *Preface,* pp. 90-91; Huppé and Robertson, *Fruyt and Chaf,* pp. 115-17.

[18] *Teseida,* ed. Roncaglia, VII, 50-66, and Notes, pp. 417, 421-22. On the authority of Tacitus (*Histories,* II, 3), Boccaccio attributes similar meanings to Venus's temple in Cyprus (*Genealogia deorum,* III, 23)—a context evoked by Venus ("Cypride") in the *Parliament* (l. 277). For other literary antecedents of the temple, see Bennett, *The Parlement of Foules,* p. 96, n. 1. The significance of the copper or brass of the temple is discussed below.

trasting implications of spiritual and carnal love. The Christian norm behind this contrast is implicit in the walled park or garden of Nature, a "blysful place" whose dominant features—its location "upon a ryver in a grene mede," the trees "clad with leves that ay shal laste," the climate without "grevaunce of hot ne cold," the birds "with voys of aungel in here armonye," the absence of sickness and old age, the endless "cler day," and the joy no man can describe—form a pattern of symbolism suggesting the garden of Paradise, an image allegorically of the Church or of man governed by the law of Nature and the spiritual Venus. To designate the corruption of God's creation through man's sin, however, Chaucer places within this paradisal setting his counterpart of Boccaccio's copper temple—a luxuriant temple of brass whose details suggest an inversion or perversion of the spiritual meanings of the garden.[19] Indicative of the will misled by carnal passion, in the vicinity of the temple appear Cupid and "Wille, his doughter," who sit "under a tre, besyde a welle" in which Wille tempers the heads of her father's arrows. Nearby are seen other allegorical figures, such as Pleasaunce, Lust, Craft, Delyt, Beute, Youthe, Curteysie, Flaterye, and Desyr—all representing aspects of

[19] The exegetical meanings of the garden and temple, along with the related symbols of Nature and Venus, are clarified by Robertson, *Preface*, pp. 69-72, 92ff., 386-88, 421-22, and Huppé and Robertson, *Fruyt and Chaf*, pp. 109ff. They observe that most of the literary gardens mirror in some way the gardens of Scripture, for example, the garden of Genesis or the *hortus conclusus* of the Canticle, and generally denote a Paradise of celestial delights or "a false paradise of earthly delights." Nature's garden in *PF* is interpreted as "neither a paradise of spiritual delights nor a paradise of earthly delights" but an image of the world in which the paradisal garden has been corrupted by the worship of the carnal Venus. In the *Roman de la Rose*, these contrasting meanings are illustrated by the garden of Deduit, where Scriptural details suggest an inversion of the spiritual Paradise, and by the garden or park later described by Genius (20,279ff.). For other literary examples, see Robertson, "The Doctrine of Charity in Mediaeval Literary Gardens," pp. 24-49.

misdirected love.[20] Appropriately, upon the temple itself perch Venus's doves, "many an hundred peyre," and around it dance gay women "in kertels, al dishevele." Inside, in "sovereyn place," sits Priapus, and in a "prive corner," sporting with her porter Richesse, reclines Venus on a bed of gold, with hair "untressed," naked "from the brest unto the hed," and the "remenaunt" covered "with a subtyl coverchef." But these tempting features of the temple, as in the *Teseida*, are offset by a portrayal of the effects of carnal love: the hot sighs engendered by desire and jealousy, and the woeful stories of lovers who worshiped in the temple, including Troilus, Hercules, Iseult, Pyramus, Thisbe, along with Dido and other victims drawn from the circle of the libidinous in the *Inferno*.

In the *House of Fame* the contrasting implications of the garden and temple are focused more directly on the temple itself. As in the *Parliament* the dominant effect is one of luxuriant and artfully contrived detail:

> But as I slepte, me mette I was
> Withyn a temple ymad of glas;
> In which ther were moo ymages
> Of gold, stondynge in sondry stages,
> And moo ryche tabernacles,
> And with perre moo pynacles,
> And moo curiouse portreytures,
> And queynte maner of figures
> Of olde werk, then I saugh ever.
> For certeynly, I nyste never
> Wher that I was, but wel wyste I,
> Hyt was of Venus redely,
> The temple . . . (119-31)

Whereas Venus's "lusty" garden is an inversion of the Garden of Paradise and related Scriptural gardens, her

[20] According to Huppé and Robertson, pp. 115ff., all of these details are indicative of the sterility and frustration of misdirected love— a meaning emphasized by the central position of Priapus, whose garden or grove is a Scriptural image of idolatry and perverted love (III Kings 15:11-13).

ornate "chirche" or temple of glass is an inversion of the Garden's allegorical equivalent, the Church of Christ, prefigured, for example, in the temple of Solomon.[21] This reversal of values is evident not only in its association with Venus but also in the details of its florid ornamentation— the glass, pinnacles, tabernacles, images, "portreytures," and "figures of olde werk"—all reminiscent of medieval churches in which the beauty of such ornaments is a reminder of the spiritual beauty of the heavenly Church or Paradise.[22] The luxuriant quality of Venus's "chirche" is portrayed most conspicuously by its glass, a feature sug-

[21] III Kings 5-8. On the temple as an image of the Church, see Bede, *De templo Salomonis liber*, *PL*, 91, cols. 757-59. Both the temple and the garden have a common referent in the exegetical meanings of Paradise, a symbol allegorically of the Church and anagogically of the heavenly city. See Augustine, *De civitate Dei*, XIII, 21, and Rabanus, *De universo*, *PL*, 111, col. 334. In *The Gothic Cathedral* (New York, 1962), pp. 37-38, 95-96, Otto von Simson relates the spiritual meanings of the temple and other Scriptural figures for the Church to medieval churches.

[22] On this aesthetic concept and the Gothic stylistic tradition suggested by Chaucer's imagery, see Simson, *Gothic Cathedral*, pp. 43, 50-51, especially 95ff., and Robertson, *Preface*, pp. 176ff. As Mâle observes (*Religious Art in France*, p. 4), ecclesiastical art is a visible embodiment and extension of the liturgy—a fact illustrated by the liturgiologists, for example, Durandus of Mende, whose *Rationale divinorum officiorum* is a compendium of traditional symbolism applied to the ritual, ornaments, and architectural features of medieval churches. Like Fame's ornate house, as we later observe, Venus's "chirche" suggests an inversion of both the Scriptural accounts of the Church and actual medieval churches, whose architectural and ornamental details point to the spiritual meanings of the heavenly Church or Paradise. From the twelfth century onward, the inversion of such details is a major device by which the poets allegorize the contrast between carnal and spiritual love. A notable example is the description of the Lover's Cave in Gottfried von Strassburg's *Tristan*, where the dimensions and other features reflect allegorical descriptions of the Church. See A. T. Hatto, *Tristan* (Baltimore, 1960), "Introduction," p. 15. A similar inversion is detectable in the jasper pillars of the temple of Venus in the *Parliament*, reminiscent of the jasper of the wall of the New Jerusalem. Cf. D. S. Brewer, ed., *The Parlement of Foulys* (New York, 1960), p. 109. Huppé and Robertson note a parallel between the inscriptions on the gate leading into Nature's garden and the inscriptions adorning the portals of medieval churches (*Fruyt and Chaf*, p. 110).

gesting both the brilliantly illuminated glass of Gothic churches and its spiritual counterpart in the Apocalypse, where it is the material to which John compares the resplendence of the New Jerusalem: "And the building of the wall thereof was of jasper stone, but the city itself pure gold, like to clear glass. . . . And the street of the city was pure gold, as it were, transparent glass" (21:18-21). Like the gold, gems, and other details describing the splendor of the holy city, glass acquires significance from the qualities making it appropriate to the spiritual meanings of the New Jerusalem. Thus the city is properly compared to glass, remarks Bersuire, because its purity and transparency denote the clarity of vision and the purity of condition in the heavenly Paradise or Church.[23] The same meanings underlie the copious use of glass in Gothic churches, where the light entering the windows corresponds mystically to the light of the celestial Church.[24] As a contrasting symbol, however, as in medieval descriptions of Fortune, the brittleness and resplendence of glass

[23] *Opera*, II, 459-60: "Glass [*vitrum*] is Paradise, where there is clearness of vision and splendor and purity of condition [*perspicuitas visionis, & claritas & puritas conditionis*], and where the images of God and the saints are seen perfectly in their true essences." Bersuire cites Apoc. 21:18. Cf. *Allegoriae in sacram scripturam*, col. 1,082. Comparable meanings are applied to crystal, for example, Apoc. 4:6, where it is the substance to which the "sea of glass" before God's throne is compared, and Apoc. 21:11 and 22:1, where it denotes the light of the Church Triumphant and the river of life.

[24] Simson relates the symbolism of the Apocalyptic glass to the glass at Chartres and St. Denis (*Gothic Cathedral*, pp. 11, 50-55, 119-23). Similar meanings are applied to the gold, gems, and other ornaments of these churches. Cf. E. Panofsky, *Abbot Suger* (Princeton, 1948), pp. 18-24, 50, 100; Paul Frankl, *The Gothic* (Princeton, 1960), p. 22; Robertson, *Preface*, pp. 177-80. Simson (p. 11, n. 27) suggests that the Gothic predilection for walls of glass may have been influenced by the Book of Enoch, in which the heavenly city is depicted as a palace "built of crystal." In literary allegory, as Patch illustrates, glass and crystal appear frequently in other world imagery suggesting the heavenly Paradise, as in *De Venus la deesse d'amors*, in which the palace is made of crystal (*The Other World*, Cambridge, Massachusetts, 1950, pp. 3, 286, 324, *et passim*).

99

are reminders of the false splendor and transience of worldly goods; for like glass, says Bersuire, these goods appear attractive and glorious but blind the eyes, and when they are destroyed they can seldom be restored.[25] In view of this contrast, we can easily distinguish the glass of the Church or heavenly city from the glass of Venus's "chirche," which is illuminated not by the light of divine wisdom and grace but by the meretricious light of idolatry. In short, as we later observe of Fame's resplendent castle, whose beryl makes everything appear more than it is, Venus's temple of glass is a false paradise or "chirche" whose glitter distorts the truth and blinds the eyes to reality.

This inversion of the spiritual meanings of the Church or Temple also appears in the many images of gold, "portreytures," and "figures" of "olde werk." Like the glass the images and "portreytures" are reminiscent of medieval churches in which the images portray the various saints and apostles and the "portreytures" (*simulacra*) are illustrations of Biblical stories, from both the Old and the New Testaments, teaching lessons of charity and man's redemption.[26] Although Chaucer does not identify the figures in

[25] *Opera*, II, 459-60. In *The Fall of Princes*, V, 587-88, Lydgate compares Fortune's favors to "brotel glas." Cf. Patch, *The Goddess Fortuna*, p. 51. The same meaning is sometimes applied to the glass in churches. See G. G. Coulton, *Art and the Reformation* (New York, 1928), p. 253. In *Allegoriae in sacram scripturam*, col. 1,082, glass is interpreted as the false allurement [*fallax blandimentum*] of this world, as in Prov. 23:31, where it designates the deceptive beauty of earthly love. Bersuire connects this meaning with the idolatrous light of worldly prosperity, which blinds the eyes and makes a "paradise" of temporal goods (IV, 296, V, 191). In *The Temple of Glas*, where Lydgate borrows his central image from Chaucer, the glass of Venus's temple, struck by the sun, blinds the dreamer's eyes.

[26] As "books" for the unlearned, paintings are condoned in churches as early as St. Gregory (*PL*, 77, col. 1,027). Cf. Honorius of Autun, *Gemmae animae*, PL, 172, col. 583, and Durandus of Mende, *Rationale divinorum officiorum*, I, 3. For a discussion of actual images and "portreytures" in fourteenth century English churches, see Tristram, pp. 15ff., who quotes Myrc's *Festial*: "I say boldly that ther ben mony

the temple of Venus, their identity may be surmised from those adorning the temples in the Knight's Tale and the *Parliament,* where they include the personified sorrows and "waymentynge" of those who worshiped in the temple and were caught in the chains of libidinous love. Among the "portreytures" in the Knight's Tale is the story of Solomon's idolatry ("the folye of kyng Salomon"), a detail bringing into sharp relief the contrast between the two temples.[27] In the *House of Fame* a similar inversion is implicit in the gold of the many "graven" images. Unlike the gold embellishing the ornaments in Solomon's temple or in medieval churches, a symbol of the light of divine wisdom, this gold mirrors the false light with which Satan blinds the eyes and leads men to idolatry; for "thow yt seme gold and schynyth rychely," comments a fifteenth-century writer on Venus's temple, "alle ys but sotelte off the fend to blere yowre ye."[28] The same contrast is suggested by the epithet "olde werk" applied to the figures, a traditional image of the church of the Jews and the Gentiles, the workers of old who built their religion without the cornerstone of Christ and the New Law.[29] In Book III, where we encounter the temple in

thousand of pepull that couth not ymagen in her hert how Christ was don on the rood, but as thei lerne hit by sight of images and payntours."

[27] III Kings 11:1ff. Bersuire contrasts true images and "portreytures" [*simulacra*] with the *simulacra Priapi,* which are those of the lecherous, "who know how to feign [*simulare*] loves and griefs to deceive women" (*Opera,* VI, 103).

[28] John Metham, *Amoryus and Cleopes,* ed. Hardin Craig (London, 1916), 1,979ff. On the contrasting gold of Solomon's temple, see Bede, *De templo Salomonis, PL,* 91, col. 752. Cf. Panofsky, *Abbot Suger,* pp. 168ff. Simson relates the gold and other ornaments at St. Denis to the temple (pp. 95, 119, 134).

[29] As opposed to the "worker" (*faber, artifex*) adorning the Tabernacle and Temple, the "worker" of graven images is an Old Testament symbol of Satan and idolaters, for example, Is. 44:8ff. See *Allegoriae in sacram scripturam,* col. 919, where *faber* is also applied, in an opposite sense, to Christ. The "graven" images in Venus's "chirche," whose "worker" Chaucer cannot name (470ff.), call up the Old Testa-

another guise, the contrast between "old" and "new," with its connotations of the Old and the New Laws, strengthens the idolatrous meanings of Fame's resplendent abode. In the present instance it is an additional reminder that those who worship in the temple of Venus live a life of cupidity, the state of captivity under the Old Law.

As a Scriptural symbol the temple is a convenient gathering point for the doctrinal ramifications of the two loves. Like the garden with which it is closely allied in Biblical commentary, the temple is a multiple symbol acquiring its fullest significance on the higher levels of exegesis. Allegorically, as most of the details suggest, the "chirche" of Venus is an inversion of the Church of Christ. On this level it may be compared to the Synagogue and the Church of the Gentiles, both symbols of the world without charity and redemption. Tropologically, the true temple is an image of the heart governed by charity or the spiritual Venus, since every man who follows the precepts of charity is said to build this temple within him. But when reason is subverted by the will and passions, this temple is besieged by the various sins and is turned into a temple of idolatry. This false temple symbolizes not only the mind's estrangement from God but also the end of such estrangement. Anagogically, therefore, it is an image of Hell, the dwelling of Satan. Conversely, the true temple signifies the heavenly Church or Paradise, the "far country" of the exiled pilgrim.[30]

---

ment context. On the idolatrous implications of "olde werk" in Old English literature, see Campbell, *The Advent Lyrics*, p. 12.

[30] Bersuire discusses the multiple meanings of the temple (*Opera*, I, 105ff.; VI, 140ff.). An important literary elaboration of the tropological meaning appears at the end of the *Psychomachia*, where Prudentius combines details of the New Jerusalem, Solomon's temple, and Wisdom's house into an allegory of the heart's triumph over the vices. On Solomon's temple as a symbol of the heavenly temple, see J. Sauer, *Symbolik des Kirchengebäudes* (Freiburg, 1924), p. 109. Simson (pp. 9, 37-38, 95-96) relates this meaning to other Scriptural figures for

These exegetical meanings of the temple suggest the rich background of Christian ideas and imagery relating the fictive details of Book I to the symbolism of the *Inferno*. Although Chaucer's visit to the temple of Venus bears little outward resemblance to Dante's visit to Hell, beneath the different *cortices* is found a subtle interplay of doctrinal meanings. As already observed, the most important connection between the two allegories is the concept of the pilgrimage, imaged in the poets themselves, who evince attitudes defining their similar roles. Thus Dante's confusion in the dark wood has its counterpart in Chaucer's confusion in the temple. Although Chaucer recognizes the temple of Venus, he does not know just where he is:

> For certeynly, I nyste never
> Wher that I was.

As we soon learn—and as the eagle confirms in Book II— the source of his confusion is his blind "reverence" for Venus and her servants. Not until he leaves the temple and sees the desert in which it is located does he gain some insight into the sterility of Venus and her "chirche." Meanwhile his preoccupation with the riches of the temple and its "olde werk" betrays his inability to see through its specious beauty. Clearly, therefore, Chaucer must learn to distinguish between appearance and reality and thereby perceive the nature and end of the wrongful love typified by Venus and her glittering temple. Book I serves this purpose. Whereas Dante witnesses the nature of cupidity and its rewards in a vision of the next life, Chaucer learns a comparable lesson in a vision of earthly love and fame.

Chaucer's equivalent of Dante's view of Hell is his own view of the events of the *Aeneid* portrayed on a "table of bras" in the temple. The idolatrous meanings of the tem-

---

the Church (for example, Ezechiel's temple, the Ark, the Tabernacle) and to medieval churches.

ple are again called up by its "table of bras," whose substance, like that of the copper and brass of the temples in the *Teseida* and the *Parliament,* has connotations of carnal love. In his Notes on the *Teseida,* Boccaccio explains the special properties making brass and copper appropriate to Venus:

In brief, he says that everything was of copper; and within he puts certain things which almost blind anyone who enters the temple. . . . The reasons that he says the temple is of copper are these. First, from the planet Venus originate copper and brass, which are the very same substance although to the sight there may be some diversity; and here what is said of copper may be said of both copper and brass. Hence it should be known that copper or brass (whichever we may wish to say) has three particular properties. The first is that it welds and joins and attaches itself to every other metal—or at least the greater part of them—as is seen by experience. The second is that brass, being polished, shines like gold. The third is that it has a very sweet sound. These properties are among the attributes of Venus because through her influence all natural unions for the purpose of creating something, especially where there is need for coming together, are done by her. Thus, just as brass may appear to be gold but is a very vile metal, so natural couplings, before they are tried, may appear to be consummate delight, whereas after the completion they are full of heavy griefs. Besides this, brass has a most sweet sound, for which reason it may well be understood that if in the acts of Venus there is some sweetness, it consists more in the mind than in the deed.[31]

In allying copper and brass with the planet Venus, Boccaccio follows the traditional astrological concept that the different metals and their properties are indicative of the qualities or influences of the planets to which they belong.[32] At the same time, as his gloss implies, both the

[31] *Teseida*, ed. Roncaglia, pp. 421-22.
[32] This concept underlies the metal–astrological imagery of Fame's pillars in Book III. Cf. the Canon's Yeoman's Tale, 825ff. As Boccaccio's gloss implies, there is little distinction between the astrological and mythographical Venuses as symbols of carnal love.

planets and their metals have become symbols of man's spiritual life. Behind Boccaccio's moralization is the familiar medieval distinction between the pure metals, gold and silver, and the base metals, such as iron, lead, tin, brass, or copper. But in Christian doctrine this distinction has become one between man in his redeemed and fallen states. Whereas gold and silver denote aspects of charity and divine wisdom, the base metals are images of sin and imperfection, as in Ezech. 22:18: "Son of man, the house of Israel is become dross to me: all these are brass, and tin, and iron, and lead, in the midst of the furnace: they are become the dross of silver."[33] This Scriptural contrast underlies the specific qualities ascribed to brass and copper in Boccaccio's gloss. Thus the sweet sound of brass—indicative of the seeming "sweetness" of carnal love—suggests St. Paul, who compares it to the appearance of virtue without charity: "If I speak with the tongues of men and of angels and have not charity, I am become as sounding brass or a tinkling cymbal" (I Cor. 13:1). Similarly, the contrast between the outward resplendence of brass and its inward vileness is a Scriptural image of the deceptive beauty attracting men to idolatry; for like hypocrites, remarks Bersuire, idols have the beauty of brass on the outside but are vile and corrupt within.[34] These Biblical meanings of brass reinforce the idolatrous connotations of the temple of Venus. As in Scripture,

[33] Cf. Num. 31:22; Is. 1:22, 25; Jer. 6:28-30; Mal. 3:3. In medieval accounts of the Earthly Paradise, the base metals are said to have been unknown. See Patch, *Other World*, pp. 158-59. In medieval alchemical treatises, the same contrast underlies the mystical identification of the philosophers' stone with Christ, the heavenly cornerstone, who frees the spirit from bodily impurities. For a discussion of this idea in relation to Chaucer, see Joseph E. Grennen, "The Canon's Yeoman's Alchemical 'Mass,'" *SP*, LXII (1965), 546-60. Cf. G. G. Fox, *The Mediaeval Sciences in the Works of John Gower* (Princeton, 1931), p. 115.

[34] *Opera*, III, 108 (on Dan. 14:6). More particularly, brass [*aes*] signifies the imperfect and sinful man [*hominem imperfectum et vitiosum*], as in Apoc. 9:20 (*ibid.*).

moreover, brass is a symbol not only of idolatry but also of its final reward—the infamy of damnation. Bersuire, commenting on the aforementioned passage from Ezechiel, glosses the brass "in the midst of the furnace" as the damned suffering torments in Hell.[35] In the Apocalypse the trumpet of the sixth angel is associated with the punishment of those who worship idols of brass—a context later called up by Fame's brass trumpet, whose infamous stench is compared to the "pit of helle." In the brass temple of the *Parliament* this anagogical meaning is more subtly evoked by the catalogue of tormented lovers, including Dido, borrowed from the circle of the libidinous in Dante's *Inferno*. Similar overtones are apparent in the contrasting gold and black inscriptions over the gate leading into the garden, suggesting the ending of the Athanasian Creed: "And those who do good shall go into everlasting life, but those who do evil shall go into everlasting fire." Whereas the gold inscription, foreshadowing the spiritual meaning of the garden, leads one "unto the welle of grace" and a "blysful place" where "dedly woundes" are healed and "grene and lusty May shal evere endure," the other, foreshadowing the temple of Venus and echoing the inscription over the gate to Dante's Hell, leads to a desert place where "nevere tre shal fruyt ne leves bere."[36] In the present instance, Dante's imagery is perhaps detectable in the "table of bras," whose substance suggests the "colore oscuro" of the words inscribed over the infernal gate.[37] But it is in the story of the *Aeneid* portrayed on the "table of bras" that Chaucer most graphically illustrates these multiple meanings of the

[35] *Ibid.* Cf. *Allegoriae in sacram scripturam*, col. 917. In the Gospel of Nicodemus, chap. XVI, brass is the substance of the gates of Hell. Cf. Ps. 106:16; Is. 45:2.

[36] Huppé and Robertson connect the inscriptions with the Athanasian Creed (*Fruyt and Chaf*, p. 111). Bennett emphasizes Dante's influence (*The Parlement of Foules*, pp. 63ff.).

[37] *Inf.*, III, 10-11. Cf. Robinson's note (*Works*, p. 780).

temple and metal of Venus. In the contrasting attitudes, actions, and fates of Aeneas and Dido, we are shown not only the nature of the two kinds of love and fame but also the eternal fame and infamy which are their final rewards.

In using Aeneas and Dido to introduce his theme, Chaucer found a precedent in Virgil, who relates the attitudes of these two characters to a spiritual conflict resembling the Christian contrast between earthly and heavenly fame. For example, both Aeneas and Dido, before their meeting, are depicted as followers of virtue and true fame: Aeneas as the pious leader and divinely appointed founder of the glory of Rome, and Dido as a responsible ruler and faithful observer of her vows of marriage and widowhood. But when Dido yields to her passion for Aeneas and neglects her duties and vows, her good name does not restrain her passion and fury. When her grief leads to despair at Aeneas' departure, she claims that it is for him she has lost the former fame ("fama prior") by which she was "approaching the stars." Jupiter's purpose in sending Mercury to Aeneas in Carthage is to remind him that both he and Dido have been forgetful of their nobler fame. Finally, Aeneas' leaving Dido is described as a return to the path of glory for which the gods have destined him. These and other passages on fame supply a meaningful context for Chaucer's use of Aeneas and Dido in introducing and exploring his theme.[38] But Chaucer's attitude toward fame is not pagan but Christian. Behind his use of the *Aeneid* is a long tradition of medieval attempts to bring Virgil's ideas into accord with the Christian contrast between two kinds of love.[39]

[38] *Aeneid*, I, 375-89; IV, 90-91, 221, 265ff., 321-23. Cf. VII, 95-106, 270-73.

[39] A convenient but largely unsympathetic account of the medieval moralizations of the *Aeneid* is found in D. Comparetti, *Vergil in the Middle Ages*, trans. E. F. M. Benecke (London, 1895). Cf. Elizabeth

The conventional view is expressed by Bernard Silvestris, who affirms that Virgil was a philosopher who concealed profound truths about the soul beneath a poetic
fiction.[40] Specifically, in Aeneas, he portrays what the
human spirit does and suffers while it is temporarily imprisoned in the body.[41] This theme is implicit in the opening lines:

Nitchie, *Vergil and the English Poets* (New York, 1919), and Armand
Gasquy, "De Fabio Planciade Fulgentio Vergilii interprete," *Berliner
Studien für Classische Philologie und Archaeologie*, VI (1887), 1-43.
One of the earliest moralizations of the *Aeneid* by a Christian is the
Virgiliana continentia of Fulgentius (ed. R. Helm, *Opera*, Leipzig,
1898), which influenced later commentators, for example, Bernard Sil-
vestris, whose *Commentum*, a moralization of the first six books, is
authoritative for the later Middle Ages and is reflected in John of
Salisbury's *Policraticus*, Dante's *Convivio*, Boccaccio's *Genealogia deorum*, and Salutati's *De laboribus Herculis*. The tradition of allegorizing the *Aeneid* persists in the fourteenth and subsequent centuries, as
Renaissance commentaries indicate.

[40] *Commentum*, p. 1. Bernard uses the terms *integumentum* and *in-
volucrum* to designate the veil concealing the philosophical truths beneath the "fabulous narrative" (p. 3). The profit gained by the reader
depends upon the state of his own intellect, for "a person acquires
utility [*utilitatem*] from this work according to his self-knowledge."
On Virgil's status as both philosopher and poet, see John of Salisbury,
Policraticus, VIII, 24, *Metalogicon*, II, 1; Boccaccio, *Genealogia deorum*, XIV, 10, 15; and Green's discussion, "Alan of Lille's *De Planctu
Naturae*," pp. 658-59.

[41] *Commentum*, p. 3. Bernard distinguishes between this "poetic"
theme, which appears *sub integumento*, and the "philosophical" theme,
which concerns "the nature of human life," each having its own order
of exposition: the natural order of philosophy and the artificial order
of poetry (pp. 1-3). Bernard regards the first six books of the *Aeneid*
as an allegory of the ages of man. In interpreting the "poetic" theme
as an allegory of the spirit, he follows Fulgentius in etymologizing
Aeneas' name as *ennos demas*, or *habitor corporis*, since the body is
the prison [*carcer*] or fetters [*vinculum*] of the spirit (p. 10). According to Boccaccio, Virgil's purpose *sub velamento poetico* is to
show "with what passions human frailty is infested, and the strength
with which a steady man subdues them" (*Genealogia deorum*, XIV, 13).
Boccaccio's phrasing, Osgood notes (p. 174), points to Petrarch, *Litterae seniles*, IV, 5. Virgil's other purposes, beyond the literal or historical sense, are to extol the family of Octavius and "to exalt the
glory of the name of Rome." The interpretation of the *Aeneid* as an
allegory of the spirit persists in the Renaissance, for example, in Douglas's *Eneados*, in which this concept exists alongside that of Aeneas as

"I wol now singen, yif I kan,
The armes, and also the man
That first cam, thurgh his destinee,
Fugityf of Troy contree,
In Itayle, with ful moche pyne
Unto the strondes of Lavyne." (143-48)

To the medieval commentators, the account of Aeneas'
flight from Troy and ultimate arrival in Italy approximates the Christian concept of the exiled pilgrim, who,
beset by the trials and temptations of the world and flesh,
finally achieves spiritual peace by bringing his will into
harmony with God. Italy, indicative of this goal, signifies
virtue or the highest degree of perfection achievable by
the spirit while still a captive in the body. More particularly, according to Bernard, it is the soul itself, with its
attributes of immortality, rationality, knowledge, and
virtue.[42] Opposed to Italy is Troy, a symbol of the body
wherein the spirit dwells and (ideally) rules. Aeneas'
flight from Troy is the flight of the spirit from the desires
of the flesh.[43] Finally, the "ful moche pyne" suffered by
Aeneas in his quest for Italy denotes the many struggles
and temptations hindering the spirit in its search for perfection.[44]

---

an ideal prince. See Bruce Dearing, "Gavin Douglas' *Eneados*: A Re-
interpretation," *PMLA*, LXVII (1952), 862.

[42] *Commentum*, pp. 20, 40, 50. Benvenuto da Imola interprets Italy
as *virtus* (*Commentum*, I, 199-200). To John of Salisbury it also
designates *beatitudo* (*Policraticus*, VIII, 24).

[43] Bernard, pp. 46, 97, 103. Benvenuto (III, 54-55) contrasts Troy
(*terra voluptatis*) and Italy (*terra virtutis*). Bernard allegorizes the
details relating to Troy. The Greek soldiers are the different vices
vexing the body (p. 98). The wooden horse is *luxuria*, which, once
admitted into the body, allows the other vices to gain control (p. 103).
The absence of reason is symbolized by the killing of Priam in his
castle. Whereas the castle [*arx*] signifies the head, the dwelling of the
intellect (p. 15), Priam is *passio*, which has subjugated the mind (pp.
99-100).

[44] The details included in Chaucer's summary are moralized by Bernard as aspects of the spirit's pilgrimage. Aeneas' bearing Anchises
"on hys bak" and rescuing the "goddes of the lond" are indicative of

Chaucer's version of the *Aeneid* is an adaptation of the conflict of the opening lines to his own theme and poetic method.[45] Although the essential outline of Virgil's narrative remains intact and provides the necessary perspective and norms for viewing the actions and attitudes of Aeneas and Dido, Chaucer has introduced significant changes—additions, omissions, as well as shifts in emphasis—to stress the themes of love and fame and to

---

pietas. Creusa, who dies but later returns in the spirit to warn Aeneas to seek Italy "as was hys destinee," denotes *concupiscentia*, the spirit's innate desire for good (p. 13). Her disappearance in the forest "at a turnynge of a wente" is the temporary loss of this desire. Aeneas' comrades ("meynee") are the powers, tendencies, or potentialities serving the spirit as long as it is guided by reason (pp. 11, 13, 17, 46, 50). The ships are various motions or inclinations of the will prompting Aeneas to act (pp. 11, 17). The tempests raised by Juno through Aeolus are the perturbations to which the spirit is often subjected. Juno is the active life (p. 46)—or Fortune, according to Neckam, *De naturis rerum*, I, 39—and the winds are the "temporal fortunes, prosperity and adversity," dealt out to man as he travels upon the sea of vices (pp. 49-50). The storm at sea is a favorite episode of medieval writers to remind the reader of Virgil's allegorical intent, for example, Boccaccio, *Genealogia deorum*, XIV, 9.

[45] The following treatment of Chaucer's version of the *Aeneid*, it should be emphasized, is not an attempt to impose the conventional moralizations on the details of his narrative. As the references to Virgil's "book" indicate, the basis of his rendering is the *Aeneid* itself, which provides the essential norms for viewing the characters and events. Nevertheless, Chaucer's view of the poem as an allegory with a moral purpose is suggested in Book III, where he includes Virgil among the pagan writers of "hy and gret sentence" (1,419ff.). From his knowledge of the *Policraticus*, we may perhaps infer his familiarity with the main outline of Bernard's interpretation. But his acquaintance with the standard commentaries seems likely from their customary use in conjunction with the original text in the schools. See G. Paré, A. Brunet, P. Tremblay, *La renaissance du XIIᵉ siècle: les écoles et l'enseignement* (Paris, 1933), pp. 116-17. Although the moralizations of Fulgentius and Bernard are standard for the Middle Ages, individual writers, for example, Petrarch and Boccaccio, sometimes offer their own interpretations of specific details. Chaucer himself, in beginning with a natural time-order, rather than *in medias res*, is obviously not following either Virgil or the concept of the ages of man. However, in his emphasis on episodes and details which are conventionally moralized, and in his basic modifications of the story to fit the symbolism of the temple of Venus, the influence of the commentaries seems clear.

adapt the story to the symbolism of the temple, which, along with its "table of bras," should be constantly borne in mind as the controlling symbol for the Christian implications of the pagan fiction. The slanting of the *Aeneid* to fit the meanings of the temple is first apparent in the treatment of Venus, whose identity with the carnal Venus depicted on the wall is emphasized by such sensual details as her being kissed by Jove, her appearing to Aeneas in the "queynt array" of a huntress with the "wynd blowynge upon hir tresse," her directing Aeneas to Dido's "faire toun," and her instigating Dido to let him do "al that weddynge longeth too."[46] Her carnality is more humorously apparent in Chaucer's addressing her with the courtly formula, "my lady dere," a conventional designation for the "dea d'amore."[47] But the most conspicuous modification of the *Aeneid* to fit the meanings of Venus and her temple is the expansion of the role of Dido, whose long lament after Aeneas' departure is the focal point of Chaucer's narrative. As the lover of Aeneas and the unhappy victim of his betrayal of the "law" of Venus and

[46] In "Chaucer in Error," *Speculum*, I (1926), 222, E. K. Rand suggests that Chaucer altered his source in order to emphasize Venus's activity, for example, in the storm at sea, where he stresses her role in ending the storm (212-21). Whereas the calming of the sea in the *Aeneid* (I, 124-56) is separated from Venus's petition by 66 lines and Aeneas' landing in Carthage occurs between these two episodes, Chaucer has him land after Venus's petition. Another change is his having Jupiter rather than Neptune end the storm, a detail perhaps designed to stress Jupiter's importance as a link between Aeneas' pilgrimage and his own. Primary emphasis, however, is upon Venus, whose appearance as a huntress calls up familiar contexts in which "hunting" is applied to carnal love, for example, Ovid, *Ars amatoria*, I, 45-46, 89, 253-54. Cf. *Aeneid*, IV, 129ff.; Bernard, *Commentum*, pp. 24-25; *Mythographus Vaticanus III*, p. 251. In *LGW*, 1,188ff., Chaucer stresses the hunt of Aeneas and the "amorous queene." On the contrasting hunts of Venus and Diana in medieval literature and art, see Robertson, "The Subject of the *De Amore*," p. 147, and *Preface*, pp. 263-64. The possible pun on the sexual meaning of "queynt" in Venus's "queynt array" and Dido's and Aeneas' "acquaintance" (225ff.) suggests the same context.

[47] Cf. Lydgate's "My Lady Dere," *The Minor Poems*, II, 420-24.

Cupid, Dido is given all the sympathy she might expect in the temple. Viewed by the norm of spiritual love, however, Dido's inordinate passion for Aeneas, culminating in her grief, despair, and suicide, exemplifies very concretely what can happen when one worships in the idolatrous temple of Venus.[48]

In emphasizing the story of Dido, Chaucer is in accord with Virgil's medieval commentators, who stress Aeneas' carnal bond with Dido as an important aspect of the spirit's pilgrimage and use it to expound the contrasting meanings of the two Venuses. Whereas Dido herself is a symbol of libidinous love,[49] Carthage, the city which she rules, is the world, or Babylon, brought to confusion by her sin.[50] Aeneas' sojourn with Dido illustrates the spirit's turning away from reason and virtue to the world and the flesh.[51] But Aeneas' worship in the temple of Venus is

---

[48] In *PF*, 284ff., the same implications are apparent in the portrayal of Dido's story in the "temple of bras."

[49] Bernard, *Commentum*, pp. 12, 24-25, 93-97, especially 95ff. Cf. Fulgentius, *Virgiliana continentia*, ed. Helm, p. 99, and Boccaccio, *Genealogia deorum*, XIV, 13. Whereas the interpretation of Dido as *libido* is based on her role in the *Aeneid*, a historical tradition represents her as the faithful widow who preferred to burn rather than to remarry. See Petrarch, "Trionfo della Pudicizia," 10-12, 154-59, and Boccaccio, *Genealogia deorum*, XIV, 13. Osgood (p. 173) finds the distinction as early as Macrobius. Although Boccaccio is aware of the historical Dido, he justifies Virgil's adapting her to his moral purpose.

[50] Bernard, p. 12: "In this city [Aeneas] finds a woman ruling—that is, the Carthaginians in servitude—for in this world such is the confusion that lust [*libido*] is in control and the virtues (which we understand by the Carthaginians, strong and valiant men) are suppressed. . . . Thus, in Holy Scripture, the world is called the city of Babylon, that is, confusion."

[51] *Ibid.*, pp. 12, 23-25. Cf. Fulgentius, *Virgiliana continentia*, p. 94; John of Salisbury, *Policraticus*, VIII, 24. For both Fulgentius and Bernard, Aeneas' affair with Dido typifies the nature of youth. Benvenuto da Imola summarizes the conventional view: "Morally speaking, Aeneas is the youthful lover (hence he is called the son of Venus), who, while sailing for Italy—that is, while pursuing virtue—and finding refuge in a haven, is suddenly shaken by the tempest of bitter love and is driven from the right path [*via recta*] to Libya, that is, libido. Thus Africa, a very hot region, properly signifies the ardor of lechery

merely temporary. His warning by Mercury and his leaving Dido and her "faire toun" symbolize the spirit's liberation from the chains of the carnal Venus and the return to deeds of glory.[52] In Chaucer's fiction these contrasting implications of the Dido–Aeneas episode are projected in the symbolism of Venus and her temple, along with the "table of bras," and in the broader framework of the *Aeneid*, in which Aeneas' piety, his glorious "destinee," Jupiter's warning through Mercury, and Chaucer's final "excuse" of Aeneas for leaving Dido bring the moral norms of Virgil's narrative into perspective. At the same time, by omitting key details suggesting Virgil's viewpoint, especially Aeneas' higher motives and Dido's less savory traits, and by a rhetorical heightening of Dido's self-pity and Aeneas' "cruelty," Chaucer creates in Dido an exaggerated picture of innocent pathos and in Aeneas a type of traitor whom neither love, vows, tears, nor death can move to pity.[53]

[*ardorem luxuriae*]; and Aeneas, enslaved there by his lustful desires, forgets his honorable goal" (I, 199-200).

[52] Like Fulgentius and Bernard, Boccaccio views Book IV as an allegory of the soul's triumph over evil concupiscence. Having illustrated "with what passions human frailty is infested, and the strength with which a steady man subdues them," Virgil "wished particularly to demonstrate the reasons why we are carried away into wanton behavior by the passion of concupiscence. . . . So he represents in Dido the attracting power of the passion of love, prepared for every opportunity, and in Aeneas one who is readily disposed in that way and at length overcome. But after showing the enticements of lust, he points the way of return to virtue by bringing in Mercury, messenger of the gods, to rebuke Aeneas, and call him back from such indulgence to deeds of glory" (*Genealogia deorum*, XIV, 13; Osgood, pp. 68-69).

[53] In *LGW*, where Chaucer acknowledges his indebtedness to Ovid's *Heroides*, the pathos of Dido's complaint is similarly heightened by the omission of unattractive traits which Virgil shows in her character, such as her anger, spite, and vengefulness (*Aeneid*, IV, 305-30, 365-87, 584ff.). For a recent reminder of the humorous exaggeration in Chaucer's and Dido's remarks on Aeneas, see William S. Wilson, "Exegetical Grammar in the *House of Fame*," *ELN*, I (1964), 244-48, who sees a deliberately comic use of medieval precepts of grammar in the moral disquisitions on male perfidy. The humor, it may be added, does not preclude the underlying seriousness of Chaucer's "sentence."

Contributing largely to this effect is the sympathy of
Chaucer the dreamer, who, as the observer of the events
depicted on the "table of bras," stands in much the same
relationship to what he sees as Dante does to the events
in the *Inferno*. Although neither is an active participant
in the drama unfolding before him, each responds posi-
tively to what he sees and expresses an attitude that frequently betrays his own confusion. In Chaucer's extrava-
gant sympathy for Dido, we may detect the ironic humor
evident elsewhere in his praise of Love's "martyrs,"
notably in the *Legend of Good Women*, where Dido is
similarly portrayed. But in this instance we may also view
his attitude as an integral aspect of his role as the mis-
guided pilgrim, whose confusion in the temple, as the
eagle's later diagnosis of his malady confirms, stems from
his blind devotion to Venus and Cupid and their servants.
Consequently, his remarks on Aeneas and Dido reflect
the distorted appearances of the temple itself. Thus Dido,
at the expense of Aeneas, is described as one who made
him

> Hyr lyf, hir love, hir lust, hir lord,
> And dide hym al the reverence,
> And leyde on hym al the dispence,
> That any woman myghte do,
> Wenynge hyt had al be so
> As he hir swor; and herby demed
> That he was good, for he such semed. (258-64)

More indicative of the humorous hyperbole that expresses
the dreamer's attitude is his own sermon on the danger of
trusting appearances—a fault aptly applied to Dido but
not inapplicable to all those, including himself, who confuse the glittering appearance of the temple with its
reality:

> Allas! what harm doth apparence,
> Whan hit is fals in existence!

For he to hir a traytour was;
Wherfore she slow hirself, allas!
Loo, how a woman doth amys
To love hym that unknowen ys!
For, be Cryste, lo, thus yt fareth:
"Hyt is not al gold that glareth." (265-72)

Chaucer's confusion stems not so much from his sympathy
for Dido, which is not altogether misplaced, as from the
fact that his absorption in her grief makes him forget the
higher love exemplified by Aeneas.[54] In condemning
Aeneas as a "traytour" for breaking his bond with Dido,
he fails to add that in breaking this carnal bond Aeneas
is re-establishing the bond of divine love, and that Dido,
in letting Aeneas do "al that weddynge longeth too,"
neglects both her sacred vows of marriage and her vows
of widowhood.[55] More obviously humorous is his cursory
dismissal of the actual circumstances of the secret love of
Dido and Aeneas because he "kan not of that faculte" and
"hyt were a long proces to telle." But if Chaucer is unable

[54] Allowing for his usual irony in portraying himself, Chaucer's
attitude as the pilgrim evinces the same irrationality that Augustine
attributes to himself as a youth when he bemoaned Dido's death for
love of Aeneas but was unmindful of his own spiritual death because
of his lack of love for God (*Confessions*, I, 13). Chaucer's attitude
might also be compared to that of Dante in the circle of the lecherous, where he faints from pity for Paolo and Francesca (*Inf.*, V,
139-42). True sympathy, according to Augustine, stems from an awareness that all men are brothers in sin. Although one should sympathize
with the sinner, he should also live in charity. Chaucer adopts this
attitude at the beginning of *Troilus*, I, 47-51. For a fourteenth century statement of the idea, see Walter Hilton, *The Ladder of Perfection*, I, 65.

[55] Dido's negligence in this respect is clear in *Aeneid*, IV, 15-19, 31-
53, 54ff., 165-72, 550-52. Dante, who puts Dido in the circle of the
lecherous, describes her as one who "broke faith to the ashes of
Sichaeus" (*Inf.*, V, 61-62). In *Amorosa visione*, XXVIII-XXIX, Boccaccio reveals Dido's longing for the pleasures of the marriage bed.
Chaucer's Parson, discussing lechery, provides the Christian norm for
viewing Dido's breaking of her vows: "And evere the gretter merite
shal he han, that moost restreyneth the wikkede eschawfynges of the
ardour of this synne. And this is in two maneres, that is to seyn, chastitee in mariage, and chastitee of widwehod" (915ff.).

to speak of Dido's "acquaintance" with Aeneas, Virgil is unequivocal in making her own eagerness for Aeneas' love the cause of her downfall.[56] This comic self-portrayal of the poet, ignorant of the "faculte" of love, is later completed in his characterization as the poet of love who, despite his praise of the "art" of Venus and Cupid, has had no part in the actual "daunce." In the temple, we might add, Chaucer cannot "speke of love" because he is so blinded by the resplendent glass and brass that he does not remember the nature of true love. Therefore he forgets the actual motives prompting the attitudes and actions of Aeneas and Dido.

Chaucer's remarks foreshadow those of Dido, whose long lament is the focal point of the attempt to adapt the *Aeneid* to the idolatrous meanings of the temple. Again by the exclusion of Aeneas' viewpoint and by an infusion of rhetorical hyperbole appropriate to the false appearances of the temple, we witness in Dido a picture of innocent pathos. But behind her exaggerated grief and self-pity lies the unattractive reality of a mind in which the image of reason has been destroyed. Enhanced by an empty and ironically incongruous use of logic, Dido's impassioned and somewhat petulant soliloquy reflects the reckless desperation of one whose worship in the temple of Venus has progressed far beyond the initial sin of carnal love. In her case inordinate love has led to uncontrolled grief, and grief to despair and suicide. The extent of her irrationality is evident in her total rejection of responsi-

[56] *Aeneid*, IV, 165ff. In *LGW* Chaucer emphasizes the scenes relating to the hunt, the tempest, and the cave where Dido seals her secret bond with Aeneas (*Aeneid*, IV, 129ff.). Bernard interprets the carnal meanings of these details: Aeneas "is driven to the cave by tempests and rains; that is to say, by fleshly agitations and the overflow of humor arising from an excess of food and drink, he is led to the uncleanness of sensuality and the flesh. This uncleanness of the flesh [*immunditia carnis*] is called a cave [*cavea*] because it darkens the clarity and discretion of the mind" (pp. 24-25).

bility for her situation. Like Chaucer the pilgrim, she blames Aeneas for his desertion, thereby appealing to a carnal bond which has no power over one who has freed himself from the chains of Venus. Her accusations take on a broader irony when her logic leads her to generalize Aeneas' treachery into the deceitfulness of all men and to reject her belief in feminine "art":

> "O, have ye men such godlyhede
> In speche, and never a del of trouthe?
> Allas, that ever hadde routhe
> Any woman on any man!
> Now see I wel, and telle kan,
> We wrechched wymmen konne noon art;
> For certeyn, for the more part,
> Thus we be served everychone.
> How sore that ye men konne groone,
> Anoon as we have yow receyved,
> Certaynly we ben deceyvyd!
> For, though your love laste a seson,
> Wayte upon the conclusyon,
> And eke how that ye determynen,
> And for the more part diffynen." (330-44)

But the height of Dido's confusion is reached in her climactic outburst against "wikke Fame." Appropriately, the motif of fame is introduced earlier when she accuses men of using women as a means of "magnyfyinge" their names. Her confusion of true and false fame becomes unquestionable when she blames Aeneas for the loss of her own good name:

> "O, wel-awey that I was born!
> For thorgh yow is my name lorn,
> And alle myn actes red and songe
> Over al thys lond, on every tonge." (345-48)

Although Chaucer follows Virgil in making Dido's fear of infamy a dominant motive behind her attitude, Virgil leaves no doubt as to where the responsibility lies for her damaged reputation: her own forgetfulness of her good name when she gave herself to Aeneas: "That day was the first day of death, that first the cause of woe. For no more is Dido swayed by fair show or fair fame, no more does she dream of a secret love: she calls it marriage and with that name veils her sin!"[57] Significantly, these lines provide the context of Virgil's description of Fame, the opening lines of which, with important additions, Chaucer attributes to Dido:

> "O wikke Fame! for ther nys
> Nothing so swift, lo, as she is!
> O, soth ys, every thing ys wyst,
> Though hit be kevered with the myst.
> Eke, though I myghte duren ever,
> That I have don, rekever I never,
> That I ne shal be seyd, allas,
> Yshamed be thourgh Eneas,
> And that I shal thus juged be,—
> 'Loo, ryght as she hath don, now she
> Wol doo eft-sones, hardely;'
> Thus seyth the peple prively." (349-60)

From a Christian viewpoint Dido's outburst against "wikke Fame" takes on particular irony; for Fame, to apply Boethius' comment on Fortune, is not in herself "wicked." Wickedness is more properly ascribed to those who place their trust in the fickle judgment of men instead of in the judgment of God. Consequently Dido feels the anxiety and fear accompanying the pursuit of Fame's unstable awards. Climaxing the irony, Chaucer calls up the Christian implications of Dido's attitude by attributing to her two lines which contain more truth than she is aware of: "O, soth ys, every thing ys wyst,/ Though hit be kevered with the myst." These lines echo Christ's warning to his disciples to beware of "the leaven of the

---

[57] *Aeneid*, IV, 169-72.

Pharisees, which is hypocrisy," for "there is nothing covered that shall not be revealed; nor hidden, that shall not be known." What follows is a pointed commentary on Dido's secret bond with Aeneas: "For whatsoever things you have spoken in darkness shall be published in the light; and that which you have spoken in the ear in the chambers shall be preached on the housetops." The contrast between two kinds of fame, heavenly and earthly, is brought forcefully home as Christ contrasts the fear of human judgment with the fear of that higher judgment which is the source of eternal fame and infamy: "And I say to you, my friends: Be not afraid of them who kill the body, and after that have no more that they can do. But I will show you whom you shall fear: fear ye him who, after he hath killed, hath power to cast into hell."[58] Blinded by despair and fearful of human judgment, Dido follows the path that leads to Hell and eternal infamy. Her despair, indeed, is itself a kind of spiritual "hell" such as Chaucer's Parson ascribes to those in a state of sloth: "Accidie is lyk hem that been in the peyne of helle, by cause of hir slouthe and of hire hevynesse; for they that been dampned been so bounde that they ne may neither wel do ne wel thynke."[59] Ending her life in suicide, Dido assures her own damnation. The pattern is completed when Aeneas descends to Hell and finds her among those who are suffering endless torments for their sins.[60]

[58] Luke 12:2-5. Cf. Matt. 10:26-33; Mark 4:22; I Cor. 4:1-5; and chap. I, n. 26, above. The verse from Luke is quoted in the margin of two of the three manuscripts of the *House of Fame*. The fear of infamy is a frequent motif in love poetry and is a distinctively medieval development of Fame and her allegorical offspring, such as Wicked Tongue in the *Roman de la Rose*. Cf. Robertson, *Preface*, pp. 396-97.

[59] Lines 686ff. Cf. *Allegoriae in sacram scripturam*, col. 969.

[60] *Aeneid*, VI, 434-76. In Christian terms, the kind of sloth leading to suicide is *tristitia*, or "worldly sorwe," which, says Chaucer's Parson (following II Cor. 7:10), "werketh to the deeth of the soule and of the body also; for therof comth that a man is anoyed of his owene lif./ Wherfore swich sorwe shorteth ful ofte the lif of man, er that

After a final rhetorical flourish in which Chaucer indignantly summons up the names of other unhappy ladies whose love and betrayal fit the pattern of Dido's fate, we return to the main line of Virgil's narrative.[61] Here the exaggerated sympathy for Dido, mirroring the distorted vision of the temple of glass and its "table of bras," is brought into perspective as Chaucer introduces Virgil's "excuse" for Aeneas' desertion:

> But to excusen Eneas
> Fullyche of al his grete trespas,
> The book seyth Mercurie, sauns fayle,
> Bad hym goo into Itayle,
> And leve Auffrikes regioun,
> And Dido and hir faire toun. (427-32)

If Dido's fate illustrates the infamy, both earthly and eternal, which rewards the worshiper in the idolatrous temple of Venus, Aeneas' forsaking Dido and his eventual achievement of his "destinee" in Italy exemplify the heavenly fame rewarding those who abandon the temple and return to the path of virtue. To both Virgil and his medieval commentators, this meaning is imaged in Mer-

---

his tyme be come by wey of kynde." If this sin "continue unto his ende," it is "cleped synnyng in the Hooly Goost" (693ff.). In the chapter from Luke to which Dido alludes, Christ warns of sinning against the Holy Spirit (12:10). In *De civitate Dei*, I, 16-19, Augustine contrasts such pagan heroines as Lucrece, who slew herself from fear of infamy, with the Christian martyrs who suffered as the others did but survived their ignominy.

[61] In the betrayal of these women (Phyllis by Demophoon, Briseis by Achilles, Medea and Hypsipyle by Jason, Dejanira by Hercules, Ariadne by Theseus)—all from the *Heroides*—the men break a carnal bond and, in some instances, return to the path of virtue, while the women subject themselves to irrational grief, which, in the stories of Dido, Phyllis, and Medea, leads to suicide. In *BD*, 714ff., Chaucer includes Dido, Phyllis, and Medea among those who subjected themselves to Fortune and "foolishly" took their own lives. The distorted viewpoint of the temple of Venus is brought into clearer focus at the end of *Troilus*, V, 1,765ff., where Chaucer juxtaposes male perfidy and Criseyde's faithlessness, which is contrasted with "Penelopees trouthe and good Alceste."

cury, whom Jupiter sends to warn Aeneas to leave "Auf-frikes regioun" and Dido's "faire toun." To follow the traditional view of Bernard, Mercury signifies reason; or to follow Boccaccio, he is the remorseful conscience which rouses the spirit from slumber, calling it back to deeds of glory and causing it to break the bonds of evil delight and spurn all flattery and tears deflecting it from its divine goal.[62] In these terms, Mercury's warning marks the beginning of the spirit's recovery from sloth.

This process of spiritual recovery is completed in Aeneas' descent to Hell:

> And also sawgh I how Sybile
> And Eneas, besyde an yle,
> To helle wente, for to see
> His fader, Anchyses the free;
> How he ther fond Palinurus,
> And Dido, and eke Deiphebus;
> And every turment eke in helle
> Saugh he, which is longe to telle;
> Which whoso willeth for to knowe,
> He moste rede many a rowe
> On Virgile or on Claudian,
> Or Daunte, that hit telle kan. (439-50)

To Bernard, as well as to many other medieval readers of the *Aeneid*, the account of Aeneas' descent to Hell contained Virgil's closest approximation to the higher truths of Christianity.[63] This higher meaning is embodied in the

[62] *Genealogia deorum*, XIV, 13. Cf. Petrarch, *Litterae seniles*, IV, 5; Bernard, p. 25. John of Salisbury, following Bernard, interprets Mercury as *ratio*. Fulgentius identifies him with *ingenium*, which Bernard defines as one of the threefold faculties of the mind: *ingenium, ratio, memoria*. Cf. chap. IV, n. 3, below. Mercury is conventionally moralized as *eloquentia* or wisdom in speech, a meaning applied by Bernard to his role of warning Aeneas to leave Dido (p. 25). In her Prologue, the Wife of Bath contrasts Mercury's "wysdam and science" with Venus's "ryot and dispence" (697-700), a contrast applicable to the Venus of the temple.

[63] Comparetti, *Vergil in the Middle Ages*, p. 112. Cf. Bernard, *Commentum*, p. 28; John of Salisbury, *Policraticus*, VIII, 24.

Sibyl, whom Aeneas consults in order to carry out his father's command that he visit him in the other world. The Sibyl, says Bernard, signifies "intelligence" or "divine counsel" whereby the mind consults itself. She is called divine because intelligence is nothing more than the comprehension of the divine.[64] Similarly, her cave denotes "religion" or "theology," for in it the mind is led to contemplate the Creator and to understand its own nature.[65] This process of education is fulfilled in the descent itself, whose meanings Bernard explains:

The descent to Hell is fourfold: one is natural, a second is virtuous, a third is sinful, and a fourth is artificial. The natural descent is the nativity of man, for at birth the soul by nature begins to be in this fallen condition and thus to descend to Hell and recede from its divine state and gradually decline to sin and assent to fleshly desires. But this descent is common to everyone. Then there is the virtuous descent which occurs when the wise man descends to worldly things through contemplation, not that he might put his trust in them but, by recognizing their fragility and casting them aside, that he might turn inwardly to things unseen and by a knowledge of created things understand the Creator more clearly. According to this descent Orpheus and Hercules, who are called wise men, went to Hell. Thirdly, there is the sinful descent by which the mind is led to worldly goods and the whole intent is placed in them and enslaved by them and never removed from them. In this manner, we read, Euridice descended to Hell. From this descent, moreover, there is no return. The fourth descent is artificial, for in necromancy the descent is performed by artifice.[66]

[64] Bernard, *Commentum*, pp. 32, 35. John of Salisbury interprets the Sibyl as "counsel of Jove" or "wisdom of God" (*Policraticus*, VIII, 25).

[65] *Ibid.*, p. 41. Those who are hidden in the cave [*spelunca*] of religion, says Bersuire, "are spiritually nourished and educated by God" (*Opera*, VI, 117).

[66] *Ibid.*, p. 30. On the fourfold meaning of the descent, see also Pietro Alighieri, *Commentarium*, pp. 11-17; Salutati, *De laboribus Herculis*, ed. Ullman, II, 483ff.; IV, 4; and chap. II, n. 74, above.

Aeneas' descent, according to Bernard, falls within the
second and fourth of these categories. On the narrative
or "literal" level, Aeneas descends by artifice when he
consults the Sibyl about the future and gains access to the
other world. Figuratively his descent is the virtuous
descent by which the mind is led to consider the world and
its temporalia and thereby turn its thoughts to the
Creator.[67] More specifically, it signifies the spirit's insight
into the nature of its own past errors. These errors are
embodied in Palinurus, Dido, and Deiphobus, symbols
respectively of sloth, lechery, and fear.[68]

Aeneas' descent to Hell brings the contrast between two
kinds of fame to a fitting climax. In Elysium, where
Anchises reveals Aeneas' glorious destiny and the mysteries of the future life, we have the goal of heavenly
fame achieved by those who remember their Creator and
forsake worldly delights. Dido's fate, on the other hand,
is the infamous goal of those who forget their nobler
duties and put their trust in earthly love and fame. Her
appearance in Hell fulfills the words of Christ which she
so ironically echoes in her outcry against "wikke Fame":
"O, soth ys, every thing ys wyst,/ Though hit be kevered
with the myst." In contrast to the fickle judgment of the
people which Dido fears, this is the judgment of him who
"hath power to cast into hell." Although Chaucer carefully adheres to the details of his pagan fiction, these

[67] *Ibid.* Cf. pp. 27-28, 50-51, 90. Bernard interprets Anchises as
the Creator, or *super omnes excelsus.* He warns Aeneas to descend to
Hell because "a knowledge of created things leads to the contemplation of the Creator" (pp. 50-51).

[68] *Ibid.,* p. 83. Cf. John of Salisbury, *Policraticus,* VIII, 24. Palinurus, who is earlier portrayed in the temple as the "sterisman" who falls
asleep and is swept overboard, is interpreted by Bernard as *errabundus
visus* (pp. 28, 32). In the *Roman de la Rose,* 13,468ff., he is an example of those falling into the realm of Morpheus, that is, slothfulness. On Dido and Deiphobus as images of Aeneas' past sins, see Bernard, pp. 95, 100. As such, they have a function comparable to that
of the souls viewed by Dante in Hell.

Christian implications are given additional weight by his appeal to Dante, along with Virgil and Claudian, as an authority on the torments in Hell.[69] The context of the *Inferno* is brought to mind not only by Dido, whom Dante views in the circle of the lecherous, but also by Aeneas, to whom Dante, not without reason, expressly compares his situation in Canto II. For Dante, too, must undergo a spiritual descent which will prepare him for a higher stage of understanding. This correspondence, as we later see, is only one instance of the meanings linking the *Aeneid* with both the *Comedy* and the *House of Fame*.[70]

In Hell, says John of Salisbury, Aeneas learns that another way must be followed by those who would attain the sweet embraces of Lavinia and the beatitude of Italy.[71] Chaucer's final scene relates how Aeneas reaches this goal. In his own fiction, as in Virgil's narrative, Italy denotes the heavenly "destinee" and rewards of true fame. In Bernard's moralization, whereas Carthage and Troy symbolize the sins of the world and flesh, Italy, the promised land of Aeneas' stormy pilgrimage, designates the highest degree of perfection achieved by the virtuous spirit while still imprisoned in the body. The life of labor and good works by which this perfection is brought about is signified by Lavinia, whom Aeneas wins as his bride.[72] Turnus, Lavinia's suitor whom Aeneas slays, is one of the many perturbations ("batayles") which the spirit must overcome before reaching its final state of beatitude.[73] Lastly, Jupi-

---

[69] The anachronism of Chaucer's Christian details, especially Dido's allusion to Scripture, seems less unusual when we recall the ending of *Troilus*, where Chaucer is more explicit about the Christian implications of his pagan tragedy. Although he is reticent about the ultimate destiny of Troilus, in *PF* he appears with Dido and other pagan worshipers of Venus drawn from the first circle of Dante's Hell.

[70] On Dante's indebtedness to the moralizations of the *Aeneid*, see E. K. Rand, *Founders of the Middle Ages* (New York, 1928), pp. 272ff.

[71] *Policraticus*, VIII, 24.   [72] Bernard, *Commentum*, p. 50.

[73] Although Bernard does not interpret the last six books, he earlier

ter, who at Venus's prayer protects Aeneas and leads him to achieve "al his aventure," is the Creator, whose divine aid is necessary to the spirit's attainment of its "destinee" of heavenly fame.[74]

The reference to Jupiter, along with Chaucer's prayer to Venus to "save us" and make "oure sorwes lyghte," is an adept transfer of the meanings of the *Aeneid* and the temple of Venus to the central allegory of the dreamer. At the same time, we may detect in Chaucer's appeal the self-directed irony and humor already apparent in his attitude toward Venus. As a symbol of heavenly love, Venus is a proper object of appeal by any pilgrim, such as Aeneas, Chaucer, or Dante, whose spirit must be brought into harmony with the divine will. But as the Venus of the temple she is the one least likely to "save" Chaucer and make his "sorwes lyghte." Not by chance, therefore, does his prayer reflect his earlier reference to St. Leonard, whose power to relieve the weary pilgrim of his chains ("to make lythe of that was hard") contrasts with Venus's enslavement of the lover with carnal chains.[75]

Unlike Aeneas, who has freed himself from Venus's chains, Chaucer is still confused by the idolatrous splendor of the temple of glass. His thoughts, consequently, are

---

moralizes Aeneas' battles as conflicts *inter spiritum et corpus* (p. 68). Fulgentius interprets Turnus as *furibundus sensus* (*Virgiliana continentia*, p. 105). In the Knight's Tale, Turnus "with the hardy fiers corage" appears among the "portreytures" in the temple of Venus.

[74] Bernard interprets the multiple meanings of Jupiter in the *Aeneid* (p. 109). As *Iupiter omnipotens*, he is to be understood as the Creator [*pro creatore*]. In *Mythographus Vaticanus III*, pp. 200-201, Jupiter is interpreted as the benevolent planet under whose protection Aeneas makes his pilgrimage.

[75] On Venus's chains as a traditional image of the spirit's captivity by the flesh, see Robertson, *Preface*, pp. 105, 394, 399, 478. As an underlying theme of the *Aeneid*, the *House of Fame*, and the *Comedy*, the motif of captivity brings the pilgrimages of Aeneas, Chaucer, and Dante into a basic thematic relationship.

again directed to its outward appearance rather than to its inward reality:

> "A, Lord!" thoughte I, "that madest us,
> Yet sawgh I never such noblesse
> Of ymages, ne such richesse,
> As I saugh graven in this chirche;
> But not wot I whoo did hem wirche,
> Ne where I am, ne in what contree." (470-75)

That Chaucer cannot identify the "worker" of these images or the "contree" in which he is lost is a tribute to Satan's ability to "bleren" men's eyes. But the truth is only too apparent when he goes through a "wiket" to see if he can find "any stiryng man" to tell him where he is. Looking about him as far as he can see, he discovers that he is in "a large feld"

> Withouten toun, or hous, or tree,
> Or bush, or grass, or eryd lond;
> For al the feld nas but of sond
> As smal as man may se yet lye
> In the desert of Lybye;
> Ne no maner creature
> That ys yformed by Nature
> Ne sawgh I, me to rede or wisse. (484-91)

Like Aeneas in Carthage and "Auffrikes regioun," Chaucer is in the sterile desert of carnal love. This meaning of the desert is suggested by the comparison of this barren land to the "desert of Lybye"—the arid country where Venus directs Aeneas to Dido and her "faire toun" and where Mercury, at Jupiter's command, rouses him from spiritual slumber.[76] This "contree," in brief, is the country

[76] *Aeneid*, IV, 256-58; 281-82. Cf. I, 384. On the connection of the "desert of Libya" with Venus and carnal love, see J. M. Steadman, "Chaucer's 'Desert of Libye,' Venus, and Jove," *MLN*, LXXVI (1961), 196-201. Benvenuto da Imola interprets Libya as *libido*, and *Affrica regio* (Chaucer's "Auffrikes regioun," l. 431) as *ardor luxuriae* (I, 199-200). Following Pliny, Bersuire locates Venus's temple at Paphos

of Dido, not the "contree of Itaylle" Aeneas finally achieves by leaving Dido and following the path of virtue and heavenly fame. These contrasting countries have a parallel in the Scriptural *patria* or *terra*, ambivalent symbols of the world or the heavenly "far country." Thus Bersuire contrasts the latter country with the country of this world, a desert place "which ought to be shunned."[77] Specifically, in Chaucer's fiction, the desert country of Dido depicts the ugly reality behind the splendor of the temple of Venus. As such it resembles the desert place associated with the temple in the *Parliament* and the many other barren spots where Venus and Fortune lead their sorrowful victims.[78] But behind them all are the numerous wastelands of Scripture, including the desert of Moses' Canticle, Ezechiel's valley of dry bones, the desert of Jericho, the Psalmist's desert and valley of the shadow of death—all indicative of spiritual death and aridity.[79] The Scriptural meanings of the desert strengthen the symbolism of the temple. Allegorically, the desert signifies the world or the present life. On this level its aridity and barrenness picture the spiritual unfruitfulness of life under the Old Law.[80] Tropologically, the desert is an image of the heart of the sinner, a projection of the mind in a state

---

next to a desert area where nothing grows—that is, *in mundo juxta venereos et luxuriosis* (*Opera*, II, 633).

[77] *Opera*, V, 203; VI, 145-50.

[78] For examples, see Patch, *The Goddess Fortuna*, pp. 99-100, and *The Other World*, pp. 183, 193, 197, 202, 210, 219.

[79] Deut. 32:10-12; Ezech. 37:1-14; Jer. 2:6; 17:6-8; 50:12-13; Ps. 62:1-3. Cf. Ps. 106:4-6; Ezech. 19:13; 29:5ff.

[80] Citing Ps. 62:3—"In a desert land [*terra deserta*], and where there is no way and no water: so in the sanctuary have I come before thee"—Rabanus Maurus interprets the desert as the spiritual need of the present life [*indigentiam praesentis vitae*]. "The Psalmist says 'in a desert land,' that is, in the dearth and unfruitful sterility of this world. This is followed by 'there is no way' because the world has no way except our Lord Saviour. . . . He adds, 'and no water,' that is, barren and unfruitful. . . . Thus, by these three phrases, the necessity [*necessitas*] of this world is shown" (*De universo*, PL, 111, col. 371).

of sloth and despair. Anagogically, it is a symbol of Hell, where "none of the elect are found" and "no assuagement of sorrow is felt."[81] In the *Inferno* these multiple meanings are mirrored in the "gran diserto" of Canto I and the arid plain of the seventh circle which Dante compares to the desert of Libya.[82] In Chaucer's allegory the Scriptural meanings are evoked by the "wiket" leading from the temple into the desert. In the *Roman de la Rose* a similar "wiket" appears as the gate of Idleness, an image of the slothfulness bringing one into the sterile garden of love. Using the same imagery, Chaucer's Parson identifies idleness as the gate "of alle harmes," the unguarded entrance by which Satan enters the heart and brings it into the captivity of Hell. In these terms, the "wiket" of Venus's temple illustrates the Scriptural contrast between the two gates: "Enter ye in at the narrow gate; for wide is the gate and broad is the way that leadeth to destruction, and many there are who go in thereat. How narrow is the gate and strait is the way that leadeth to life; and few there are that find it."[83]

Like Dante in the sterile waste of Hell, Chaucer in the desert of Venus undergoes an experience that marks the

[81] *PL*, 79, col. 355. Cf. Bersuire, *Opera*, IV, 39, 361, who cites Ezech. 29. On the desert as an image of the heart of the sinner [*cor peccatoris*], see *PL*, 174, col. 986; 193, col. 268. These meanings are reflected in the Wife of Bath's Prologue, 371-72 ("Thou liknest eek wommenes love to helle,/ To bareyne lond, ther water may nat dwelle"), where the source is St. Jerome, *Epistola adversus Jovinianum*, I, 28 (*PL*, 23, col. 250). On the desert as a literary image of the despair of lovers—for example, in Deschamps' *Lay du desert d'amours* —see Patch, "Chaucer's Desert," *MLN*, XXXIV (1919), 321-28.

[82] *Inf.*, I, 64; XIV, 8-15; XXIV, 82ff. Cf. Benvenuto's gloss (n. 76, above) and Lucan, *Pharsalia*, IX, 411ff., which Dante echoes. Bersuire (*Opera*, IV, 361, 591) associates the desert of Libya with Hell.

[83] Matt. 7:13. In *The Other World*, Patch relates the Scriptural passage to the numerous wickets and gates in medieval literary allegory. On the connection of the wicket with idleness and Satan, see the Parson's Tale, 713ff., the Second Nun's Prologue, 1-28, and Bersuire, *Opera*, V, 264. Robertson (*Preface*, pp. 92-93) discusses the carnal implications of the gate of Idleness in the *Roman de la Rose*.

beginning of his spiritual education. Here he gains insight
into the reality beneath the beauty of Venus and her
temple, as well as Dido's deceptive pathos. Now his confusion gives way to fear—the fear that turns the mind
to God. Like the fearful Dante in the "gran diserto,"
Chaucer can still ask for aid and receive it.[84] His appeal
to Christ to save him from the illusions of Satan—

> "O Crist!" thoughte I, "that art in blysse,
> Fro fantome and illusion
> Me save!" (492-94)

is a symbolic act of the mind turning to God for spiritual
remedy. In conjunction with the desert, Chaucer's fear and
petition for divine aid echo the Psalmist: "The sorrows
of death surrounded me, and the torrents of iniquity
troubled me. The sorrows of hell encompassed me. . . .
In my affliction I called upon the Lord, and I cried to
my God. And he heard my voice from his holy temple,
and my cry before him came into his ears."[85] In this
Scriptural context it is no coincidence that when Chaucer
lifts his eyes to heaven "with devocion" he should see an
eagle soaring "faste be the sonne":

> Thoo was I war, lo! at the laste,
> That faste be the sonne, as hye
> As kenne myghte I with myn ye,
> Me thoughte I sawgh an egle sore,
> But that hit semed moche more
> Then I had any egle seyn. (496-501)

Although the eagle acquires more particular connotations in the allegory of Book II, his appearance in the

[84] *Inf.*, I, 64. In *De doctrina Christiana*, II, 5ff., Augustine describes the fear that turns the mind to God and begins the process of
purgation whereby the malady of sin is eradicated.

[85] Ps. 17:5-7. Cf. Ps. 106:4-6 ("They wandered in a wilderness [*in
solitudine*], in a place without water. . . . And they cried to the Lord
in their tribulation, and he delivered them out of their distresses") and
Rabanus' gloss on the *terra deserta* of Ps. 62:3 (n. 80, above).

desert of Venus summons up a rich background of meanings, both mythographical and Scriptural, which define
his basic function as a symbol. In the pagan fiction the
eagle performs his conventional role as the *armiger* or
intermediary of Jupiter. Bearing immediately on the
imagery at the end of Book I, he is linked in medieval
mythography with the desert of Libya, where Jupiter,
under the name of Ammon, is said to have a temple and
to bring relief to those lost in the sterile waste. Along with
other mythographers, Bersuire interprets Jupiter's role in
this instance as an aspect of his charity and benevolence.
He is said to have a temple in the desert of Libya because
in such a place of evil and adversity divine aid and charity
are especially needed.[86] In this context the eagle is an instrument of Jupiter's benevolence; for, says John Ridewall, just as birds of prey cease their predatoriness from
fear of the eagle, so Satan and other evil spirits (sometimes designated as birds in Scripture) fear nothing in
man so much as charity.[87] This moralization is influenced

---

[86] *Ovidius moralizatus*, ed. Ghisalberti, p. 95. Bersuire cites Fulgentius
as authority that "by Jupiter is designated benevolence or charity
[*benivolencia vel caritas*]." Ridewall attributes the same meanings to
Jupiter, who has a temple in the desert of Libya [*in arenis Libie*] since
it is "the nature of true love and benevolence to show themselves in a
place and time of hardship and need [*necessitatis et indigencie*]"
(*Fulgentius metaforalis*, III, ed. Liebeschütz, pp. 79ff.). In "Chaucer's
'Desert of Libye,' Venus, and Jove," pp. 196-201, Steadman relates the
mythographical tradition of Jupiter and the desert to the details of
Chaucer's fiction.

[87] *Fulgentius metaforalis*, pp. 80-81: "For the poets represent the
eagle as the armor-bearer [*armigerum*] of the god Jupiter; and for this
reason he is depicted by the poets as surrounded on all sides by eagles,
just as a great lord is usually surrounded by his armor-bearers. This
agrees, in a fashion, with the power of charity, as learned authors well
teach; for, as Pliny says in his *Natural History* [x, 6, 14], other birds
are frightened by the sight and sound of the eagle, and from terror
birds of prey give up their predatoriness. Applying this therefore to
the power of charity, Hugh of St. Victor, in his exposition of the Rule
of St. Augustine [*PL*, 176, col. 883], tells us how wicked spirits, who
in Scripture are sometimes called birds, . . . fear nothing in men so
much as charity. . . . Significantly, therefore, the power of charity is

by Scriptural commentary, where the eagle is also associated with the desert and divine protection. Thus in the
Canticle of Moses the eagle's appearance in the desert is
an image of God's liberation of Israel from its captivity
in Egypt:

He found him in a desert land, in a place of horror, and of
vast wilderness. He led him about, and taught him; and he
kept him as the apple of his eye. As the eagle enticing her
young to fly, and hovering over them, he spread his wings, and
hath taken him and carried him on his shoulders. The Lord
alone was his leader, and there was no strange god with him.[88]

Following earlier commentators, Rabanus Maurus interprets the desert as the world or Babylon and connects it
with idolatry. The eagle is a symbol of divine grace and is
likened to Christ because "by his death he snatched away
the prey of Satan and after the resurrection of his body,
which he assumed for the redemption of mankind, he
ascended to heaven, exhorting us to follow by faith and
devotion where he ascended in the flesh."[89] In a gloss on
the same passage, Wyclif compares the wings of the eagle
to the "two wyngis of Charite" by which Christ sustains
us in our weariness and ravishes our hearts to heaven so
that we may see the sun that "nevere schal have set-
tinge."[90]

Similar exegetical meanings inform the more specific
attributes ascribed to the eagle in Scripture, bestiaries, and
encyclopedias. On the authority of Psalm 102:5—"Thy

---

depicted as surrounded by eagles because of the fear produced on all
sides in demons and wicked spirits." Cf. Bersuire, *Ovidius moralizatus*,
p. 95.

[88] Deut. 32:10-12. Cf. Ex. 19:3-6.

[89] *Enar. super Deut.*, PL, 108, col. 973. Cf. *Allegoriae in sacram
scripturam*, col. 862: "The eagle is Christ, as in the Canticle of Deuter-
onomy." On the Ascension, Rabanus quotes Luke 17:37: "Wheresoever
the body shall be, thither will the eagles also be gathered together."
Cf. *De universo*, PL, 111, col. 243; Bersuire, *Opera*, VI, 245.

[90] *Select English Works*, ed. T. Arnold (Oxford, 1871), III, 35. Cf.
Rabanus, *De universo*, PL, 111, col. 242.

youth shall be renewed like the eagle's"—the eagle in the bestiaries is a symbol of the rejuvenation of the sinner. Thus his alleged practice in old age of flying into the sphere of the sun, burning off his feathers and falling into a fountain, is said to signify the regeneration of the Old Man, who through repentance and the mercy of Christ (the Sun of Justice) renews himself in the fount of baptism. The same meaning is attached to his practice of ridding himself of his old beak by striking it on a rock— a symbol of Christ and the Church.[91] But the most recurrent moralizations of the eagle stem from two characteristics distinguishing him most notably from other birds: his keenness of vision and the high altitude of his flight. The first of these traits—which is related etymologically to the eagle's name ("Aquila dicitur quasi habens acutos oculos")—acquires significance from three traditional beliefs about his powers of vision: the ability to detect fish in the sea from afar; the power to look directly at the sun; and the practice of exposing his young to the sun in order to test their ability to fly.[92] Because the eagle can see even the smallest fish from a great height, he is compared to Christ, who looks from heaven into the hearts of men and rescues them from the sea of vices.[93] Similarly,

[91] *Physiologus: A Metrical Bestiary . . . by Bishop Theobold,* trans. A. W. Rendell (London, 1928), pp. 8-12. For similar moralizations, see Florence McCulloch, *Mediaeval Latin and French Bestiaries* (Chapel Hill, 1960), pp. 113-15. Cf. Neckam, *De naturis rerum,* I, 23.

[92] Isidore, *Etymologiae,* XII, 7 (*PL,* 82, col. 460). These and other traditionally moralized traits of the eagle are discussed by John M. Steadman, "Chaucer's Eagle: A Contemplative Symbol," *PMLA,* LXXV (1960), 153-59, where Bersuire is a source for the etymology of *aquila* (p. 153, n. 6). For some of the exegetical material that follows, I am indebted to this useful assemblage of conventional symbolism relating to the eagle.

[93] Bersuire, *Opera,* II, 170: "The eagle is Christ, who, from the heights of Paradise, sees sinners, like fish, wandering in the sea of the world, and feeling compassion suddenly descends to them through His Incarnation, and having seized them and converted them to the faith, he raises them heavenward to the state of grace and glory."

his power to fix his gaze on the sun is symbolic both of Christ, who by his wisdom (*sapientia*) looks directly at the Father, and of the intellect or reason, which through contemplation penetrates the mysteries of heavenly truth.[94] This tropological meaning also informs the eagle's practice of exposing its young to the rays of the sun—a symbol, says Alexander Neckam, of "contemplative men, who by meditation and devotion fix their eyes on the glory of eternal light."[95] As an image of the intellect, the eagle's acute sight is related to the high altitude of his ascent. St. Gregory, commenting on Isaiah 40:31 ("But they that hope in the Lord shall renew their strength; they shall take wings as eagles"), interprets the eagle's flight as a flight of contemplation. The same meaning is attributed to the eagle in Job 39:27-29: "Will the eagle mount up at thy command, and make her nest in high places? . . . From thence she looketh for the prey, and her eyes behold afar off." Just as the eagle builds its nest on high, says Gregory, so the saints and other faithful, following God's precepts, build their desires on celestial, rather than worldly, considerations.[96] Rabanus Maurus, also citing Job, compares the eagle's flight to the soul exalted by contemplation and, like Gregory, connects it with his power to gaze at the sun. Both Gregory and Rabanus, on the authority of Ezechiel, identify the eagle with John the Evangelist, "who left the earth in his flight, because, through his subtle understanding, he penetrated, by be-

[94] McCulloch, pp. 114-15. Steadman ("Chaucer's Eagle," pp. 154ff.) includes examples from Gregory, Rabanus, Hugh of St. Victor, Bartholomeus, and Bersuire. In *Policraticus*, I, 13, John of Salisbury attributes the eagle's ability to gaze at the sun and see fish from afar to the prophetic gift given him by Jove to penetrate the mysteries of nature and heaven.

[95] *De naturis rerum*, I, 23.

[96] *Moralia, PL*, 76, cols. 625-26. Commenting on Job 9:25-26 ("My days have . . . passed by . . . as an eagle flying to the prey"), Gregory interprets the eagle's flight as the height of man's reason before the Fall (*PL*, 75, cols. 884-86).

holding the Word, inward mysteries."[97] Following the
same tradition, Neckam equates the eagle with Philosophy; for Philosophy, "which can be designated by the
name of the eagle because of its keen sight and many other
worthy qualities," looks with contempt "on those who can
not direct their minds to the subtleties of lofty things."
On the other hand, "she regards boastfully as her own
those who penetrate hidden mysteries by their acuteness
of intellect."[98]

In Book II the eagle's function as a symbol of reason
and contemplation is called up explicitly when Chaucer,
at the climax of his ascent, thinks of Boethius' flight with
the "feathers" of Philosophy. But the particular imagery
describing the eagle comes from Dante:

> But this as sooth as deth, certeyn,
> Hyt was of gold, and shon so bryghte
> That never sawe men such a syghte,
> But yf the heven had ywonne
> Al newe of gold another sonne;
> So shone the egles fethers bryghte. (502-507)

The eagle's feathers, their gold, and the comparison to
the sun are an amalgamation of closely associated images
in the *Purgatorio* and *Paradiso*. The golden feathers are
borrowed from the eagle appearing to Dante in a dream
and identified with Lucia, the heavenly lady who, Dante
learns upon waking, has borne him in his sleep to the
entrance of Purgatory. On Scriptural authority the commentators interpret both the eagle and Lucia as the intellect illumined by grace and connect the eagle with St.
John.[99] The golden plumes designate divine love, emanat-

---

[97] Gregory, *PL*, 76, cols. 625-26; Rabanus, *De universo*, *PL*, 111,
cols. 243-44. Cf. *Allegoriae in sacram scripturam*, col. 862.

[98] *De naturis rerum*, I, 23.

[99] Benvenuto da Imola, III, 248; Jacopo della Lana, *Commento*, II,
98, 103; Pietro Alighieri, *Commentarium*, pp. 60-61. Cf. Steadman,
"Chaucer's Eagle," p. 156.

ing from the Holy Spirit and lifting the mind to contemplation.[100] The sun, to which Chaucer compares the brightness of the eagle's wings, appears in Canto I of the *Paradiso*, where Dante compares Beatrice's fixed gaze at the sun to that of an eagle. Just as it seems to Chaucer that in the eagle heaven has won "another sonne," so it seems to Dante, following Beatrice's gaze, that "He who has power" has adorned heaven "with another sun" ("d'un altro sole"). The sun, as elsewhere in the *Comedy*, is a symbol of Christ (the eternal sun) and *sapientia*.[101] Benvenuto da Imola, glossing this passage, compares Beatrice's eyes to the eyes of the intellect, nourished by the light of divine wisdom, and repeats the conventional interpretation of the eagle's ability to look unhindered at the sun.[102]

These richly interacting meanings of the eagle from Scripture, mythography, encyclopedias, bestiaries, and Dante should clarify the symbolic pattern underlying Chaucer's appeal to Christ and the simultaneous appearance of the eagle. In conjunction with the desert, the eagle reminds us that Chaucer's dream is under the auspices of Jupiter, the "well-willing" planet, lord of the house of faith and religion, who brings relief to the pilgrim caught in the desert of the world or Babylon. More particularly, like Dante's golden eagle, he is a symbol of the intellect infused with grace, turning to God with devotion. As such he performs a role comparable to that of Mercury and Virgil—both images of reason awakening the mind from sloth and initiating a pattern of spiritual recovery. In the *Aeneid* and the *Inferno* this pattern begins with Aeneas' and Dante's descents to Hell; in Chaucer's allegory it begins with his experience in the

[100] Francesco da Buti, II, 200.
[101] Benvenuto, IV, 302. For Beatrice's association with the sun, see *Par.*, III, 1; XXX, 75.
[102] *Commentum*, IV, 312ff. Cf. Francesco da Buti, III, 20.

desert, whose exegetical meanings, especially as an image of Hell, are a further link between Book I and the symbolism of the *Inferno*. Like Aeneas and Dante in Hell, Chaucer in the desert undergoes an experience preliminary to a higher stage of understanding. Just as Aeneas and Dante view the eternal infamy rewarding the various sins, so Chaucer views the nature and reward of one of these sins, carnal love, symbolized by the temple and desert of Venus and more concretely by Dido and her sterile "contree." At the same time, in Aeneas and his "contree" of Italy, he views the heavenly fame achieved by the spirit that follows the path of virtue and true love. These contrasting countries, images of two kinds of love and fame, foreshadow the contrasting tidings of his "verray neyghebores" and of a "fer contree" which are to be the goal of his flight to the House of Fame. But first, like Aeneas and Dante—and we must also include Boethius, whose physician, Philosophy, soon adds her feathers to the eagle—Chaucer must learn the nature of his malady and complete a process of education which will prepare him for these tidings. The allegory of Book II dramatizes this process.

CHAPTER IV

THE HOUSE OF FAME—
PURGATORY

THE large amount of exposition, especially in the
eagle's lengthy discourse, is indicative of the
pivotal function of Book II. Here the related
themes of love and fame, introduced in the story of
Aeneas and Dido, take on broadening Christian connotations which become the basis for the allegory of Fame
and her awards in Book III. Aside from the humor of the
eagle, not the least of Chaucer's achievements in this book
is his skillful fusion of the eagle's subject matter with
the central allegory of the pilgrimage. While the exposition establishes the necessary machinery for the later exploration of fame, its immediate motivation is the instruction of the dreamer, whose spiritual state is clearly
manifested at the end of Book I.

Chaucer's flight with the eagle develops the Scriptural
pattern underlying his rescue from the desert of Venus.
At the same time, parallels with Boethius and Dante add
further dimensions to the allegory of the pilgrimage. In
Book I the *Consolation* is echoed not only in the circumstances of the eagle's appearance and rescue of Chaucer
but also in the central problems of love and fame. Boethius' confused attitude toward Fortune and her gifts has
its equivalent in Chaucer's confusion in the temple of
Venus, where he is blinded by the idolatrous light and
fails to distinguish between the true and false love and
fame prompting the attitudes and actions of Aeneas and
Dido. In Book II these parallels continue in the eagle's
diagnosis of Chaucer's malady and in the process of instruction by which his mind is prepared for a clearer understanding of heavenly love and fame. But if the ideas

and imagery of the *Consolation* are closely woven into the basic pattern of Book II, Dante's pilgrimage remains a constant point of reference for the major stages of Chaucer's spiritual journey. The most obvious connection with the allegory of the *Comedy* is the eagle, whose mission from Jove and function as the intellect reveal his kinship with both Virgil and the golden eagle of the *Purgatorio*. But these parallels acquire their fullest import from the rich aura of meanings which Dante's two symbols bring with them into the *House of Fame*. Chaucer's garrulous bird, admonishing and lecturing his fat and somewhat befuddled passenger, contrasts amusingly with Virgil and the mysterious eagle bearing Dante to the threshold of Purgatory. Behind the differences, however, lies a common area of Christian symbolism relating Book II to the *Purgatorio*.

The context of the *Comedy* is called up at the beginning by Chaucer's Invocation, borrowed, with the exception of the initial appeal to Venus, from Dante's opening invocation:

> Now faire blisfull, O Cipris,
> So be my favour at this tyme!
> And ye, me to endite and ryme
> Helpeth, that on Parnaso duelle,
> Be Elicon, the clere welle.
> O Thought, that wrot al that I mette,
> And in the tresorye hyt shette
> Of my brayn, now shal men se
> Yf any vertu in the be,
> To tellen al my drem aryght.
> Now kythe thyn engyn and myght! (518-28)

According to Dante's medieval commentators, the three-fold appeal

> O Muse, o alto ingegno, or m'aiutate!
>   O mente, che scrivesti ciò ch' io vidi,
>   qui si parrà la tua nobilitate. . . (*Inf.* II, 7-9)

invokes the three qualities of the mind necessary for the perfection of the poet's work. The Muses symbolize knowledge, or *scientia* (the "noteful sciences," Chaucer elsewhere glosses them), which, if not the highest wisdom (*sapientia*), signified by Apollo, is the preliminary stage to such wisdom.[1] This meaning is further imaged in Parnassus, a symbol of contemplation, and in Helicon, the "clere welle" by which they are said to dwell, a symbol of the divine source of doctrine.[2] As an aspect of the mind, the Muses, along with the other two objects of Dante's appeal, form the trinity of intellect, will ("ingegno"), and memory ("mente")—or, as Chaucer calls them, "intellect," "engyn," and "memorie"—which corresponds to the heavenly Trinity and which must work in harmony if the mind is to function rationally.[3] Chaucer's Invocation is an adaptation of these meanings to his own pagan fiction. His originality lies in his substituting Venus for Dante's "ingegno" or "will." But the true Venus, as observed earlier, is synonymous with the power of divine love (*amor*) which moves the will and directs it to God.[4] Whereas Venus in Book I functions as a symbol

[1] Benvenuto da Imola interprets Dante's Muses as *scientiae profunditas* (*Commentum*, I, 75-76). Cf. Pietro Alighieri, *Commentarium*, pp. 51-52; Francesco da Buti, *Commento*, I, 60. Bernard Silvestris equates each of the Muses with a quality of the intellect (*Commentum*, p. 35). For Chaucer's gloss on Philosophy's Muses, see *De consolatione philosophiae*, I, Pr. 1.

[2] Benvenuto, III, 4ff. Cf. Bersuire, *Ovidius moralizatus*, p. 102: "Truly, those who wish to escape the depths of the vices should ascend Mount Parnassus, that is, the heights of contemplation."

[3] Pietro (pp. 51-52) quotes Peter Lombard and Augustine, *De trinitate*, IX, 4. In the Second Nun's Tale, 338-41, Cecilia compares the three "sapiences" of the mind to the Trinity. In the *Legenda Aurea*, these appear as *ingenium*, *memoria*, and *intellectus* (cf. Robinson's note, *Works*, p. 759). Benvenuto interprets Dante's *mente* as *memoriae vivacitas* (I, 75-76). The terms *voluntas* and *ingenium* (Dante's *ingegno*, Chaucer's "engyn") appear variously for the "will."

[4] Quoting Peter Lombard, Pietro identifies Dante's *ingegno* with love [*amor*] (pp. 51-52). Cf. *PL*, 192, cols. 530-31, where Lombard follows Augustine (*De trinitate*, IX): "For the mind remembers itself,

of carnal love, in Book II, under the ironic guise of "Cipris," she is implicitly invoked as the power of divine love.[5]

If Chaucer's Invocation expresses his higher purpose as a poet, for Chaucer the pilgrim it marks a higher stage in his spiritual education. As such it may be contrasted with his earlier Invocation to Morpheus, whose fantasies and illusions depict the mind in a state of sloth. In logical progression, the Invocation to Book II is an appeal to the three powers of will, memory, and intellect which must be brought into accord before the dreams of Morpheus can be dispelled and the image of reason restored to its pristine likeness to the Trinity. It is this restoration of the divine image to which St. Augustine likens the process by which the spirit, turning to God through fear, is purged of the malady of sin and prepared for the contemplation of heavenly light and wisdom.[6] In Scripture, remarks Pierre Bersuire, this process of purgation appears in many guises:

Since to purge (*purgare*) is nothing else than to make some-

---

understands itself, and loves itself; if we perceive this, we perceive the Trinity. . . . For here appears a kind of trinity of memory, understanding, and love [*memoriae, intelligentiae et amoris*]." Traditionally, the Holy Spirit is equated with *amor*, the power moving the will (for example, Augustine, *De trinitate*, xv, 18). As Robinson notes (*Works*, pp. 822-23), Chaucer's invocation to Venus in *Troilus*, iii, 1ff., is colored by the Christian–Boethian concept of the divine chain of love, which Bernard associates with the spiritual Venus. In *Teseida*, i, 3, *Amorosa visione*, ii, 1ff., and *Ameto* (Proem), Boccaccio connects *ingegno* with Venus as a source of inspiration. Chaucer's alteration of Dante's *ingegno* was perhaps suggested by *Purg.*, i, 19, where the invocation to the Muses is followed by a reference to Venus, the "fair planet" which quickens love [*ad amar conforta*].

[5] D. S. Brewer (*Chaucer*, p. 74) observes that Chaucer calls Venus "Cipris" only when he is referring to the wanton Venus. If so, the irony seems clear, since the central image in the eagle's discourse in Book ii is the power of love ("kyndely enclynyng") that prompts every object to seek its "kyndely stede."

[6] *De civitate Dei*, xi, 2, 26. In *De doctrina Christiana*, ii, 7, Augustine describes this process at length.

thing clean, to make it free of sordidness, and to restore it to purity, we can note briefly that in Scripture we come upon many things that purge the soul and purify it from sin. Just as the physician purges the body to restore it to health, and the maid-servant purges the house to make it clean, and the smith purges metals to restore their colors, so man truly ought to purge and purify his heart so that he can receive the health of grace, obtain cleanliness in the sight of God, and recover and maintain the color of a virtuous life.[7]

The Christian concept of purgation underlies both the *Purgatorio* and Book II of the *House of Fame*. Dante's purgation is mirrored in his ascent of the mountain of Purgatory and in the instruction of Virgil, a symbol of knowledge or reason which disciplines the passions and directs the mind to God. Chaucer's purgation is imaged in his flight above the earth and his instruction by the eagle. Although the symbols differ on the surface, a common meaning is found in the Scriptural concept of the flight (*volatus*), which is likened to the eagle's ascent and is interpreted as the process by which the spirit frees itself of bodily impurities and flies mentally to Paradise.[8] Thus Dante, describing his ascent with Virgil, uses the same image: "But here a man must fly, I mean with the swift wings and with the plumes of great desire, behind that Leader, who gave me hope, and was a light to me."[9] Like

[7] *Opera*, v, 351.
[8] *Ibid.*, vi, 245: "There is a certain desirable and virtuous flight by which spiritual birds [*spirituales volucres*] fly upwards mentally to Paradise, and by which even the angels rise to God through love." Bersuire illustrates this meaning with the wings of the eagle in Apoc. 12:14. On the common doctrine underlying Chaucer's and Dante's imagery, cf. Boccaccio, *Genealogia deorum*, xiv, 7: "The poets would declare with their own lips under whose help and guidance they compose their inventions when . . . they raise flights of symbolic steps to heaven . . . or go winding about mountains to their summits."
[9] *Purg.*, iv, 27-30. Cf. *Par.*, xv, 53-54; xxv, 49-51. Francesco da Buti interprets Dante's details as an allegory of the intellect. Whereas the swift wings [*ali snelle*] designate faith and hope, the plumes [*piume*] designate the charity and love [*la carità e l'amore*] by which the spirit is raised to the heights of penitence (ii, 82-83).

Virgil—and also Philosophy, in whose feathers Boethius makes his flight—Chaucer's eagle functions primarily as a symbol of the intellect or reason by whose guidance and instruction the mind is purged of its worldly desires and is led to the contemplation of higher spiritual truths. At the same time, in the details of his descent, he reveals his affinity with the eagle of the *Purgatorio*, a symbol of the mind, illumined by grace, turning to the guidance of reason. This parallel is strengthened by imagery common to Dante and Chaucer: the swiftness of the descent and the lightning or thunderbolt to which the swiftness is compared—symbols respectively of the mind and the divine power bringing it to devotion.[10]

The symbolic pattern underlying the eagle's descent and flight is humorously completed as Chaucer compares himself to a lark—a conventional image of the spirit filled with grace, rising joyfully above the earth to Paradise to sing God's praise.[11] But Chaucer, unlike the lark, is hardly ready to sing at heaven's gate. His fear and confusion at his sudden ascent—

> so astonyed and asweved
> Was every vertu in my heved,
> What with his sours and with my drede,
> That al my felynge gan to dede. . . (549-52)

[10] On the eagle's swiftness, see Deut. 28:49; II Kings 1:23; Jer. 4:13; Lam. 4:19. In *De consolatione philosophiae*, IV, Pr. 1, the image is applied to the mind's ascent with Philosophy's wings. Cf. Steadman, "Chaucer's Eagle," p. 158. In Ex. 19:16, thunder and lightning are indicative of divine power. As iconographic details, they are associated with Jupiter and his eagle and interpreted as aspects of divine benevolence, for example, in Ridewall, *Fulgentius metaforalis* (ed. Liebeschütz), pp. 8off. Benvenuto relates Dante's imagery of the eagle's descent to this tradition (*Commentum*, III, 253).

[11] Citing Is. 12, Bersuire interprets the lark [*alauda*] as man praising God; for "when clearness of conscience and the splendor of divine grace abound, and when he rises above the earth, that is, above earthly things, condemning them, and ascends heavenward to Paradise, he then is set free in spiritual joy and glories happily in God" (*Opera*, II, 174-76).

are paralleled in Dante, who, awakening from his dream
of ascent with the eagle, grows pale as a man "frozen
with terror." In both instances the poet's fear and confusion are denoted by "sleep," an image of spiritual slumber.[12] Significantly, it is just after Dante has left Hell
"full of sleep" and the Old Adam that the eagle appears
to him.[13] Chaucer's state of mind is dramatized with amusing onomatopoetic effect in the eagle's admonishing him
"in mannes vois" to awaken and not to be "agast":

> "Awak!
> And be not agast so, for shame!"
> And called me tho by my name,
> And, for I shulde the bet abreyde,
> Me mette, "Awak," to me he seyde,
> Ryght in the same vois and stevene
> That useth oon I koude nevene;
> And with that vois, soth for to seyn,
> My mynde cam to me ageyn,
> For hyt was goodly seyd to me,
> So nas hyt never wont to be. (556-66)

Chaucer might well indeed compare the "vois" of the
eagle to that of one he "koude nevene"; for this "goodly"
voice, awakening him from slumber, is the same voice
with which Christ and the apostles admonish men to
awaken from their sleep and follow the path of salvation:
"Rise, thou that sleepest, and arise from the dead, and
Christ shall enlighten thee."[14] But the eagle's "goodly"

[12] On this meaning of sleep [*dormitio*], see *Allegoriae in sacram
scripturam*, col. 913. In *Piers Plowman and Scriptural Tradition*
(Princeton, 1951), pp. 37ff., Robertson and Huppé relate the image to
the dreamer in that poem.

[13] *Purg.*, IX, 10-12. In *Aeneid*, IV, 554ff., Mercury similarly appears
to Aeneas in a vision, accuses him of slumber, and prompts him to
remember his divine destiny.

[14] Eph. 5:14. Rabanus glosses sleep, in this instance, as the dullness
[*stupor*] of the mind, whose alienation from the true way "is a kind
of death from which it is reminded to awaken, so that, upon re-
viving, it will recognize the truth, which is Christ" (*PL*, 112, col.
451). Cf. Luke 22:46; Rom. 13:11; I Cor. 15:34; I Thes. 5:6. On

voice also brings to mind another physician, Lady Philosophy, who, from her "sovereyne sete," descends to Boethius in his "solitaire place" of exile and gently rebukes him for his "astonynge":

"Knowestow me nat? Why arttow stille? Is it for schame or for astonynge? It were me levere that it were for schame, but it semeth me that astonynge hath oppressid the." And whan sche say me nat oonly stille, but withouten office of tunge and al dowmb, sche leyde hir hand sooftly uppon my breest, and seide: "Here nys no peril," quod sche; "he is fallen into a litargye, which that is a comune seknesse to hertes that been desceyved. He hath a litil foryeten hymselve, but certes he schal lightly remembren hymself, yif so be that he hath knowen me or now; and that he may so doon, I will wipe a litil his eien that ben dirked by the cloude of mortel thynges" (I, Pr. 2).

Philosophy's gentle rebuke, her consoling voice, and her promise to remedy Boethius' "litargye" are paralleled in the eagle's similar rebuke of Chaucer for his fear and "dumbness" and in his assuring him that he is his "frend" and that the flight is for his "lore" and profit.

The extent of Chaucer's "litargye" is evident in his conclusion that he is about to be "stellified"—that is, made one of God's elect. But this bold assumption is tempered somewhat by his admission that he is neither an Enoch nor an Elias, both of whom, Scripture tells us, were translated bodily to the Earthly Paradise because of their exceptional faith.[15] In this Scriptural context Chaucer's

---

vox as a symbol of Christ's voice, see *Allegoriae in sacram scripturam*, col. 1,083.

[15] Gen. 5:24; IV Kings 2:11; Ecclus. 44:16; Heb. 11:5. According to traditional commentary, Enoch and Elias prefigure Christ and his Ascension and, by extension, all the faithful who follow the path of salvation. See Augustine, *De civitate Dei*, xv, 19; *PL*, 76, col. 1,217; *PL*, 109, cols. 206-207. In *The Other World*, p. 151, Patch notes the portrayal of Enoch and Elias in visions of the Earthly Paradise. On the stars [*sidera*] as a symbol of the elect, see Rabanus, *PL*, 111, col. 272, who refers to I Cor. 15—a meaningful context for the symbolism of sleep and the ascent. Cf. Lydgate, *Pilgrimage of the Life of Man*, 18,835ff.

recollection of Ganymede, Jove's "botiller," is humorously ironic, although Ganymede's flight with Jupiter's eagle is frequently interpreted as a flight of contemplation and related to John's flight to the holy mountain and city. This moralization is followed by Dante, who compares his ascent with the golden eagle to the ascent of Ganymede.[16] But Chaucer's attitude and phraseology are both reminiscent of the *Inferno*, where Dante questions his worthiness to follow the path of St. Paul or Aeneas:

> But I, why go? or who permits it? I am not
> Aeneas, am not Paul; neither myself nor
> others deem me worthy of it. (II, 31-33)

Both Dante and Chaucer are still too full of sleep to know the extent of their fantasy. As the eagle must remind Chaucer, he is not about to be stellified. Like Boethius, before he can become one of "God's knights" his eyes must be cleared of the "cloude of mortel thynges." This ultimate purpose of his flight is implicit in the continued parallel with Dante. Just as Virgil, to free Dante of his fear and confusion, recounts how Beatrice, through pity, has sent him to rescue Dante from the "gran diserto," so the eagle, for the same reason, explains how Jove, through his "routhe," has sent him to rescue Chaucer from the desert of Venus. Suggesting Philosophy's role as physician, the eagle's account of his mission from Jove assumes the form of a detailed diagnosis of Chaucer's malady.

He has been sent, the eagle begins, because Jove pities Chaucer for having "so longe trewely"

> ". . . served so ententyfly
> Hys blynde nevew Cupido,

---

[16] *Purg.*, IX, 22-24. Ganymede is mentioned along with Enoch and Elias in the *Ecloga Theoduli*, 65-68, 217-80, a work probably known by Chaucer and glossed by Odo of Picardy, who interprets Ganymede as St. John and the eagle as clarity of wisdom [*limpitudo sapientiae*]. See Steadman, "Chaucer's Eagle," p. 157, who quotes relevant passages from Odo and Bersuire.

> And faire Venus also,
> Withoute guerdon ever yit." (614-19)

The picture developed in the next few lines is the amusing one of the poet of love, who despite his confusion as to the nature of true love (in his "hed ful lyte is") sets his "wit" to making "bookys," "songes," and "dytees"—in rhyme "or elles in cadence"—

> ". . . in reverence
> Of Love, and of hys servantes eke,
> That have hys servyse soght, and seke." (624-26)

Chaucer's "reverence" for the servants of Venus and Cupid was amply illustrated in the temple of Venus, where he extravagantly sympathized with Dido and other "victims" of faithless men. Moreover, his lack of "guerdon" for his service is clear enough when he finds himself in the sterile desert of love. But despite his devotion to Venus and Cupid, the eagle implies, Chaucer is still subject to divine pity; for Jove considers it "gret humblesse" and "vertu eke" that the poet writes "ever mo" of Love's "folk" and furthers their cause even though he himself is in the "daunce" of those whom Love "lyst not avaunce."[17] This portrait of Chaucer in his "studye"— writing "humbly" of Love's servants without any reward for himself—is completed in the description of his going home at night after all his "labour" and sitting as "domb as any stoon" at another book until his "look" is "fully daswed." Both the picture of Chaucer with his books and the tone of the eagle's rebuke parallel Philosophy's description of Boethius in his library "wrought with yvory and with glas":

"I seie that the face of this place ne moeveth me noght so mochel as thyn owene face, ne I ne axe nat rather the walles

---

[17] On the carnal implications of "daunce" in this context, see Robertson, *Preface*, pp. 130-31.

of thy librarye, apparayled and wrought with yvory and with glas, than after the sete of thi thought, in which I put noght whilom bookes, but I putte that that maketh bokes wurthy of prys or precyous, that is to seyn the sentence of my bookes." (I, Pr. 5)

Like Boethius, Chaucer has become so absorbed in the "matere" of his books that he has failed to gain the solace that comes from understanding their "sentence." Or more particularly in Chaucer's case, while he has read of "Loves folk" and praised them in his writings, he does not know

> ". . . yf they be glade,
> Ne of noght elles that God made." (645-46)

In the eagle's words, Chaucer lacks "tydynges"—both tidings of his "verray neyghebores" who dwell almost at his door and tidings of a "fer contree."

A knowledge of these twofold tidings needed by Chaucer is necessary for an understanding of the remainder of the allegory; for they motivate the flight to the House of Fame and control the action and subject matter of Book III, including the puzzling ending. Although their full meaning is deliberately obscured on the surface, it is implicit in the very nature of Chaucer's malady. As his earlier attitude toward Dido reveals, he has become so enmeshed in the praise of Venus and her servants that he has forgotten the nature and end of true love. Or as the eagle later diagnoses his "seknesse," he is full of "hevynesse" and "distresse" and is "disesperat of alle blys" because he feels that Fortune has turned against him. Like Boethius, therefore, in order to free himself from Fortune's snare, he needs to remember God, who wields the rewards of both true and false love, and thereby view the world in proper perspective, that is, from the vantage point of reason. The dual tidings promised Chaucer for his "lore" and profit are symbolic of this goal.

Whereas the tidings of his "verray neyghebores" are tidings of the world or earthly love, the tidings of a "fer contree" are tidings of that heavenly country which, Philosophy reminds Boethius, is the source of all true felicity.[18] Unlike the desert country of the Psalmist and the sterile "contree" of Venus from which he has just been rescued by the eagle, this is the "contree" of Aeneas, the *terra longinqua* of Scripture, the true home of the exiled pilgrim. The Scriptural basis of the imagery is found in Proverbs 25:25 where the far country is associated with good tidings: "As cold water to a thirsty soul, so is good tidings from a far country."[19] In his commentary on Proverbs, Rabanus Maurus relates this verse to Psalm 41: "As the hart panteth after the fountains of water, so my soul panteth after thee, O God." For, he explains, just as cold water slakes the heat of thirst, so the divine sweetness ("dulcedo divinae") consoles the languishing spirit and restores freedom from the heat of present tribulations. Thus heavenly ministers descend daily to the world as messengers from a far country ("de terra longinqua"), bringing hope to those caught in temptation.[20] In Scripture the tidings of a far country are asso-

---

[18] *Consolation*, I, Pr. 5, 9ff.; IV, Pr. 1, 70; Met. 1, 44.

[19] For other Scriptural references to the "far country," see Is. 46:10-11; Jer. 46:27; III Kings 8:41-43; II Par. 6:32-33. In "Amors de terra londhana," *SP*, XLIX (1952), 574, Robertson illustrates another literary use of the image. As in the *Consolation*, this is the native home or country [*patria*] which Augustine calls the goal of the exiled pilgrim (for example, *De doctrina Christiana*, I, 4). Cf. Heb. 11:13-16. "All these died according to faith, not having received the promises, but beholding them afar off, and saluting them and confessing that they are pilgrims and strangers on the earth. For they that say these things do signify that they seek a country. And truly, if they had been mindful of that from whence they came out, they had doubtless time to return. But now they desire a better, that is to say, a heavenly country. Therefore God is not ashamed to be called their God; for he hath prepared for them a city."

[20] *PL*, 111, col. 764. Rabanus' gloss derives from Bede (*In proverbia Salomonis*, *PL*, 91, col. 1,015).

ciated not only with angelic messengers but also with the
many prophets, preachers, and apostles who bring the
good news of Christ and the New Law of charity by
which men might achieve salvation and the peace of Jerusalem.[21] Among such tidings were those of the Old Testament prophets, such as Daniel, Ezechiel, and Isaiah, who
foretold the coming of Christ and the final destruction of
Babylon, as in the prophecy of Isaiah: "My counsel shall
stand, and all my will shall be done; who call a bird from
the east, and from a far country the man of my own will"
(46:10-11). In III Kings 8:41-43 Christ may also be
identified figuratively with the stranger from a far country
whom God will send to spread tidings of his name.[22] In
the New Testament these tidings are fulfilled in the "new
doctrine" of redemption and future judgment preached
by Christ in his divine role of authority and spread by St.
Paul and other apostles.[23] These Scriptural connotations
of "tydynges" of a "fer contree" establish the symbolic
pattern behind the eagle's diagnosis of Chaucer's malady
and his need for tidings. Ensnared by Fortune and blinded
by his long and unrewarded service to Venus and Cupid,
Chaucer must be reminded of true felicity—the heavenly
love and fame prefigured in Aeneas' quest for Italy and
opposed to the worldly love and fame sought by Dido
and, the eagle implies, by his "verray neyghebores." Although Chaucer has temporarily forgotten the country
which is the source of these glad tidings, his mind is not

[21] For example, Is. 40:9; 41:27; 52:7; Nah. 1:15; Luke 2:10; Rom.
10:15 ("How beautiful are the feet of them that preach the gospel of
peace, of them that bring glad tidings of good things"); Eph. 1:13
("In whom you also, after you had heard the word of truth, the gospel
of your salvation, in whom also believing, you were signed with the
holy Spirit of promise"); Eph. 2:17; 3:8. In the sense employed here,
the concept of good (glad) tidings or news is conveyed in the Vulgate
by *evangelium* (*evangelizare*) or, as in Prov. 25:25, *numtius bonus*.

[22] Cf. II Par. 6:32-33, and Jer. 46:27: "I will save thee from afar
off [*de terra longinqua*], and thy seed out of the land of thy captivity."

[23] Mark 1:27; Acts 17:19-21.

149

so devoid of grace that he cannot be prompted to remember it. Or as Philosophy assures Boethius: "Al be thow fer fro thy cuntre, thou n'art nat put out of it, but thow hast fayled of thi weye and gon amys."[24]

The eagle's explanation of his mission, especially his promise of "glad" tidings, reminds us once more that Chaucer's pilgrimage is under the divine auspices of Jupiter, lord of the house of faith and religion, who sends tidings of heavenly bliss beneath the guise of dreams. At the same time, the eagle introduces the elaborate machinery of Fame and her abode by which these tidings are to be revealed in Book III. Just as Virgil explains his heavenly mission to guide Dante to the threshold of Paradise, so the eagle explains that Jove, through his "grace," has commanded him to take the poet to a place called the House of Fame where he will be afforded "som disport and game" as well as "good chere" in compensation for his service and devotion—"loo causeles"—to "Cupido, the rechcheles." In this house, he assures Chaucer, many a tiding will be heard of Love's folk, both "sothe sawes and lesinges,"

> And moo loves newe begonne,
> And longe yserved loves wonne,
> And moo loves casuelly
> That ben betyd, no man wot why,
> But as a blynd man stert an hare;
> And more jolytee and fare,
> While that they fynde love of stel,
> As thinketh hem, and over-al wel;
> Mo discordes, moo jelousies,
> Mo murmures, and moo novelries,
> And moo dissymulacions,
> And feyned reparacions. . . (675ff.)

In this foretaste of the tidings to be heard in the House of Fame, we can recognize the mingled truth and false-

---

[24] *Consolation*, I, Pr. 5, 9-11.

hood, the happiness and sorrow, the "discordes," "jel-ousies," "murmures" and "dissymulacions" which are the rewards of the worshiper in the temple of Venus. But Chaucer, we recall, is to hear not only the unhappy tidings of earthly love but also the consoling tidings of a "fer contree." Or as he later informs the mysterious stranger in Book III who asks his reason for coming to the House of Fame, he is to learn some "newe thinges" of love "or suche thynges glade." In short, as the image of the *terra longinqua* implies, he is to hear those tidings of "new things" (*nova*) which Christ and St. Paul identify as the "new doctrine" of charity and man's future salvation and bliss. Implicit in the eagle's description of Fame and her abode is a pattern of Scriptural imagery pointing to this higher Christian meaning.

This less patent function of Chaucer's pagan fiction may be illustrated by the eagle's account of the location of Fame's house and his explanation of why all earthly speech, "either privy or apert," must ascend there. Like the other basic features of Fame's abode, its location is borrowed from Ovid, who also places it

> Ryght even in myddes of the weye
> Betwixen hevene, erthe, and see. (714-15)

For Chaucer, just as for Ovid, the central position of Fame's dwelling derives its appropriateness from the god-dess herself, whose vigilant eyes and ears (like rumor) are said to detect all words and deeds in the world below. At the same time, as a means of contrasting earthly and heavenly fame, this detail takes on a more important func-tion. For in Christian cosmography the trinity of heaven, earth, and sea denotes the world (*mundus*), the temporal sphere created by God,[25] and its mid-point, or center, ac-

[25] "The world [*mundus*] is heaven, earth, and sea, and all the works of God within them" (Isidore, *Etymologiae*, XIII, 1).

quires significance from the contrasting implications of this concept (*medium* or *centrum*) in Scripture and Christian doctrine. Pierre Bersuire, commenting on the Scriptural image of the mid-point, identifies it allegorically with the world, or Babylon, a false paradise whose center is found in temporal rewards and prosperity. It is indicative of worldly prosperity, he explains, because just as heavy objects by their nature seek the center of the earth, so all sinners seek their center in the transitory goods and bliss of this world.[26] As a contrasting symbol, however, the mid-point is an image of the Earthly Paradise, which symbolizes the Church and is placed by medieval tradition in a middle region between heaven and earth.[27] For a similar reason, it may also designate Jerusalem, which according to Scripture is located in the center of the world and, like Paradise, betokens Holy Church, the spiritual center of man's pilgrimage.[28] Anagogically, like both Jerusalem and the Earthly Paradise, the mid-point is symbolic of the heavenly Paradise or Church Triumphant, the "far country" of Scripture, the beginning and end of God's creation. On this level, it is the seat of divine judgment, the center of providence, the eternal "poynt" around which, says Boethius, the temporal order moves.[29] Conversely, as an image of cupidity, it may designate Hell, whose location in the center of the earth, remarks Bersuire, typifies the false goal of the spirit weighted by

[26] *Opera*, v, 38. Bersuire cites Jer. 50:8: " 'Remove out of the midst [*de medio*] of Babylon,' that is, of the world." Cf. v, 36 ("The world is in the middle [*in medio*], ensnaring the wicked in its vices") and III, 38: "Sometimes by the middle [*medium*] is understood the world or worldly prosperity itself [*mundus vel prosperitas ipsa mundana*]."

[27] On the location of the Earthly Paradise, see Patch, *The Other World*, p. 135. Bersuire identifies the midpoint with Paradise, the center of highest felicity [*summae foelicitatis*] (*Opera*, v, 36).

[28] This familiar concept of the medieval Church is reflected in the topographical setting of the *Divine Comedy*. For the Scriptural basis of the image, see Ezech. 5:5, and Jerome, *PL*, 25, col. 54.

[29] *De consolatione philosophiae*, IV, Pr. 6. Cf. Bersuire, *Opera*, v, 36.

sin.[30] Anagogically, therefore, the mid-point is symbolic of the contrasting goals of man's pilgrimage, eternal fame and infamy. Finally, at such a mid-point in the world, we are told, all souls will gather at the Last Judgment and receive the awards of Christ the Judge according to their earthly thoughts and deeds.[31]

In the light of these Scriptural connotations of the mid-point, we may easily identify the location of Fame's house with the false "center," or paradise, of this world, and her gifts with the temporal fame having its center in the unstable judgment of men, not in the stable judgment of God. As we later see, Fame's house is itself an inversion of the Scriptural house of God, the divine center of man's spiritual life. But in the immediate context the Scriptural meanings of the mid-point add a significant dimension to the eagle's explanation of why all speech—in heaven, earth, or sea—must ascend to the mid-point of the House of Fame:

> ". . . what so ever in al these three
> Is spoken, either privy or apert,
> The way therto ys so overt,
> And stant eke in so juste a place
> That every soun mot to hyt pace,
> Or what so cometh from any tonge,
> Be hyt rouned, red, or songe,
> Or spoke in suerte or in drede,
> Certeyn, hyt moste thider nede." (716-24)

Although the eagle again echoes Ovid, the particular imagery describing the ascent of speech evokes a body of

---

[30] *Ibid.*

[31] Bersuire cites Joel 3: "Just as a judge must place his seat of justice in a central and accessible place so that he can be approached from every direction, so, truly, Christ places his seat of judgment in an accessible and central place—indeed, in Jerusalem in the valley [of Josaphat], where the middle of the world is said to be—so that the dead might arrive in an equal manner [*aequaliter*] from every region of the world" (*Opera*, IV, 420).

Christian doctrine which reinforces the symbolism of the mid-point. That we are to look beneath the surface for the eagle's fullest meaning is suggested by his reply to Chaucer's objection to the idea that Fame, even if she had all the "pies" and "spies" in "al a realme," can hear every word spoken on earth. "O yis, yis!" he replies:

> ". . . that kan I preve
> Be reson worthy for to leve,
> So that thou yeve thyn advertence
> To understonde my sentence." (706-10)

In warning Chaucer to understand his "sentence"—a warning twice repeated in his discourse—the eagle reveals his kinship not only with Mercury, the other messenger of Jove in whom wisdom and eloquence unite, but also with the divine eagle whom Dante confronts in the sphere of Jupiter in the *Paradiso*. Dante's intellectual doubts and their resolution by the eagle's lengthy disquisition on divine justice are amusingly paralleled in Chaucer's questioning attitude and in the reply of his erudite and loquacious bird.[32] But the eagle's "sentence" relates him more closely to Lady Philosophy, whose instruction of Boethius lies behind his opening remarks:

> "Geffrey, thou wost ryght wel this,
> That every kyndely thyng that is
> Hath a kyndely stede ther he
> May best in hyt conserved be;
> Unto which place every thyng,
> Thorgh his kyndely enclynyng,
> Moveth for to come to,
> Whan that hyt is awey therfro." (729-36)

The eagle's explanation of the doctrine of "natural place" is the essence of Philosophy's teaching in the first three

[32] On this parallel with Dante (*Par.*, XIX-XX), see A. Rambeau, "Chaucers *Hous of Fame* in seinem Verhältnis zu Dantes *Divina Commedia*," *Englische Studien*, III (1880), 233-34; Sypherd, pp. 55-56; Steadman, "Chaucer's Eagle," pp. 156-57.

books of the *Consolation*. The concept is introduced in Book I when she asks Boethius if he remembers "the ende of thynges, and whider that the entencion of alle kynde tendeth." What follows is in large part an exposition of the Christian doctrine of divine love or charity which moves every object to seek its natural place and prompts man to remember his heavenly country.[33] The eagle's examples of stones, lead, fire, sound, and smoke, each going upward or downward according to its weight, suggest similar statements of Augustine, Boethius, and other Christian writers for whom such phenomena symbolize the soul which rises or does not rise above the earth to God according to the degree that it is weighted by sin. Just as fire mounts upward and stones sink downward, says Augustine, so the body is borne downward by its heaviness and the spirit is borne upward by its love of God.[34] It is this natural motion of love—or "kyndely enclynyng," to use the eagle's phrase—which directs the devout mind to the divine "center" of God's house. For God has ordained that all things, animate and inanimate, should "conserve" the natures given them.[35] Only in man, whose soul longs

---

[33] *De consolatione philosophiae*, I, Pr. 6; III, Pr. 11. Cf. III, Met. 2, 39-42: "Alle thynges seken ayen to hir propre cours, and alle thynges rejoysen hem of hir retornynge ayen to hir nature."

[34] *Confessiones*, XIII, 9. Cf. *De civitate Dei*, XI, 28: "If we were stones, or waves, or wind, or flame, or indeed anything of that nature without sensation and life, we still would not lack a kind of longing [*appetitus*] for our own proper place and condition. For the motions of bodies are, as it were, their loves, whether they are carried downward by their heaviness, or upward by their lightness. For the body is borne by its weight, as the spirit by love, in whatever direction it is borne." See also Boethius, *De consolatione philosophiae*, III, Pr. 11, 134-52; Alanus, *De planctu naturae*, PL, 210, col. 453; Bersuire, *Opera*, V, 38, 78; Dante, *Purg.*, XVIII, 28; *Par.*, I, 103ff.; *Convivio*, III, 3; *Roman de la Rose*, 16,761ff.

[35] In *De consolatione philosophiae*, III, Pr. 11, Philosophy states the principle of "conservation" by which even objects without sense seek to fulfill "the entencioun of nature" or "by semblable resoun to kepyn that that is hirs (*that is to seyn, that is accordynge to hir nature in conservacioun of hir beynge and endurynge*." Although Chaucer refers to

to conserve its immortal nature, has this divine motion been deflected; for through cupidity the spirit seeks its center in the world, that is, in such unnatural ends as carnal love, fame, honors, and riches.[36] In these terms Philosophy portrays Boethius as one who is "pressyd with hevy cheynes, and bereth his chere enclyned adoun for the grete weyghte, and is constreyned to loken on the fool erthe."

Although the doctrine of natural place provides an ingenious and ironic basis for the eagle's otherwise "scientific" explanation of how all speech, by a process of "multiplicacioun" and reverberation of air, must ascend to the mid-point of Fame's house, its relevance to the Christian symbolism of the mid-point is found in Scripture, where we are told that no word uttered by man— "privy or apert," "foul or fair," to use the eagle's terms— is lost to God, who perceives all things said or done in the world below and records them for future judgment: "No thought escapeth him, and no word can hide itself from him."[37] But the ascent of speech to heaven, as Augustine explains, expresses a human-divine relationship that has little to do with the "multiplicacioun" of air. Speech, to pursue this doctrine, is but the outer manifestation of an inner spiritual state; it is the outward sound of words,

---

Plato and Aristotle, both the doctrine and the imagery are Christian. Cf. Augustine, *De civitate Dei*, XI, 27.

[36] "For just as all heavy things naturally seek the middle [*medium*], that is, the center which is in the middle of the earth, so all sinners seek and long for this world" (Bersuire, *Opera*, V, 38). Man's departure from "the entencioun of nature" through the worship of the wrongful Venus underlies Nature's complaint in *De planctu naturae*. Cf. *Roman de la Rose*, 19,021ff., and chap. III, n. 6, above.

[37] Ecclus. 42:20. Cf. Ecclus. 15:19-20; 39:24; Pss. 33:16; 89:8; and Heb. 4:13, which the eagle's phrase, "open and apert," perhaps echoes: "Neither is there any creature invisible in his sight; but all things are naked and open [*nuda et aperta*] to his eyes, to whom our speech is."

which in turn are the signs of the things men think. In this sense, speech includes words that are spoken inwardly as well as outwardly by sounds. When we speak inwardly, says Augustine, speech and sight are the same, and to say that God "hears" or "sees" man's speech is merely a figurative expression of his omniscience.[38]

The contrast between inward and outward speech is developed by Augustine and later writers in terms of St. Paul's distinction between the inner and the outer man. The speech of the inner man expresses the spiritual harmony between man and God, as in an attitude of prayer and devotion. The word of the inner man is an image of the divine Word, or wisdom, and this word can neither be uttered in sound nor be conceived in the likeness of sound. Therefore, says Augustine, anyone who would attain the likeness of the divine Word must disregard the word that sounds in the ears.[39] In Scripture this distinction is symbolized by two mouths, one of the body, another of the heart. The mouth of the heart is indicative of one's spiritual state, because if the heart is turned to God, so are the things one says. Otherwise, remarks St. James in his Epistle, the tongue is "an unquiet evil, full of deadly poison." With it "we bless God and the Father," and with it "we curse men," who have been made after the likeness of God. "Out of the same mouth proceedeth blessing and cursing."[40] From the spiritually estranged

---

[38] *De trinitate*, XV, 10-11. Cf. *De civitate Dei*, XI, 2: "For God speaks with a man not by means of some bodily creature making sounds in bodily ears so that the intervals of air are vibrated between speaker and hearer; . . . rather he speaks by the truth itself, if one is worthy of listening with the mind instead of with the body."

[39] *De trinitate*, XV, 11. Cf. *In Joannis Evangelium, Tract I, PL*, 35, col. 1,383; Neckam, *De naturis rerum*, I, 20.

[40] Jas. 3:2-10. Augustine contrasts the two mouths (*De trinitate*, XV, 10): "Thus, certain thoughts are speeches [*locutiones*] of the heart, where there is also a mouth, as the Lord shows when he says: 'Not that which goeth into the mouth defileth a man; but what cometh out of the mouth, this defileth a man' [Matt. 15:11]. This one sentence describes two 'mouths' of a man, one of the body, the other of the heart.

heart come all those abuses of the tongue—false rumor, jangling, detraction, and murmuring—which defile the spirit and lead it to eternal infamy. For God in his omniscience reads the hearts of men and inscribes all speech, inward and outward, for judgment at the end of the world. Therefore, says the Book of Wisdom, "he that speaketh unjust things cannot be hid":

. . . neither shall the chastising judgment pass him by. For inquisition shall be made into the thoughts of the ungodly, and the hearing of his words shall come to God, to the chastising of his iniquities. For the ear of jealousy heareth all things, and the tumult of murmuring shall not be hid. Keep yourselves therefore from murmuring, which profiteth nothing, and refrain your tongue from detraction; for an obscure speech shall not go for nought, and the mouth that belieth killeth the soul.[41]

At the end of Book II, these Scriptural implications of the doctrine of speech are embodied fictively in the eagle's description of the personified words, clothed in truth and falsehood, which ascend to the mid-point of Fame's house in the likeness of their earthly speakers. In Book III, where these "images" appear as the self-spoken words appealing to their earthly deeds and receiving the goddess's judgments, this doctrine provides the basis for an elaborate inversion of the Last Judgment which enables Chaucer to explore the deepest ramifications of the Christian contrast between earthly and heavenly fame. In the mean-

---

For that which his listeners thought man is defiled by enters the mouth of the body; however, that which the Lord says defiles the man comes from the mouth of the heart." In *De mendacio*, XVI (*PL*, 40, cols. 508ff.), Augustine relates the verse from Matthew to Wis. 1:11 ("and the mouth that belieth killeth the soul").

[41] Wis. 1:8-11. On God's punishment of evils of the tongue, see Ps. 51:1-7, a favorite source of portrayals of detraction in manuscript illumination. On similar portrayals of "jangling" in wall painting of Chaucer's period, see Tristram, p. 109. Robertson and Huppé discuss the doctrinal implications of the contrast between true and false speech (*Piers Plowman*, pp. 22ff.).

time, as the eagle concludes his explanation of the ascent of speech, the contrast between his "sentence" and what he calls his "palpable" meaning is brought home with amusing irony when he inquires if he has not proved his point simply and without "subtilite" of speech. Chaucer's laconic reply—"Yis"—indicates well enough his lack of understanding at this point. So too does his bewildered acquiescence when the eagle requests an opinion as to the "conclusyon" of his "sermon":

> "A good persuasion,"
> Quod I, "hyt is; and lyk to be
> Ryght so as thou hast preved me." (872-74)

Like Boethius in the early stages of Philosophy's instruction, Chaucer is still too enmeshed in worldly things to grasp the less "palpable" meaning of what he has been told. To adapt the eagle's words, he must have "proof" and "experience" of "thys sentence" by exercising his powers of understanding. In brief, he must turn his thoughts upward, contemplate God's works, and thereby view the world in true perspective. The remainder of the flight symbolizes this process.

Whereas the eagle's remarks on "natural place" parallel Philosophy's exposition in the first three books of the *Consolation*, the flight itself parallels her instruction in the last two. In order to demonstrate the just providence behind the fickleness of Fortune's gifts, Philosophy promises to "fycchen fetheris" in Boethius' thought so that "it mai arisen in heighte" and bring him "hool" and "sownd" to his true "contree." This process is foreshadowed in an allegorical description of the mind's flight above earthly things to the contemplation of God:

"I have, forthi, swifte fetheris that surmounten the heighte of the hevene. Whanne the swifte thoght hath clothid itself in tho fetheris, it despiseth the hateful erthes, and surmounteth

159

the rowndnesse of the gret ayr; and it seth the clowdes by-
hynde his bak, and passeth the heighte of the regioun of the
fir, that eschaufeth by the swifte moevynge of the firmament,
til that he areyseth hym into the houses that beren the sterres,
and joyneth his weies with the sonne, Phebus, and felawschipeth
the weie of the olde colde Saturnus; and he, imaked a knyght
of the clere sterre (*that is to seyn, whan the thought is makid
Godis knyght by the sekynge of cleer trouthe to comen to the
verray knowleche of God*)—and thilke soule renneth by the
cercle of the sterres in alle the places there as the schynynge
nyght is ypainted. . . . And whan the thought hath don there
inogh, he schal forleten the laste hevene, and he schal pressen
and wenden on the bak of the swifte firmament, and he schal be
makid parfit of the worschipful lyght of God. There halt the
lord of kynges the septre of his myght and atemprith the
governementz of the world, and the schynynge juge of
thinges, stable in hymself, governeth the swifte wayn (*that is
to seyn, the circuler moevynge of the sonne*). And yif this
wey ledeth the ayein so that thou be brought thider, thanne
wiltow seye that that is the contre that thou requerist, of which
thou ne haddest no mynde—'but now it remembreth me wel,
here was I born, her wol I fastne my degree. . . .' " (IV,
Met. 1, 1-38)

Not without reason does Chaucer, at the climax of his
flight, recall these lines. Indeed, allowing for a common
doctrinal source, we might say that his flight is essentially
a dramatization of Boethius' intellectual flight. Philosophy's feathers, here transferred to the eagle, illustrate
the principle of natural place whereby the mind seeks its
heavenly country and arrives at an understanding of God's
providence. Chaucer's flight parallels the first six of the
seven stages of Boethius' ascent. But the confused tidings
in Fame's house are a far cry from the peace and stability
of God's "hous." This difference, however, is one of both
thematic emphasis and poetic method. Whereas Boethius'
higher meaning is embodied in a rhetorically brilliant exposition of the relationship between temporal and eternal,
Chaucer's "sentence" is clothed in a dramatic and richly

concrete allegory whose component symbols point to the contrast between earthly and heavenly fame.

In order to strengthen the symbolism of the flight, Chaucer borrows details not only from Boethius but also from Dante, Scripture, and other sources, both pagan and Christian. Thus his looking downward at the earth at the eagle's bidding is reminiscent of Dante, who at Beatrice's behest surveys the vast distance he has ascended through the heavenly spheres and smiles at the earth and its "sorry semblance."[42] But the imagery describing the earth as it diminishes in size again echoes Philosophy, who in demonstrating the vanity of worldly fame compares the earth to a pin's point ("prykke"):

> But thus sone in a while he
> Was flowen fro the ground so hye
> That al the world, as to myn yë,
> No more semed than a prikke;
> Or elles was the air so thikke
> That y ne myghte not discerne. (904-909)

In Scipio's dream the same image is applied to the world as viewed from a mid-point in the air where Scipio is instructed in the vanity of earthly glory.[43] His dream is called up explicitly as the eagle compares Chaucer's ascent with other famous flights:

> ". . . for half so high as this
> Nas Alixandre Macedo;
> Ne the kyng, Daun Scipio,
> That saw in drem, at poynt devys,
> Helle and erthe and paradys;
> Ne eke the wrechche Dedalus,
> Ne his child, nyce Ykarus,

[42] *Par.*, XXII, 135. This parallel is strengthened by Beatrice's earlier instruction of Dante in the doctrine of "natural place" (*Par.*, I, 97ff.).

[43] Macrobius, *Commentary*, II, 9. Cf. Cicero, *De re publica*, VI, 16. In the *Parliament of Fowls*, 57-58, 64-66, Chaucer uses imagery from this portion of the dream to foreshadow the contrast between earthly and heavenly love underlying the main allegory. Cf. Huppé and Robertson, *Fruyt and Chaf*, pp. 105ff.

That fleigh so highe that the hete
Hys wynges malt, and he fel wete
In myd the see, and ther he dreynte,
For whom was maked moch compleynte." (914-24)

The flights of Scipio and Alexander—the latter of whom
was carried to the Earthly Paradise and similarly shown
the vanity of worldly fame—both emphasize the symbolism of Chaucer's flight. All three, that is, illustrate the
process by which the mind rises above the world and perceives its vanity.[44] But the flight of "nyce Ykarus" illustrates another kind of flight—the flight of cupidity. Bersuire uses the Ovidian legend to contrast the flight of the
virtuous, who through good works fly above the earth to
Paradise, with the flight of those like Icarus who through
vainglory fly so high that the heat of ambition melts their
wings and causes them to fall into the sea of vices.[45]

This contrast is developed in the description of the
"regioun of the air" to which the eagle next directs Chaucer's attention:

"Now turn upward," quod he, "thy face,
And behold this large space,
This eyr; but loke thou ne be
Adrad of hem that thou shalt se;
For in this region, certeyn,

---

[44] On this connotation of Alexander's flight, see M. M. Lascelles, "Alexander and the Earthly Paradise in Mediaeval Writings," *MÆ*, v (1936), 31-46. Cf. Patch, *The Other World*, pp. 157ff. Although Alexander was sometimes a medieval model of the virtues, his ascent to the skies, borne up by gryphons, was a favorite illustration of pride and vainglory. The subject appears in medieval art, even in misericords. See M. D. Anderson, *Misericords* (Harmondsworth, 1954), p. 19 and Pl. 30.

[45] *Opera*, VI, 246-47: "There is a wicked and abominable flight, and this is the flight of evil persons, who are like Icarus, the son of Daedalus." In *Inf.*, XVII, 111, Dante associates the flight of Icarus with the "way of evil" [*mala via*]. Cf. Benvenuto's gloss (*Commentum*, I, 582): "Allegorically, Daedalus, who was an ingenious man, is the prudent father admonishing his son not to fly to excessive heights, that is, beyond the limits of his powers, nor yet remain in the lowest regions, that is, in earthly things and vices."

Duelleth many a citezeyn,
Of which that speketh Daun Plato.
These ben the eyryssh bestes, lo!"
And so saw y all that meynee
Boothe goon and also flee. (925-34)

Chaucer's looking upward, like his looking downward at
the earth, is a symbolic act marking a stage in the mind's
purgation. The "large space" of air now seen corresponds
to the "gret ayr" which Philosophy says the mind must
pass through on its journey to God's "hous." Although the
eagle appeals to Plato as his authority, the description of
this region and its "citizens" is also Scriptural.[46] In Christian cosmography this is the *locus aerius* between earth
and heaven proper wherein dwell the evil spirits which
try to prevent the mind's ascent to God. According to St.
Paul, their leader is Satan, the "prince of the power of
this air," who works on the minds of unbelievers and
others who live in the fashion of the world.[47] In *The City
of God* Augustine discusses at length the false and deceitful mediators who, instead of showing men the way
to God, strive to conceal that way from them. Although
God allows these "eyryssh bestes" to deceive men, they
have no power over the spirit when it has faith. For just
as the birds of the air are inferior to us by virtue of our
reason, so these airy spirits are subject to us because our
faith transcends their despair.[48]

[46] Augustine refers to Plato, along with Apuleius, in the same connection (*De civitate Dei*, VIII, 15ff.).

[47] Eph. 2:2-3. Cf. Eph. 6:12; Col. 2:8, 20. The Scriptural passages
underlie Prudentius' account of this region (*Hamartigenia*, 517-22).
On "citizens" [*cives*] as a designation for evil spirits, see *Allegoriae
in sacram scripturam*, col. 898. In the similar flight and description of
"alle the hevenes region" in the *Anticlaudianus*—referred to by Chaucer
at the climax of his ascent (985ff.)—Alanus applies the terms *aerios
cives*, *cives superi*, and *superos cives* to the aerial powers (IV, 5; V,
7, 9). Chaucer's phrase "eyryssh bestes," Robinson notes (*Works*, p.
783), finds a basis in Augustine's *animalia . . . corpore aeria* (*De civitate
Dei*, VIII, 16).

[48] *Ibid.*, VIII, 15. Cf. IX, 18. In *Hamartigenia*, 517ff., Prudentius

In cautioning Chaucer not to fear the "eyryssh bestes," the eagle performs the role of reason which controls the perturbations of the will. What can happen when reason succumbs to fear and passion is illustrated by the story of Phaeton, introduced by the eagle to explain how the Milky Way, now in sight, was once "ybrent with hete." Chaucer is viewing the region through which, Philosophy says, the mind ascends into "the houses that beren the sterres" and "joyneth his weies with the sonne, Phebus, and felawschipeth the weie of the olde colde Saturnus." From this region, says Dante, two things become visible: the multitude of stars and the Galaxy—"that white circle which is popularly called the Way of St. James."[49] Like its earthly counterpart—the road to the shrine of St. James at Compostela—the Milky Way is a symbol of man's heavenly pilgrimage. John of Salisbury, recalling Ovid's account of Phaeton, associates it with the "via virtutis" or "beatitudinis." Similarly, Bersuire contrasts the "via virtutis" with the "via criminalis" and refers to Phaeton's story.[50] Like the Milky Way, the Phaeton legend is moralized in the Middle Ages. Phaeton, who insists upon driving the "carte" and horses of his father, Phoebus, is

---

asserts the efficacy of reason and faith over the airy demons, who, though instigators of men's sins, have power only to perturb and mislead.

[49] *Convivio*, II, 15.

[50] *Opera*, VI, 193: "For this way [of virtue] and its beauty are imaged in the way that Phaeton took to the palace of the Sun [*Metamorphoses*, II, 31ff.]. . . . This road [Ovid] calls the sublime way, the milky way, and the shining way, the way inclining toward the east, the way containing the twelve signs; for without doubt the way of virtue is sublime and lofty, sweet and admirable, milk-like, beautiful, delightful, and shining." Cf. *Policraticus*, VIII, 25. In the *Parliament*, 43-56, Chaucer follows Macrobius (*Commentary*, I, 15) in identifying "the Galaxye" with eternal bliss, the meeting place and reward of those that loved "commune profyt." In view of the connection of the Galaxy with the pilgrimage to St. James, the eagle's appeal to "seynt Jame," as he begins to soar (884-86), is perhaps not fortuitous.

interpreted as "pride," "ambition," or "vainglory."[51] The Scorpion, the zodiacal sign inciting Phaeton's fear and causing him to lose his "wyt" and "let the reynes gon," may be likened to the "fals, flaterynge beste" which Chaucer elsewhere compares to Fortune and in Scriptural commentary is identified with Satan and other evil spirits.[52] As an astrological symbol, Scorpio is called "the darkest house" or "the house of death," and like Mars, whose malevolence is especially powerful in this house, it is indicative of fear, anxiety, strife, and worldly tribulations.[53] The unfortunate aspects of Scorpio are illustrated by the disaster of Phaeton, whose punishment by Jupiter typifies the divine justice overtaking those who through pride or

[51] John of Garland interprets Phaeton as the proud [*superbi*], who "prefer themselves to others" (*Integumenta Ovidiana*, ed. F. Ghisalberti, Milan, 1933, p. 44). According to Giovanni del Virgilio, Phaeton's driving his father's horses illustrates vainglory and the dangers of vain and futile speculation (*Allegorie librorum Ovidii Metamorphoseos*, ed. Ghisalberti, p. 47). Cf. Ridewall, *Fulgentius metaforalis*, pp. 56-57; Bersuire, *Ovidius moralizatus*, p. 107; and Panofsky, *Studies in Iconology* (New York, 1962), p. 219.

[52] The scorpion is an image of Fortune in the *Book of the Duchess*, 636-41, and the Merchant's Tale, 2,057-60. Cf. Patch, *The Goddess Fortuna*, p. 52. In Scripture, the scorpion is a figure for Satan and his followers (Luke 10:19) or detractors (Ezech. 2:6), meanings exemplified in the Man of Law's Tale, 404-406, and the Manciple's Tale, 271-72. Cf. *Allegoriae in sacram scripturam*, col. 1,060; Bersuire, *Opera*, II, 401.

[53] On the attributes of Scorpio and its connection with Mars, see Curry, *Chaucer and the Mediaeval Sciences*, p. 177. Cf. chap. II, n. 43, above. Bersuire identifies Scorpio with the house [*domus*] of this world (*Opera*, IV, 88): "According to Messahala, this is the house of death, fear, crime, toil, war, and misfortune. So, too, the world can be called a house of death, because it will bring one to everlasting death: 'For her house inclineth unto death' [Prov. 2:18]. Similarly, it is the house of fear, for in the world there is no security. . . . Furthermore, the world is the house of crime, toil, war, and misfortune, because in the world there is nothing, literally, except wickedness and corruption, toil and hardship, war and dissention, misfortune and ruin. Hence this is the house spoken of in Jer. 9: 'For death is come up through our windows: it is entered into our houses.' " In the Man of Law's Tale, 295ff., the unfortunate aspects of Scorpio provide a meaningful background for the misfortunes of Constance and the wicked actions of the Sultaness, who is compared to Satan and the "scorpioun."

vainglory depart from the path of virtue, "let gon" the "reynes" of reason, and yield to the wiles of Satan or Fortune.[54] With characteristic understatement, the eagle himself is careful to point out a moral in the story:

> "Loo, ys it not a gret myschaunce
> To lete a fool han governaunce
> Of thing that he can not demeyne?" (957-59)

After the lesson of Phaeton's unhappy end, the effect of the eagle's instruction can be seen in Chaucer's progression from an attitude of fear, such as he felt in the desert and at the beginning of his ascent, to one of faith and acceptance of the teachings of the eagle, who, as he continues to soar, gladdens the poet by his "faithful" speech. At this point Chaucer can at least look downward without fear and view in clearer perspective all the temptations and perturbations he has left behind him:

> Tho gan y loken under me
> And beheld the ayerissh bestes,
> Cloudes, mystes, and tempestes,
> Snowes, hayles, reynes, wyndes,
> And th' engendrynge in hir kyndes,
> All the wey thrugh which I cam. (964-69)

These clouds, mists, and tempests are the elements of the air which Philosophy says the mind must rise above if it is to reach the stability of God's house. For the mind, too, says Prudentius, has clouds and mists which hinder its contemplation of truth.[55] Just as Chaucer's earlier appeal to Christ marked the beginning of his spiritual recovery, so his appeal to God and recollection of Boethius' similar

---

[54] John of Garland moralizes Phaeton's death as the punishment by which God humbles the proud (*Integumenta Ovidiana*, p. 44). Or to follow Giovanni del Virgilio, it is the reward of those whose vain speculations sow errors in the world (*Allegorie librorum*, II, 1-3, p. 47).

[55] *Hamartigenia*, 89-92. These are the "elements of the world" which St. Paul (Col. 2:8-11) and Augustine (*De civitate Dei*, IX, 18) associate with the wicked powers of the air.

flight through the elements climax a higher stage of insight:

> "O God!" quod y, "that made Adam,
> Moche ys thy myght and thy noblesse!"
> And thoo thoughte y upon Boece,
> That writ, "A thought may flee so hye,
> Wyth fetheres of Philosophye,
> To passen everych element;
> And whan he hath so fer ywent,
> Than may be seen, behynde hys bak,
> Cloude,"—and al that y of spak. (970-78)

As an indication of Chaucer's attitude at this point, the appeal to God "that made Adam" is an affirmation of the power of grace that opens up to faith and reason a path by which the spirit might transcend the burden of Adam's sin. The symbolism of the flight, now explicit in the reference to the "fetheres of Philosophye," is further strengthened by Chaucer's recollection of the intellectual flights described by Alanus de Insulis and Martianus Capella, whose accounts of "alle the hevenes region" he now can believe as far as he can see the "proof."[56]

Chaucer, it would seem, has reached the stage of contemplation necessary for understanding the tidings promised him by the eagle. Nevertheless we can still detect traces of the confusion which earlier led him to compare himself to Enoch and Elias and other elect whom God has "stellified." In this instance, excited by his speculations on the heavenly regions, he views himself as another St. Paul carried up to Paradise:

[56] On the Christian implications of the symbolism of the flight in the *Anticlaudianus*, see Green, "Alan of Lille's *De Planctu Naturae*," p. 655, and Mâle, *Religious Art in France*, pp. 8 off., who discusses the influence of the allegories of Martianus and Alanus on medieval Christian art. The similar doctrine underlying the eagle's flight and Mercury's flight in *The Marriage of Philology and Mercury* is evident in the glosses of Remigius of Auxerre, John the Scot, and Alexander Neckam.

Thoo gan y wexen in a were,
And seyde, "Y wot wel y am here;
But wher in body or in gost
I not, ywys; but God, thou wost!"
For more clere entendement
Nas me never yit ysent. (979-84)

Chaucer's vain but amusing speculation and the eagle's
forceful rebuke—"Lat be ... thy fantasye!"—both parallel
the *Paradiso*, where Dante, likewise elated by his new
experience of heavenly phenomena and desiring to know
their cause, also alludes to St. Paul and is admonished
by Beatrice: "Thou thyself makest thyself dense with false
imagining, and so thou seest not what thou wouldst see,
if thou hadst cast it off."[57] Reminding Dante that he is not
on the earth, Beatrice explains to him the principle of
"natural place" by which he has transcended the heavenly
bodies—a lesson Chaucer has just received from the eagle.
The eagle's answer to Chaucer's confusion is an offer to
teach him the names of the stars and the heavenly signs;
but Chaucer rejects the offer with the excuse that he is
"now too old," that he prefers to believe those who have
already written on these matters, and, finally, that the
stars shine so brightly they might harm his sight. This
last excuse again suggests Dante, whose vision at the beginning of the *Paradiso* is still too dim to confront the
light of divine wisdom.[58] At the same time, we may perhaps read into this amusing colloquy between Chaucer
and the eagle a brief debate between faith and reason.
Chaucer's argument that he prefers to believe those who
have already written about the stars and heavenly bodies

[57] *Par.*, I, 82-90. Cf. II Cor. 12:2-4: "I know a man in Christ;
above fourteen years ago (whether in the body, I know not, or out of
the body, I know not; God knoweth), such a one . . . was caught up
into paradise and heard secret words which it is not granted to man
to utter."

[58] *Par.*, I, 58; IV, 139-42; V, 1ff. Cf. *Purg.*, XXVII, 50-60; XXXII,
10-12; *Par.*, XXIII, 31-33, 76-78.

reflects an attitude also appearing in the *Legend of Good Women*, where he again extols "the doctrine of these olde wyse" in books as opposed to the futile probing for "preve."[59] In any event, the eagle's rebuke apparently has had its proper effect. At least the eagle's response—"That may wel be"—is indicative of the soundness of Chaucer's attitude.

Such is the state of Chaucer's understanding when sounds from a distance announce his approach to the House of Fame. Like Boethius at the beginning of Book IV and Dante at the beginning of the *Paradiso*, Chaucer is ready to contemplate higher truths. But the noise he hears is in ironic contrast to the stability of Boethius' heavenly "hous" or the harmonious sounds greeting Dante in Paradise. The subdued murmuring issuing from Fame's house fulfills all the expectations of the eagle's earlier account of what Chaucer would hear. Instead of the praise of God which should be heard from the "triune compass" of earth, sea, and sky, what he hears at this mid-point of the world is a mixture of "feir speche" and "chidynges," both "fals and soth compouned."[60] In reply to the eagle's inquiry—"And what soun is it lyk?"—Chaucer again appropriates images from Ovid's description of Fame's abode:

"Peter! lyk betynge of the see,"
Quod y, "ayen the roches holowe,
Whan tempest doth the shippes swalowe;
And lat a man stonde, out of doute,
A myle thens, and here hyt route;
Or elles lyk the last humblynge
After the clappe of a thundringe,
Whan Joves hath the air ybete. . ." (1034-41)

Although the image of the tempest is from Ovid, Chau-

[59] Prol. F, 1-28.
[60] Cf. the Second Nun's Tale, Prol., 45-47.

169

cer's appeal to St. Peter brings to mind a particular tempest in which the apostle, "tossed" by waves, calls upon Christ and is saved.[61] But in this tempest of sounds emanating from Fame's house the voice of faith and reason is lost in that of the "unbridled tongue," the "blessing and cursing" proceeding from the same mouth. What Chaucer hears, in short, is the confusion of Babylon, the "confusion of tongues" which stems from the heart of the sinner and which will persist until the end of the world, when truth and falsehood—Jerusalem and Babylon—will be forever separated.

These Apocalyptic implications underlie the concluding imagery of Book II. Here the Christian doctrine of speech, implied throughout the eagle's earlier account of the ascent of words to the House of Fame, takes on additional Scriptural connotations which in Book III become the basis for an ironic inversion of the Last Judgment. The immediate link is the eagle's reply to Chaucer's question as to whether the "noyse" in Fame's house comes from "folk that doun in erthe duellen" and has traveled here in the manner already described and whether the "living" bodies of these "folk" are also here. Again the eagle must correct Chaucer's "fantasye." "Noo," he exclaims—"by Seynte Clare!"—

> "Loo, to the Hous of Fame yonder,
> Thou wost now how, cometh every speche;
> Hyt nedeth noght eft the to teche.
> But understond now ryght wel this,
> Whan any speche ycomen ys
> Up to the paleys, anon-ryght
> Hyt wexeth lyk the same wight
> Which that the word in erthe spak,
> Be hyt clothed red or blak;
> And hath so verray hys lyknesse
> That spak the word, that thou wilt gesse

[61] Matt. 14:24-33. Cf. 8:23-26.

> That it the same body be,
> Man or woman, he or she. . ." (1070-82)

The eagle's rebuke and his oath by St. Clare both echo the *Paradiso*, where Dante's similar misconception of the angelic "images" appearing before him must be corrected by Beatrice, who explains that these images, although "true substances," are merely accommodations to the imperfect sight of mortals.[62] But as the confused sounds from the House of Fame make clear, the "images" of which the eagle speaks are to be part of no supramundane sphere as in the *Paradiso* but of the very worldly sphere where Fame has her abode and wields her fickle awards. Indeed, as we discover in Book III, these words appearing in the likeness of their earthly speakers are nothing less than the throngs of suppliants gathering before Fame's throne and receiving her judgments of praise, slander, and oblivion. Although the contrast between Dante's and Chaucer's "images" might again suggest parody, we may more profitably seek in this parallel another instance of Chaucer's use of Dante to convey the doctrine underlying his allegory.

Viewed in this light, these "images" may be considered as an extension of the eagle's earlier "sentence." Although their literal basis is found in Ovid's account of the personified rumors crowding Fame's dwelling, they have become more than a personification of rumor. As the eagle's remarks on "natural place" indicate, these words ascending so "naturally" to the mid-point of Fame's house have become images of the soul itself, whose "inward speeches," whether true or false, rise to the divine center

[62] *Par.*, III, 19-30; IV, 22ff. Except for the possible reference to St. Clare in *Par.*, III, 97ff., this parallel is noted by Paul Ruggiers, "Words Into Images in Chaucer's *House of Fame*: A Third Suggestion," *MLN*, LXIX (1954), 34-37. Another parallel to Chaucer's fiction is found in Scipio's dream, where Scipio, inquiring if his father and Africanus are "living," is told that he is viewing spirits who have flown from their bodies as from a prison.

of God's house.[63] With further reason, therefore, must the eagle correct Chaucer's belief that these words ascend in the "living" bodies of their speakers. For the essence of this doctrine is that the ascent of speech has to do not with a bodily ascent but with a human-divine relationship. Thus understood, the eagle's explanation that the words ascend not in the living bodies of their speakers but in their "likeness" or "image" is merely an elaboration of the same concept. For according to Christian doctrine all speech, by its very nature, is an "image" or "likeness" of the mind that conceives it. Just as thoughts are expressive of the state of the spirit, so are words images of the thoughts thus conceived. Speech itself, therefore, is but an image of the spirit.[64] The ascent of the images themselves to a divine mid-point develops this concept. Chaucer's "wynged words," rising in the likeness of their earthly speakers and petitioning Fame before her throne, have a doctrinal basis in the words of prayer or devotion which fly to God.[65] In the Apocalypse the prayers themselves are presented to God by one of the angels (Christ,

[63] In "Two Notes on J. T. Williams' 'Words Into Images in Chaucer's *House of Fame*,'" *MLN*, LXIV (1949), 73-76, Julian Ziegler discusses the parallel between Chaucer's "words" and Boethius' personified thoughts ascending with the feathers of Philosophy.

[64] "Truly, all words by which we speak—that is, think—anything in the mind are likenesses and images [*similitudines et imagines*] of the things of which they are the words; and every likeness, or image, to the extent that it is true, is to the same extent an imitation of the thing whose likeness it is" (St. Anselm, *Monologium*, XXXI, *PL*, 158, col. 184). Cf. cols. 187-88: "When the rational mind understands itself by thinking, an image of itself is born in its thought; indeed, this thought of itself is its image, . . . this image of itself being its word." In *De trinitate*, IX, XV, Augustine elaborates upon the concept of the human word [*verbum*] as an image of the spirit.

[65] For example, Ps. 87:3; Ecclus. 35:20-21; II Par. 30:27; Acts 10:4. In *The Pilgrimage of the Life of Man*, 22,807ff., Lydgate personifies this concept in Lady Prayer, who flies up to God to present prayers "made in good entente" and "grownded on resoun." In *Teseida*, VII, a similar personification appears in the self-spoken prayers ascending to the deities of Palamon, Arcita, and Emilia.

the High Priest), who offers them with incense upon the altar before the throne.[66] The implicit personification of these prayers, which are said to be "seen" as well as "heard" by God, is applicable to all speech—"foul or fair," "privy or apert"—which, together with one's works, ascends to God to be recorded in the books of judgment and to be manifested before Christ the Judge at the end of the world.[67]

In this Scriptural context it is but a short step from Chaucer's personified words to the related concept of their clothing; for, according to Christian doctrine, the body in which one's image or likeness outwardly appears is nothing more than the clothing (*vestimentum*) of the spirit.[68] As such men's clothing is indicative of the degree of inward purity or corruption. Accordingly, clothes have a twofold meaning. On the one hand, there are *vestes virtuales* or *spirituales*, the clothing of the "word" of the inner man; or there are *vestes criminales*, the clothing of the "word" of the outer man.[69] If one's words or thoughts (inward speeches) emanate from charity, as in an attitude of prayer or devotion, they are clothed in truth; if they are expressive of cupidity, however, they are clothed in

[66] Apoc. 8:2-4. In *Paradise Lost*, XI, 14ff., Milton develops the implicit personification of the Scriptural passages by contrasting the prayers of Adam and Eve, which, clad in incense, appear before God's throne, with the prayers of the wicked, which, like Chaucer's "wynged wondres" (2,117ff.), are blown about by the wind. In "Words Into Images in Chaucer's *House of Fame*," *MLN*, LXII (1947), 488-90, J. T. Williams discusses a thirteenth century Hebraic analogue to Milton's passage in which words converted into images before God's throne bear a close resemblance to Chaucer's self-spoken words before Fame's throne.

[67] Cf. Acts 10:4; Rom. 2:15-16; II Cor. 5:10; Heb. 4:13; Apoc. 20:11-13. For the doctrine underlying the symbolism, see chap. V, n. 106, below.

[68] Bersuire, *Opera*, VI, 188.

[69] *Ibid*. Together these are the *vestes temporales* in which the spirit is clothed in its earthly condition. For a discussion of the Scriptural imagery of clothing, see Robertson and Huppé, *Piers Plowman*, pp. 24-26, 51-52, especially 168ff.

falsehood.[70] Anagogically, the clothes of the inner man
are the *vestes superales* which Christ provides as a suitable
garment for the divine Word in man: "For he hath
clothed me with the garments of salvation" (Is. 61:10).
Behind this concept is the doctrine of Incarnation: "And
the Word was made flesh, and dwelt among us."[71] Just
as the Word of God became flesh, so the flesh of the elect
will be purified as a proper garment for the "word" in
man. Or, as Augustine says, just as Christ was conformed
to men by assuming mortality, so men will be conformed
to Christ by immortality, that is to say, by the resurrection
of the body. However, he adds, the conformity to the
image of Christ or the divine Word is to be understood
only of the inner man; for the ascent to God must be by
a spiritual likeness, not by corporal elevation.[72] This spiritual ascent is true also of the outer man, who conforms
not to Christ but to Satan, who provides the spirit with
garments stained in sin, the *vestes infernales* in which it
will rise to the seat of final judgment and be condemned
to eternal infamy.[73]

The conformity of the inner man to Christ is sym-

[70] Cf. Boethius, *De consolatione philosophiae*, I, Pr. 6: ". . . and
the nature of thoughtes desceyved is this, that, as ofte as they casten
awey sothe opynyouns, they clothen hem in false opynyouns, of the
whiche false opynyouns the derknesse of perturbacion waxeth up, that
confowndeth the verray insyghte."

[71] John 1:14. In *De trinitate*, Augustine discusses the analogy between the human "word" and the Incarnate Word, for example, XV,
11: "Just as our (inner) word becomes, as it were, a sound [*vox*] of
the body, assuming this sound so that it may be manifested to the
senses of men, so the Word of God was made flesh, assuming the flesh
so that he might manifest himself to men's senses. And just as our
word becomes sound but is not changed into sound, so the Word of
God was made flesh but was not changed into flesh. Therefore, whoever wishes to attain some kind of likeness of the Word of God should
disregard the word that sounds in the ears."

[72] *De civitate Dei*, XXII, 16 (on Rom. 8:29; 12:2); IX, 18.

[73] Bersuire, *Opera*, VI, 188. For an elaboration of the concept of the
spirit's conformity to the image of Christ or Satan, see Walter Hilton,
The Ladder of Perfection, I, 52ff.; II, 1ff.

bolized in the Apocalypse by the white garments of the elect who congregate about the thrones of God and the Lamb.[74] These spirits clothed in white have their ironic counterpart in Chaucer's words clothed in "red or blak." In each instance the color symbolism is merely a figurative extension of the meaning of the clothing; for the color of one's clothing, like the clothing itself, is an outward manifestation of one's spiritual state and is said to conform to the image or word within.[75] Thus red, in reference to cupidity, may signify carnal love, as in the Apocalypse, where it is the color of the apparel of the Whore of Babylon, or in Isaiah, where it is contrasted with the purity of white: "If your sins be as scarlet, they shall be made as white as snow; and if they be red as crimson, they shall be white as wool."[76] But red may also denote the ardor of charity itself, as again in the Apocalypse and in Isaiah, where the red in Christ's garment symbolizes his humanity or passion and the martyrdom by which he redeemed mankind.[77] As applied to speech, moreover, red is expressive of the truth of the inner man. For this reason, says Bersuire, all speech should be clothed in red: "For just as the tongue is by nature red, so our speech should be colored with the truth or red of charity."[78] Such words clothed in red have their opposite in words clothed in black. Although black, as a Scriptural

[74] Apoc. 7:9-10. Cf. 3:5.

[75] On "color" as a symbol of the spiritual state of man, see Rabanus, *De universo*, col. 563. Bersuire illustrates this doctrine by the chameleon; for just as the chameleon's color conforms to its interior condition, so man's conduct [*conditio conversationis*] conforms to the inward state of the heart or conscience (*Opera*, II, 389-90). Cf. II, 541.

[76] Apoc. 17:4; Is. 1:18.

[77] Apoc. 19:13; Is. 63:1-2. Alanus interprets the red apparel in the latter passage as *humana Christi natura* (*Distinctiones*, PL, 210, col. 999). On "red" [*rubor*] as a symbol of charity, see Rabanus, *De universo*, col. 563; Bersuire, *Opera*, II, 541; III, 321.

[78] *Ibid.*, IV, 471. In Apoc. 19:13, "red" is an image of the clothing of the Divine Word: "And he was clothed with a garment sprinkled with blood. And his name is called: *The Word of God.*"

figure, may pertain to charity, it is above all the color of cupidity, the color in which Satan clothes the sinner and leads him to damnation. Whereas red is indicative of true speech, black signifies the false speech of the wicked—the lies, slander, and detraction emanating from the heart of the sinner:

The tongue of detractors and slanderers is like the tongue of a serpent, which is exceedingly venomous. Hence on account of its malice it seems black with poison and likewise moves quickly, because it seems to be double-tongued; for the speech or tongue of slanderers and detractors, which is especially black, is to those whom it bites deadly and poisonous and, loving to defame others, swift and sharp.[79]

Although black is preeminently the color of falsehood, sometimes, as in the speech of hypocrites and janglers, falsehood may be clothed in the color of truth. For, says Lydgate, when tongues are "to wyde vnlooke," speech is "clad in dowbill hue" to "compace thynges" that were never meant.[80]

Chaucer's words clothed in "red or blak" would appear to be an adaptation of these Scriptural–exegetical meanings to his own thematic purpose. Viewed in this light his personified words or images betray the same ambivalence of his other Scriptural symbols. As an aspect of earthly fame, these words clothed in red or black denote the truth or falsehood, or both combined, of the confused tidings of his "verray neyghebores." As such they illustrate the fickle judgment of the people feared by Dido and other worshipers in the temple of Venus. At the same time, as the Christian doctrine of speech implies, the ascent of these images to Fame's house in the likeness of their earthly

---

[79] *Opera*, IV, 471. Cf. II, 541; III, 321; V, 104. In Hilton's *Ladder of Perfection*, I, 52-54, "black" is applied to the image of the soul clothed in sin, which, though hidden from men's eyes, appears clearly in the sight of God.

[80] *The Minor Poems*, II, 797.

speakers is an ironic inversion of the Scriptural accounts of the Last Judgment, when every soul—"man or woman, he or she," to quote the eagle—will reclaim his "living" body and rise to the mid-point of Christ's tribunal in the image of charity or cupidity. At that time all words recorded in the books of judgment—"foul or fair," "privy or apert," clothed in the "red" of truth or the "blak" of falsehood—will be visibly manifested, along with one's works, as testimony of the conscience.[81] These ironic implications are dramatically fulfilled in Book III as the self-spoken words before Fame's throne appeal to their earthly deeds and receive the goddess's fickle awards of praise and infamy. In this inverted Apocalyptic setting, the implied contrast between Christ's and Fame's judgments points toward the tidings of a "fer contree" which are the goal of Chaucer's flight. The prophetic nature of these tidings is again suggested as the eagle, reminiscent of Virgil at the threshold of the Earthly Paradise, arrives with Chaucer at the House of Fame, bids him farewell, and asks "God of heven" to send him "grace" to learn "some good."[82]

[81] An interesting analogue to Chaucer's color imagery is found in the *Annales Bertiniani* of Prudentius of Troye, where a priest, led by a heavenly guide, visits a church where he sees books in which deeds of good and evil are recorded in red and black letters respectively. See A. B. Van Os, *Religious Visions* (Amsterdam, 1932), p. 33.

[82] Cf. *Purg.*, XXVII, 124-42. Although Virgil remains briefly with Dante in the Earthly Paradise, his function as divine guide ends with his "crowning" Dante—an action symbolizing the will made free and sound by the rule and guidance of reason.

CHAPTER V

THE HOUSE OF FAME—
PARADISE

> But thou, son of man, show . . . them the form of the
> house and the fashion thereof, the goings out and the
> comings in, and the whole plan thereof, and all its
> ordinances, and all its order, and all its laws, and thou
> shalt write it in their sight, that they may keep the whole
> form thereof, and its ordinances, and do them. This is
> the law of the house upon the top of the mountain: All
> its border round about is most holy: this then is the law
> of the house.
>
> —Ezech. 43:10-12

T HE promise of a vision of prophetic import inspires the opening lines of Chaucer's "lytel laste bok," borrowed, with additions, from Dante's invocation to the *Paradiso*:

> O God of science and of lyght,
> Appollo, thurgh thy grete myght,
> This lytel laste bok thou gye!
> Nat that I wilne, for maistrye,
> Here art poetical be shewed;
> But for the rym ys lyght and lewed,
> Yit make hyt sumwhat agreable,
> Though som vers fayle in a sillable;
> And that I do no diligence
> To shewe craft, but o sentence. (1091-1100)

Chaucer's higher purpose is expressed not only by the distinction between his "craft" and his "sentence"—that is, the doctrine beneath his "art poetical"—but also by Apollo, who as god of "science and of lyght" is grouped with the Muses as the source of the "sentence" of poetry. As distinguished from the Muses, Apollo signifies *sapientia*, or divine wisdom, a distinction conveyed in Dante's invoca-

178

tion by the two yokes of Parnassus, the higher and the
lower, images respectively of the wisdom (*sapientia*) and
knowledge (*scientia*) which stem from doctrine.[1] As a
symbol of the higher reason, Apollo is identified with the
sun, the divine "lyght" of wisdom, and also with Christ,
the "true wisdom of the Father," and in this capacity he is
attributed with the power to reveal prophetic truths.[2] This
power is particularized in the laurel, a tree said to bring
dreams of doctrinal content and to make manifest the hidden truths of poetry. Because of its fragrance, moreover,
the laurel symbolizes good fame, that is, fame based on
virtue; and its enduring qualities—its shade, incorrupti-
bility, eternal verdure, and immunity to lightning—denote
the persistence of such fame and its immunity to age.[3] To
these powers of the laurel Chaucer presumably alludes in
the remainder of his invocation:

> And yif, devyne vertu, thow
> Wilt helpe me to shewe now
> That in myn hed ymarked ys—
> Loo, that is for to menen this,
> The Hous of Fame for to descryve—

[1] Pietro Alighieri, *Commentarium*, p. 545. Cf. Benvenuto da Imola,
IV, 299-300. On Apollo as a symbol of *sapientia*, see also Neckam,
De naturis rerum, II, 70, and Bernard Silvestris, *Commentum*, pp. 9-10,
who summarizes his multiple meanings: "Apollo sometimes designates
the sun, sometimes divine wisdom [*divinam sapientiam*], sometimes
man."

[2] Benvenuto, IV, 302. On Apollo's prophetic power, see *Mythographus
Vaticanus III*, p. 129, which follows Fulgentius, *Mitologiae*, I, 23. In
Genealogia deorum, V, 3, Boccaccio identifies Apollo in this role with
the sun, the planet through which "many future things are shown to
mortals."

[3] These and other properties of the laurel, along with their significations, appear in Petrarch's "Coronation Oration," translated by E. H.
Wilkins, *PMLA*, LXVIII (1953), 1,241-50. On Dante's laurel, see Benvenuto, *iv*, 302ff.; Francesco da Buti, III, 16. Cf. Neckam, *De naturis
rerum*, II, 170; *Mythographus Vaticanus III*, p. 219; Boccaccio, *Genealogia deorum*, V, 3. Bersuire identifies the laurel with the Cross, for
Phoebus (Christ) himself, spiritually, "claims this tree, that is, the
wood of the Holy Cross, as his own" (*Ovidius moralizatus*, II, ed.
Ghisalberti, p. 103).

> Thou shalt se me go as blyve
> Unto the nexte laure y see,
> And kysse yt, for hyt is thy tree.
> Now entre in my brest anoon! (1101-1109)

If Apollo and his laurel embody the higher purpose and subject matter of Chaucer the poet, for Chaucer the pilgrim they mark the culmination of his spiritual education. Apollo's significance in this regard may best be understood if we relate the invocation to the two earlier ones. As a mirror of Chaucer's spiritual state, the invocation to Morpheus is indicative of the mind in a condition of sloth; for in Morpheus' cave, as Boccaccio remarks, the light of Apollo's wisdom is never seen.[4] In contrast to Apollo's prophetic power, Morpheus' dreams are an image of the fantasies and illusions of Satan and as such foreshadow the allegory of the temple and desert of Venus and more particularly the drama of Hell unfolding in the story of the *Aeneid*. Like Aeneas' and Dante's experiences in Hell, Chaucer's sojourn in the temple and desert marks the initial stage which the mind must undergo before it can be purged of earthly thoughts and prepared for the contemplation of higher truths. The process of purgation, beginning with the appeal to Christ and the appearance of the eagle, underlies the invocation to Book II—an appeal to the three powers of will, memory, and intellect which must work in harmony before reason can fulfill its proper function. This higher stage, symbolized by the flight with the eagle, culminates in the invocation to Apollo, whose "science" and "lyght" are the source of the contemplation of heavenly truth. In the *Paradiso* this stage of contemplation is figured in Beatrice, who, like Apollo, signifies *sapientia* or divine revelation, as distinguished from Virgil, a symbol of *scientia* or the natural light of reason. Chaucer's eagle, it would seem, combines these two functions,

---

[4] *Genealogia deorum*, I, 31.

as his association with Beatrice and the sun at the end of
Book I suggests. However, this association, along with the
appeal to Apollo, is ironic on the surface; for Chaucer's
vision, unlike Dante's, is to be of no spiritual Paradise but
of the very worldly "paradise" of Fame. Nevertheless,
Chaucer's "lytel laste bok" is indeed his own *Paradiso*.
Like Dante in his "ultimo lavoro," Chaucer in Book III
is Chaucer the contemplative, and the goal of his contemplation is to be not only the worldly tidings symbolized
by Fame and her fickle decrees but also the "glad" tidings
of a "fer contree"—the *terra longinqua* of Scripture and
of Dante's *Paradiso*. In preparation for these tidings, the
Apocalyptic symbolism, especially apparent at the end of
Book II, acquires an increasingly important function.

In keeping with the higher subject matter of Book III,
the symbolism of the flight takes on broadening Scriptural connotations. At the very beginning the ascent with
the eagle is linked with the mountain in a pattern foreshadowing the "apocalyptic" vision which is to follow.
Chaucer's flight to the mountain and house of Fame
parallels several Biblical flights, the most obvious being
John's flight with "one of the seven angels" to the holy
mountain and city of Jerusalem: "And he took me up in
spirit to a great and high mountain, and he showed me the
holy city Jerusalem, coming down out of heaven from
God, having the glory of God." Tropologically, John's
flight is interpreted as the process by which the intellect,
freed from the body, contemplates the mysteries of heaven
and the next life. The angel bearing him to the mountain
is a symbol of Christ or the intellect, as is also the eagle,
with whom John is traditionally identified.[5] Similar meanings underlie Ezechiel's flight to the holy mountain and
city:

[5] Haymo, *Expositio in Apocalypsin*, PL, 117, cols. 1,197-98 (on
Apoc. 21:10-11). Cf. *PL*, 165, col. 720.

In the five and twentieth year of our captivity, in the beginning
of the year, the tenth day of the month, the fourteenth year
after the city was destroyed, in the selfsame day the hand of
the Lord was upon me, and he brought me thither. In the
visions of God he brought me into the land of Israel, and set
me upon a very high mountain, upon which there was as the
building of a city, bending towards the south.[6]

If the eagle relates Chaucer's flight more closely to John's
flight to the holy mountain and city, the date of his dream
connects it with Ezechiel's vision on "the tenth day of the
month." Moreover, the "tenth day of the tenth month"—
the Biblical equivalent of December 10—is associated in
Ezechiel's vision and elsewhere in Scripture with one of
the most significant events in Old Testament history: the
siege and capture of Jerusalem by Nabuchodonosor, King
of Babylon.[7] The special importance of the date for Ezechiel's vision is apparent earlier in his prophecy: "And the
word of the Lord came to me in the ninth year, in the
tenth month, the tenth day of the month, saying: Son of
man, write thee the name of this day, on which the king of
Babylon hath set himself against Jerusalem today"
(24:1-2). Both the date and the events of the siege are
found, among other places, in the fourth book of Kings:

And it came to pass in the ninth year of his reign [i.e., of
Sedecias], in the tenth month, the tenth day of the month,
that Nabuchodonosor king of Babylon came, he and all his

---

[6] Ezech. 40:1-2.

[7] The "tenth day of the tenth month" is referred to in Zach. 8:19
as one of the four fast days to be observed by Israel in commemorat-
ing its captivity and deliverance. In *De clericorum institutione*, PL, 107,
col. 334, Rabanus Maurus places the date in December: "The tenth day of
fasting is in the tenth month, which we call December, when all the
captives of Babylon learned that the temple had been destroyed in the
fifth month." In the Jewish calendar the tenth day of the tenth month
is the tenth day of Tebet, roughly equivalent to December, the time of
the winter solstice, and along with Tamuz (the summer solstice) one
of the two most unlucky months. Since the sack of Jerusalem by Titus
in A.D. 70, the tenth of Tebet has remained a fast day in the Jewish
calendar.

army against Jerusalem. And they surrounded it, and raised works round about it. And the city was shut up and besieged till the eleventh year of king Sedecias.[8]

The importance of these events to the medieval reader, as well as their possible bearing on Chaucer's allegory, may be found in Scriptural commentary, where the siege and capture of Jerusalem acquire special meaning in reference to the pilgrimage of the spirit. Allegorically, the conquest of Jerusalem by Babylon signifies the siege and captivity of Holy Church by the forces of the world or Satan. Nabuchodonosor, the "king of kings from the north" (Ezech. 26:7), is Satan himself, the arch-enemy of Christ and the Church, the "princeps carceris" who brings mankind into chains of captivity. Tropologically, Jerusalem symbolizes the heart or spirit, led into captivity by the sins of the world, flesh, or devil. Anagogically, the capture of Jerusalem denotes the soul's captivity in Hell.[9] To follow an exegetical tradition deriving from St. Jerome, the events on "the tenth day of the tenth month" prefigure the final destruction of the world. For, says Rabanus Maurus, just as the imperfection of the number nine is a Scriptural image of the afflictions of the present life, so the perfection of the number ten designates the clemency with which Christ will relieve these afflictions at the Last Judgment when Babylon will be forever destroyed.[10]

---

[8] IV Kings 25:1ff. Cf. Jer. 39:1; 52:4. The date also appears in Josephus, *Historia Judaeorum*, X, 6-7.

[9] Bersuire, *Opera*, I, 133-34, summarizes the exegetical meanings of the siege and captivity. Cf. Eucherius, *Com. in lib. regum*, PL, 50, col. 1,206: "Jerusalem and the land of Israel designate the city of Christ, that is, Holy Church; on the other hand, Babylon and the Chaldees, or Philistines, designate the city of the devil, that is, the whole multitude of evil spirits, either men or angels." On Nabuchodonosor, see Rabanus, PL, 111, col. 1,177, and Honorius of Autun, PL, 172, cols. 855-56: "Nabuchodonosor is the devil, Babylon this world. Nabuchodonosor led the people captive into Babylon, and the devil led the human race astray in this world." The tropological meanings of the siege and captivity are developed in *De David li prophecie*, ed. G. E. Fuhrken (Halle, 1895).

[10] *Commentaria in Ezechielem*, PL, 110, col. 752 (on Ezech. 40:1). Cf.

These eschatological meanings find symbolic expression in the prophetic imagery of Book III, especially at the end of the vision. But whether or not we apply these meanings to Chaucer's date, his dream on "the tenth day of the tenth month" evokes a Scriptural context that brings the details of his allegory into a broader symbolic relationship with John's and Ezechiel's visions. The motif of spiritual captivity—noted earlier in the astrological connotations of December 10, in the imagery of winter and Advent, in the pilgrimage to St. Leonard's shrine, in Venus's connection with chains, in the theme of the *Aeneid*, and in the symbolism of the flight—here acquires an inclusive referent in the contrast between Jerusalem and Babylon, the opposing ends of man's spiritual pilgrimage.[11] In Book III this contrast is brought to a focus in the imagery of the mountain and house—ambivalent symbols which in Chaucer's allegory are reversals of the holy mountain and house of John's and Ezechiel's visions. Since these are the central symbols around which Chaucer develops his contrast between earthly and heavenly fame, an awareness of their traditional meanings should bring the details of his allegory into clearer perspective.

Allegorically, in reference to charity, the city on the mountain signifies the Church Militant of which Christ is the foundation and cornerstone. Thus the mountain may be identified with the rock that Christ designated to Peter

---

Jerome, *PL*, 25, col. 238. Citing Apoc. 2:10, Bersuire interprets "ten" as eternal punishment (*Opera*, IV, 12). Augustine identifies the number with the millennium, since it is cubed to one thousand (*De civitate Dei*, XX, 7). On winter and December as images of the Last Judgment, see above, chap. II, n. 57. On the authority of Matt. 24:20ff., in which Christ foretells the signs preceding the destruction of Babylon and the Last Judgment, Rabanus connects winter with the captivity of Jerusalem and the end of the world (*De universo*, *PL*, 111, col. 303).

[11] In both the *House of Fame* and the *Comedy*, where Dante's release from captivity is mirrored in the symbolism of Easter, the Scriptural, liturgical, and astrological connotations of the date of the vision do not exclude but rather reinforce one another.

as the foundation of his Church: "Upon this rock I will build my Church, and the gates of hell shall not prevail against it."[12] On this level the city of Jerusalem may be equated with the Earthly Paradise, which exegetical tradition places on a high mountain top and likewise interprets as the Church.[13] Tropologically, both Paradise and the city on the mountain are images of the heart turned to God. In Dante's allegory this meaning is mirrored in the Earthly Paradise at the summit of the purgatorial mountain, the latter symbolizing the faith and penitence by which the spirit regains the blissfulness of Paradise in this life.[14] Anagogically, Jerusalem and Paradise signify the heavenly country or Church Triumphant, the *visio pacis* or eternal bliss whose foundation is the truth and stability of God.[15] On all levels the mountain is allied with the symbolism of the house, and with similar meanings:

Domus est patria coelestis, ut Psalmis: *Ut inhabitem in domo Domini* [22:6], id est, vivam in patria coelesti. *Domus*, Ecclesia, ut in Psalmo: *Domum tuam decet sanctitudo* [92:5], quod oportet, ut sanctitas sit in Ecclesia.[16]

[12] Matt. 16:18-20. Cf. *Glossa ordinaria, PL*, 114, col. 746 (on Apoc. 21:9-11): "The mountain [*mons*] is Christ. . . . And on that mountain he revealed the foundation of the Church." Similar meanings are applied to the mountain in Is. 2:2-3; Ps. 47:2-4; Matt. 5:14. Cf. Augustine, *PL*, 35, col. 2,450; Bersuire, *Opera*, IV, 235-36.

[13] Rabanus, *De universo, PL*, 111, col. 334: "Paradise, that is, the garden of delight, signifies spiritually the present Church or the land of the living, where those who are deserving through faith and good works will live eternally. . . . Paradise is the Church, as we read of her in the Canticle: 'My sister, my spouse, is a garden enclosed [*hortus conclusus*].' " Cf. Augustine, *De civitate Dei*, XIII, 21, and Jerome, *PL*, 25, col. 272, who relates Ezechiel's holy mountain to Paradise and Mount Sion. On the use of this imagery in literary allegory, see Patch, *The Other World*, pp. 135, 142, 151, *et passim*; Dante, *Purg.*, XXVIII, 97ff.

[14] For these tropological meanings of Paradise and Jerusalem, see Augustine, *De civitate Dei*, XIII, 21; Rabanus, *PL*, 112, col. 331.

[15] Rabanus, *PL*, 112, col. 331; Peter Lombard, *PL*, 191, col. 167. Cf. Heb. 12:22: "But you are come to Mount Sion, and to the city of the living God, the heavenly Jerusalem."

[16] *Allegoriae in sacram scripturam*, col. 911. Cf. Bersuire, *Opera*, IV,

St. Paul contrasts this heavenly house with its opposite, the house of the world or flesh: "For we know, if our earthly house of this habitation be dissolved, that we have a building of God, a house not made with hands, eternal in heaven."[17] In the Sermon on the Mount, Christ also contrasts two houses: one built upon the rock of wisdom and charity, the other built upon the shifting sands of the world:

Everyone therefore that heareth these my words, and doth them, shall be likened to a wise man that built his house upon a rock. And the rain fell, and the floods came, and the winds blew, and they beat upon that house, and it fell not, for it was founded on a rock. And everyone that heareth these my words, and doth them not, shall be like a foolish man that built his house upon the sand. And the rain fell, and the floods came, and the winds blew, and they beat upon that house, and it fell, and great was the fall thereof. (Matt. 7:24-27)

Augustine, commenting on Christ's Sermon, identifies the house built on sand with the house of this world, a place full of misery and tribulation. The rain and floods menacing this house are the various temptations of the world or flesh, and the winds are the vain rumors and murmurings of men.[18] These exegetical meanings, along with imagery from the Sermon, appear in Boethius' contrast between two houses:

What maner man stable and war, that wol fownden hym a

---

88. For other Scriptural examples, see Is. 2:2-3; Ezech. 43:12; II Cor. 5:1ff. On the related symbolism of the house, city, and temple, cf. Augustine, *De civitate Dei*, XV, 19: "Whether it is called the house of God, the temple of God, or the city of God, it is one and the same." Similar meanings are applied to the tower or tabernacle on the mountain. See Robertson and Huppé, *Piers Plowman*, pp. 35-37, who refer to commentaries on Ps. 14:1, Luke 9:28-33, and Apoc. 21:2-11.

[17] II Cor. 5:1.

[18] *De sermone Domini in monte*, I, 7. Cf. Rabanus, *De universo*, *PL*, III, col. 281; Bersuire, *Opera*, IV, 88. On the winds and storms besetting this house, see Heb. 12:18 (cited below, n. 20).

perdurable seete, and ne wol noght ben cast doun with the
lowde blastes of the wynd Eurus, and wole despise the see
manasynge with flodes; lat hym eschuwen to bilde on the cop
of the mountaigne, or in the moyste sandes; for the felle wynd
Auster tormenteth the cop of the mountaigne with alle his
strengthes, and the lause sandes refusen to beren the hevy
weyghte. And forthi, yif thou wolt fleen the perilous aventure
(*that is to seyn, of the werld*) have mynde certeynly to fycchen
thin hous of a myrie site in a low stoon. For although the wynd
troublynge the see thondre with overthrowynges, thou, that art
put in quiete and weleful by strengthe of thi palys, schalt leden
a cler age, scornynge the woodnesses and the ires of the eyr.
(II, Met. 4)

Boethius' high mountain, beset by winds and floods, becomes the medieval setting for Fortune's house or palace—
a false Earthly Paradise where the goddess dispenses her
fickle gifts.[19] This mountain has its Scriptural prototype
in the high mountain of Satan, not of Christ, and the house
on its summit is not the Church or heavenly city but the
world or Babylon. In contrast to the holy mountain, whose
foundation is firm and fixed, the foundation of this house
is vainglory or cupidity, the unstable basis of all worldly
goods, such as fame, which are sought for their own sake.[20]
To the top of this high mountain Christ was carried by
Satan and tempted with "all the kingdoms of the world

[19] Patch, *The Goddess Fortuna*, pp. 124ff., especially 132ff. Patch
notes the imagery from Christ's Sermon in Boethius' description.

[20] Bersuire, *Opera*, V, 71, connects the lofty mountain of cupidity
with the haughtiness, arrogance, and exaltation of proud men or sinners [*fastus et arrogantia superborum, vel fastus et eminentia pecca-
torum*]. Although this mountain has many foundations, three especially
weak ones are hypocrisy, avarice, and pride (IV, 236). In Is. 13:1-2,
Babylon is designated as the "dark mountain" [*montem caliginosum*].
In Heb. 12:18-24, Mount Sinai—a symbol of the Old Law and its
afflictions—is contrasted with Mount Sion, a symbol of the New Law
and the stable foundation of the Church and heavenly Paradise: "For
you are not come to a mountain that might be touched, and a burning
fire, and a whirlwind, and darkness and storm, and the sound of a
trumpet, and the voice of words. . . . But you are come to Mount
Sion and to the city of the living God, the heavenly Jerusalem."

and the glory of them." Whereas Christ set the pattern whereby mankind might resist this glory, those who seek the heights of "windy fame," says Prudentius, have already enchained themselves in the prison of Satan.[21]

Chaucer leaves no doubt as to the temporal nature of Fame's mountain and house. Like the temple of Venus, this castle or "palys" is an inversion of the spiritual Paradise, and its location at the mid-point of the world is the opposite of the divine center from which God wields the temporal order and hears all speech below.[22] The emphasis throughout is upon its transitoriness. Thus the comparison of the castle to "castles in Spain" suggests the *Roman de la Rose*, where such airy castles are equated with the joy that "shall no while laste."[23] But the ephemeral nature of Fame's house is best revealed by its icy foundation:

> For hyt was lyk alum de glas,
> But that hyt shoon ful more clere;
> But of what congeled matere
> Hyt was, I nyste redely.
> But at the laste aspied I,
> And found that hit was every del
> A roche of yse, and not of stel. (1124-30)

As a reversal of the holy mountain, Fame's "roche of yse" is appropriately characterized by its material; for ice, like winter, is a Scriptural image of spiritual frigidity

---

[21] *Hamartigenia*, 437ff. Cf. Prov. 17:16 ("He that maketh his house high, seeketh a downfall"). For Satan's "high mountain," see Matt. 4:8-9. In traditional commentary, Satan [*diabolus*] is identified with the mountain in Matt. 17:19: "You shall say to this mountain, Remove from hence hither, and it shall remove." See *Allegoriae in sacram scripturam*, col. 1,001.

[22] In *De amore*, 1, 6 (Fifth Dialogue), Andreas Capellanus locates the Palace of Love *in medio mundi*, an inversion emphasized by details suggesting Ezechiel's description of the heavenly Temple. For examples of the castle as an image of the heavenly city, see Tristram, p. 20, and Robertson, "Amors de terra londhana," *SP*, XLIX (1952), 576.

[23] Mid. Eng. trans., 2,568-2,579. Cf. R. M. Smith, "Chaucer's 'Castle in Spain,'" *MLN*, LX (1945), 39-40.

—a connotation further implied by the contrast between "yse" and "stel"—the latter a symbol of the strength and unity of Holy Church and its elect.[24] Because it lacks durability, moreover, ice, like the glass of Venus's temple, may also signify the transiency of worldly goods, as in the *Panthère d'Amours*, where the steep and icy approach to Fortune's house typifies the perils and vanity of seeking her gifts.[25] The vanity of seeking one of these gifts, earthly fame, becomes apparent as Chaucer climbs Fame's mountain and observes its "feble fundament":

> "By seynt Thomas of Kent!
> This were a feble fundament
> To bilden on a place hye.
> He ought him lytel glorifye
> That hereon bilt, God so me save!" (1131-35)

Chaucer's comment reveals his initial insight into the nature of fame. Like Dante's arduous ascent of the mountain of Purgatory, Chaucer's "painful" ascent is part of his spiritual education. Although he has yet to see through all the gilt and guile of Fame and her abode, his mind has been sufficiently cleared of clouds and mists for him to perceive the unstable basis of her awards. His increasing insight is reflected in his remarks on the contrasting names engraved on the south and north sides of the "roche of yse." On the south side, where he sees the names of "famous folk" who were once "in mochel wele" and whose renown was "wide yblowe," so many letters have melted that the names can scarcely be read:

---

[24] *Allegoriae in sacram scripturam*, cols. 853-54. In *The Fall of Princes*, v, 587-88, Lydgate contrasts "stele" and Fortune's "brotel glas." On ice [*glacies*] as a symbol of cupidity, see Rabanus, *PL*, 111, col. 327 ("For ice signifies the hardness [*duritiam*] of sinners") and Neckam, *De naturis rerum*, II, 15.

[25] Ed. H. A. Todd (Paris, 1883), 1,958ff. Cf. Sypherd, pp. 114ff., and Patch, *The Goddess Fortuna*, pp. 133-34. For Venus's similar mountain, see Patch, *The Other World*, pp. 176ff. In the *Temple of Glas*, Lydgate, imitating Chaucer, locates her temple on a craggy rock frozen like ice.

> . . . for, out of drede,
> They were almost ofthowed so
> That of the lettres oon or two
> Was molte away of every name,
> So unfamous was woxe hir fame. (1142-46)

On the north side, however, the names are still intact.
Even though they are the names of famous people of
"olde tyme," their letters are still

> As fressh as men had writen hem here
> The selve day ryght, or that houre
> That I upon hem gan to poure. (1156-58)

Viewed on the surface, the contrasting names on the "roche
of yse" are an obvious reminder of the fickleness of Fame's
gifts. In the melting names on the south side we can
detect the spirit of the fourteenth century lyric: "Truste
ȝe raþir to lettirs writen in þ'is,/ þan to þis wrecchid world,
þat ful of synne is."[26] Boethius uses similar imagery to
express the fading renown of the great: "Where wonen
now the bones of trewe Fabricius? What is now Brutus
or stierne Caton? The thynne fame yit lastynge of here
idel names is marked with a fewe lettres."[27] Implicit in
both examples is the Scriptural warning: "And our name
in time shall be forgotten, and no man shall have any remembrance of our works" (Wis.2:4). But behind this
warning lies an implication of much deeper import about
the fickleness of worldly fame. For as Philosophy reminds Boethius, the unequal distribution of fame and
other temporal goods is to be attributed not to the willful
play of time, chance, or fortune but to God, who dispenses
all earthly awards with a just intent. As Augustine says,
the seeming confusion of such awards is part of the divine
plan for man's salvation.[28] In allowing some names to

---

[26] *Religious Lyrics of the Fourteenth Century*, ed. Carleton Brown
(Oxford, 1924), p. 237. Cf. Petrarch, "Trionfo del Tempo," 127ff.
[27] *De consolatione philosophiae*, II, Met. 7.
[28] *De civitate Dei*, I, 8. Cf. XX, 2.

prosper and others to be forgotten, God teaches the vanity of trusting worldly goods. If many who deserve fame seem to die unremembered, their reward will come in heaven, where they will receive eternal fame. Conversely, if others appear to achieve a lasting fame on earth, it is often a false, deceptive fame with which God allows Satan to tempt men and thereby test their virtue.

This less obvious implication of Chaucer's imagery provides an ironic commentary on the contrasting names on Fame's mountain. For it reminds us that the "permanence" of the names on the north side is merely another indication of the false appearance of earthly fame. The Christian norm underlying the irony is suggested by Neckam's gloss on Cant.4:16: "The north wind, from which spreads all evil, constricts the waters, but the south wind, which blows through the garden of delight, melts the ice."[29] Just as ice signifies the spiritual frigidity of the life of sin, so the north is conventionally associated with Satan, the prototype of all evil.[30] Thus the north wind, as Neckam indicates, designates the force of cupidity constricting the hearts of sinners and bringing them into spiritual captivity. On the other hand, the south wind, which blows through the garden of delight, is symbolic of the divine warmth of charity and grace with which the Holy Spirit relaxes the frigidity of the heart and frees it of sin: "And in justice thou shalt be built up, and in the day of affliction thou shalt be remembered; and thy sins shall melt away as the ice in the fair warm weather."[31] These meanings also ap-

---

[29] *De naturis rerum*, II, 15.

[30] Augustine connects ice with Satan and the north [*aquilo*]: "Therefore the devil and his angels, having turned away from the light and heat of charity, and having progressed too far in pride and envy, were sluggish as if in icy hardness [*velut glaciali duritia torpuerunt*]. And for this reason they are located figuratively in the north" (*Epistola CXL, PL*, 33, col. 561).

[31] Ecclus. 3:17. Cf. Ecclus. 43:17-23 and Ps. 147:17-18: "He sendeth his crystal like morsels: who shall stand before the face of his cold?

pear in Gregory's gloss on Ezechiel's vision of the holy
city, "bending towards the south":

For it is customary, as those who are learned in Holy Writ
are aware, to designate the Holy Spirit in the figure of the
south wind, just as the devil, conversely, is often designated
by the north wind, since the one relaxes in warmth and the
other binds in coldness. . . . This city bends toward the south
gate because the grace of the Holy Spirit relaxes the torpor of
the mind. . . . For our captive minds, which in the coldness
of sloth are slow to turn to God, are relaxed by the warmth of
the Holy Spirit so that they might hasten to the love of God.[32]

Applied to the mountain, these contrasting connotations of
north and south are especially referable to Mount Sion,
another figure of the Church or heavenly Paradise and
the spiritual opposite of Mount Sinai, a symbol of the
Old Law; for its location is said to be opposite to the
north, the location of Satan and his followers, the Jews
and the Gentiles, although by God's grace, we are told,
"these infidels can be, and in part have been, converted

He shall send out his word, and shall melt them: his wind shall blow,
and the waters shall run." Augustine relates these passages to the Bride's
response in Cant. 4:16 ("Arise, O north wind, and come, O south
wind: blow through my garden, and let the aromatical spices thereof
flow"): "She says, 'and come, O south wind,' invoking the spirit of
grace, blowing from the south, as though from a hot and luminous
region, so that the aromatical spices might flow. Wherefore the Apostle
says: 'We are the good odour of Christ' [II Cor. 2:15]. Hence it is
also said in one of the Psalms [125:4], 'Turn again our captivity, O
Lord, as a stream in the south': truly, the captivity under the devil by
which they were bound, as it were, in the north, where, with iniquity
abounding, they were cold and, in a manner of speaking, frozen. On
this matter the Gospel also speaks: 'And because iniquity hath abounded,
the charity of many shall grow cold' [Matt. 24:12]. But when the
south wind blows, the ice is melted and the streams flow; that is to
say, when released from their sins, the people run to Christ in charity.
Hence it is written elsewhere [Ecclus. 3:17]: 'And thy sins shall melt
away as the ice in the fair warm weather'" (*Epistola CXL*, *PL*, 33,
col. 561).

[32] *PL*, 76, cols. 939-40. Cf. col. 1,019. Gregory refers also to Is.
14:13; Jer. 6:7; Matt. 24:12.

to the true faith and aligned with the city of God."[33] In medieval church architecture this contrast is visibly expressed in those churches, oriented from the rising to the setting sun, in which the north, the region of dark and coldness, is devoted to the Old Testament, and the south, warmed by the Sun of Justice, is consecrated to the New.[34]

Against this Scriptural–exegetical background, the contrasting names on the two sides of Fame's mountain are more easily identified. Whereas the "famous folk" of "olde tyme" whose names are preserved on the north side are those who achieved renown as Gentiles or as Jews under the Old Law, the state of man without charity, the melting names on the south side are those in whom the ice of cupidity or the desire for renown has been removed by the heat of the Holy Spirit and who have achieved a living name in God.[35] Their names, therefore, have been erased not by the fortuitous winds of chance or Fortune but by the heat of divine grace. Or as Chaucer himself thoughtfully observes, their names

> . . . were molte awey with hete,
> And not awey with stormes bete. (1149-50)

But his comment—"What may ever laste?"—might apply

---

[33] Cassiodorus, *Expositio in Psalterium*, *PL*, 70, col. 337 (on Ps. 47:3). Cf. Panofsky, *Abbot Suger*, pp. 210ff. In Is. 14:13, the north side of the mountain likewise denotes Satan and the Old Law.

[34] Durandus of Mende, *Rationale divinorum officiorum*, IV, 23-24. Cf. Rabanus, *De universo*, IX (Prol.). Mâle, *Religious Art in France*, p. 5, gives examples from Notre Dame, Rheims, and Chartres, where the heroes of the Old Law are depicted on the north side and those of the New Law on the south side. Cf. Panofsky, *Abbot Suger*, p. 11, and Sauer, *Symbolik des Kirchengebäudes*, pp. 88, 90-92, both of whom relate the symbolism to medieval churches.

[35] Chaucer's imagery also suggests the names written on the gates of the wall of the New Jerusalem (Apoc. 21:12), symbolic of the apostles or all who have achieved a living name in Christ. In *Glossa ordinaria*, *PL*, 114, col. 747, this meaning is applied to II Cor. 3, in which the glory of the letters engraved upon the stone of the Old Law is contrasted with the greater glory of the letters written upon the heart by the Holy Spirit.

equally well to the names on the north side; for their seeming permanence, like that of the mountain and castle, is part of the deceptive appearance of fame. Although the renown of these people of "olde tyme" seems to be lasting, the "writynge," Chaucer carefully notes, is preserved only by the shade of the castle itself, which stood on "so cold a place" that "hete myghte hit not deface." The Scriptural inversion of the castle is also implicit in its shade. Unlike the shade or shadow (*umbra*) which signifies the divine protection of Christ and his Church, the shade of Fame's house is the false protection of worldly prosperity, an image of the present life untouched by the heat of divine grace: "For when the Sun, that is, Christ, is remote from us because of our sins, then the shadow of worldly prosperity seems even greater. But when Christ the Sun approaches man through grace and illuminates him with wisdom, then he considers such prosperity as nothing."[36] In short, the shadow of Fame's castle is the spurious protection of Satan, who tempts men with the false security of earthly renown.

Chaucer's insight into the transitoriness of Fame's abode continues as he nears the top of the mountain and views the castle itself. On the surface, nothing could be more beautiful:

> al the men that ben on lyve
> Ne han the kunnynge to descrive
> The beaute of that ylke place. (1167-69)

But the irony of Chaucer's comments becomes apparent in the profusion of Scriptural imagery describing the beauty and riches of the castle:

[36] Bersuire, *Opera*, II, 121, who quotes Wis. 5:9. Cf. I Par. 29:15. In Wis. 2:5, the image expresses the transitoriness of fame (see above, chap. I, n. 24). On the contrasting shadow of Christ and the Church, see Ps. 16:8, Is. 32:2, and *Allegoriae in sacram scripturam*, col. 1,085. "*Shadow* [*umbra*], the protection of Christ, as in the Canticle [2:3]: 'I sat down under his shadow, whom I desired,' that is, 'I found refuge in the protection of Christ, whom I love.'"

> But natheles al the substance
> I have yit in my remembrance;
> For whi me thoughte, be seynt Gyle!
> Al was of ston of beryle,
> Bothe the castel and the tour,
> And eke the halle and every bour,
> Wythouten peces or joynynges. (1181-87)

Like many other features of the castle, its beryl is reminiscent of John's and Ezechiel's visions, where beryl is said to be one of the gems adorning the garden of Paradise and the New Jerusalem.[37] Collectively, according to Bede and other commentators, these gems are symbolic of the various virtues found within the Church. By meditating upon these virtues, says Abbot Suger of the gems in his church at St. Denis, the mind is led from the material beauty of the gems to the immaterial beauty of the heavenly Paradise.[38] Like the other Scriptural gems, beryl has particular qualities defining its spiritual value. Thus Marbodus of Rennes, whose *Lapidarium* is the source of many of the later medieval lapidaries, compares its resplendence and warmth when touched by the sun to the mind illuminated by the grace and charity of Christ.[39] As

---

[37] Apoc. 21:20-21; Ezech. 28:13.

[38] Panofsky, *Abbot Suger*, pp. 62, 64. Cf. Simson, pp. 119, 134. On the symbolism of the gems, see Bede, *PL*, 93, col. 197. Cf. Bruno Astensis, *PL*, 165, col. 725 (on Apoc. 21:19-21): "We may say, therefore, that the apostles signify the foundations [*fundamenta*]; but the gems with which they are adorned signify virtues and clean habits [*virtutes et mores honestos*]."

[39] *PL*, 171, col. 1,771. Cf. Mâle, *Religious Art in France*, p. 30, and Joan Evans and Mary Serjeantson, *English Mediaeval Lapidaries* (London, 1933), pp. 28, 48. The lapidaries borrow from the Scriptural commentators, for example, Bede, who interprets the Apocalyptic beryl as the mind infused with the light of grace (*PL*, 93, col. 200). Cf. *PL*, 165, col. 727: "The eighth gem is beryl, whose color is similar to the color of water reflecting the sun, by which we may understand true intelligence and the sound doctrine of Scripture, which, unless illuminated by the sun of justice, becomes easily darkened by the deformity of error. Accordingly, when the sun shines on the waters, the color of beryl is produced, for when the waters of Scripture are illumined by Christ our Lord, a sound and true intellect is formed."

a quality of the intellect, therefore, beryl symbolizes contemplation, by which the mind perceives not only heavenly truth but also the falseness beneath the beauty of worldly goods. The falseness of one of these goods, earthly fame, is Chaucer's own conclusion after he has "imused longe while" upon

> these walles of berile,
> That shoone ful lyghter than a glas
> And made wel more than hit was
> To semen every thing, ywis,
> As kynde thyng of Fames is. (1288-92)

Like the glass of Venus's temple, Fame's beryl shines with an idolatrous splendor which blinds the eyes, just as earthly fame, Chaucer concludes, distorts the truth and makes it seem more than it is.[40] This inversion of the Scriptural beryl brings to mind the other characteristic of Fame's gem, its lack of "peces or joynynges," a feature mentioned in the lapidaries, where Biblical authority is cited that "berill shulde not be shape, but hit behoueth to be plain and polished." In medieval accounts of the Church, this feature is attributed to Solomon's temple, whose artfully wrought "turnings and joints" are said to signify the perfection of Holy Church and the unity of its members in Christ.[41]

---

[40] The comparison of Fame's beryl to "a glas" (1. 1,288) connects the false light of Venus's temple with that of the castle. On the use of beryl in a transferred sense for crystal or glass, see Robinson's note (*Works*, p. 784). On the association of beryl with love, see Sypherd, p. 133, n. 2. The light of Chaucer's beryl and glass illustrates the *lux opulentiae terrenae* which, says Bersuire, blinds the eyes with worldly prosperity and leads men to evil actions (*Opera*, IV, 296). Cf. above, chap. III, n. 25.

[41] III Kings 6:18. Cf. Eph. 2:21-22; Col. 2:19. In *Psychomachia*, 823ff., this Scriptural idea appears in the description of the temple of Wisdom. In *The Shepherd of Hermas*, the tower of Holy Church is said to have been built of stones evenly shaped and closely fitted together at their joints so that the structure seems to be built of one stone. On the relevance of this feature to beryl see Evans and Serjeantson, pp. 28, 48, 72. Cf. Patch, *The Other World*, pp. 89, 219. In

The other outward details of the castle—its many images, pinnacles, "babewynnes," tabernacles, and windows—may also be viewed as inversions of aspects of the Church or heavenly city. In medieval churches the "babewynnes" are the various monsters or grotesques reminding us of the vices perverting the intellect and transforming men into beasts.[42] The windows—as many as "flakes falle in grete snowes"—suggest both the numerous windows in Gothic churches and their spiritual equivalent in Ezechiel's vision of the heavenly Church, symbols of the light of contemplation and divine wisdom.[43] But the high point of this ironic inversion is the catalogue of minstrels and "gestiours" who inhabit the pinnacles and "habitacles" outside the castle and perform in honor of Fame. Since these entertainers are a conspicuous feature of the setting for the drama of fame that soon follows, we should bear in mind the careful disposition of details within the overall pattern. It is worth noting, for instance, that these figures are located outside the inner chamber or "halle" where the goddess is enthroned and where her

---

Douglas's *Palice of Honour*, the palace, a symbol of the dwelling place of God, is wrought of polished "beriall stone" which shines like crystal.

[42] On the importance of "babewynnes" in medieval carving, wall painting, stained glass, and manuscript illumination, see Tristram, pp. 17-18, who quotes Chaucer. Robertson (*Preface*, pp. 151-56, 250-57) discusses their moral significance.

[43] *Allegoriae in sacram scripturam*, col. 924, which cites Ezech. 40:16. Bersuire interprets windows [*fenestrae*] as *divina Scriptura*, through which faith illuminates the world and through which the law of God enters the Church. In contrast to these windows are those (Jer. 9:21) through which "the devil hurls his darts to slay the soul with temptation" (*Opera*, IV, 192). Durandus of Mende applies similar meanings to the glass windows in churches, for, like Holy Scripture, they expel the wind and rain—that is, all things harmful—but transmit the light of the true sun (Christ) into the hearts of the faithful. They also signify the bodily senses, which ought to be shut to worldly vanities and open to spiritual gifts (*Rationale divinorum officiorum*, I, 1, 24). On the connection between windows and the symbolism of light in Gothic churches, see Simson, pp. 3-5, 50ff.

most famous devotees appear. Their position thus corresponds to that of the saints of lesser glory who adorn
the "habitacles" or niches on the pinnacles and buttresses
of the Church.[44] On this basis we might also contrast them
with those "singing men" who in Ezechiel's vision inhabit
the court outside the sanctuary of the temple and sing
to God's glory. These heavenly minstrels have their
counterpart in all those minstrels and entertainers of men
who perform for the sake of charity. Opposed to them
are the false minstrels who, as in *Piers Plowman*, "feynen
hem fantasies" for temporal gain or, like those in Fame's
castle, direct their minstrelsy to worldly praise.[45]

Appropriately, Chaucer's catalogue begins with the
harpers, for the harp is above all the instrument denoting
fame, both heavenly and earthly. This meaning is exemplified in the Old Testament by the harp of David,
whose harmonious music prefigures the "new song" of
charity and the spiritual harmony of Holy Church. Thus
in the Apocalypse it is the instrument to which John compares the song of the redeemed before the throne of the
Lamb: "And the voice which I heard was as the voice
of harpers, harping on their harps. And they sung as it
were a new canticle before the throne."[46] Contrasting with
this harp is the harp which plays not for God's glory but
for earthly glory. In Scripture this harp typifies the

[44] On this parallel, see Skeat, *The Complete Works of Geoffrey
Chaucer*, III, 267. Durandus interprets the pinnacles as the heavenly
aspiration of prelates' minds.

[45] B, *Prol.*, 35-39. Fame's minstrels may be compared to the "flow-
tours," "mynstrales" and "jogelors" who perform in honor of physical
love in the *Roman de la Rose* (Mid. Eng. trans., 763ff.). Cf. the
Merchant's Tale, 1,709ff. The spiritual opposite of these minstrels is
illustrated by St. Francis' concept of his disciples as "God's minstrels"
[*joculatores Dei*].

[46] Apoc. 14:2-3. Cf. 5:8-11. On David's harping as a prefiguration
of the New Law, see Augustine, *De civitate Dei*, XVII, 14, and Rabanus,
PL, 109, cols. 49-50 (on I Kings 16:16-23). The symbolism pervades
the Psalms, for example, 97, 150.

music of all those worldly musicians and entertainers who inhabit Babylon. Unlike the song of David—a prefiguration of Christ's "new song"—the song of these musicians is the "old song" of cupidity, and its mellifluous sounds denote the sweet persuasiveness with which Satan tempts men to worship worldly delights.[47] In view of this contrast, it is not surprising that David, the most famous of all harpers, should be absent from the company of Fame's musicians. In Orpheus, however, Chaucer has chosen an appropriate symbol for contrasting the two kinds of fame. As one whose harping is said to have combined wisdom and eloquence, Orpheus is traditionally associated with good fame. At the same time, his harping is a familiar medieval illustration of how true fame may be deflected by an irrational love for earthly things. This meaning underlies Boethius' moralization of Orpheus' rescue of Euridice from hell by the power of his harping: "Whoso that evere be so overcomen that he ficche his eien into the put of helle (*that is to seyn, whoso sette his thoughtes in erthly thinges*), al that evere he hath drawen of the noble good celestial he lesith it, whanne he looketh the helles (*that is to seyn, into lowe thinges of the erthe*)."[48] To this aspect of Orpheus' harping Nature apparently alludes in *De planctu naturae* when she laments that man alone of

[47] On the contrast between the "new" and "old" songs in medieval art and literature, see Robertson, *Preface*, pp. 126-30. In *De civitate Dei*, XVII, 14, Augustine distinguishes David's music from the music serving vulgar delight. Cf. John of Salisbury, *Policraticus*, I, 6. Bersuire, citing Job 21:12 and Is. 5:12, identifies the harp of cupidity with the harp [*cithara*] with which sinners sing of worldly glory or joy, which is empty and sterile [*inanis est, et sterilis*] and ultimately disappears (*Opera*, III, 307). For other Scriptural examples of this harp, see Ezech. 26:13; Apoc. 18:22.

[48] III, Met. 12. For similar moralizations of Ovid's story (*Metamorphoses*, X, 1-63), see Giovanni del Virgilio, *Allegorie librorum Ovidii Metamorphoseos*, p. 89; Bernard, *Commentum*, pp. 53ff.; Salutati, *De laboribus Herculis*, IV, 7. Giovanni connects Orpheus with good fame [*hominem bone fame*]. On Orpheus' harping as a symbol of wisdom and eloquence, see Boccaccio, *Genealogia deorum*, V, 12; Ridewall, *Fulgentius metaforalis*, pp. 107-108.

all God's creatures has rejected the music of her harp and raves under the harp of "the frenzied Orpheus."[49] The same note of disharmony may be detected in the music of Fame's other harpers—Arion, Chiron, and Bret Glascurion. Thus Ovid in the *Ars amatoria* includes Arion and Chiron, along with Orpheus, among the harpers whose music leads to the delights of Venus. Directed to the same end was the music of Bret Glascurion, the Welsh harper who played so hard (so the ballad tells us) that the "ladies waxed wood."[50]

The music of the harpers sets the pattern for the next group of minstrels, the pipers and the trumpeters, all of whom bear some taint of worldliness. This is true of the piper Marsyas, who

> loste her skyn,
> Bothe in face, body, and chyn,
> For that she wolde envien, loo!
> To pipen bet than Appolloo. (1229-32)

Ovid's story, to which Chaucer refers, relates how the satyr Marsyas challenged Apollo to a musical contest and was defeated and punished for his presumption. Whereas Apollo is moralized as divine wisdom (*sapientia*), Marsyas is interpreted as ignorance or folly (*insipientia*), and his contesting Apollo's wisdom is an example of vainglory.[51]

[49] Pr. IV, 87ff. John of Salisbury contrasts the good and bad aspects of Orpheus' harping (*Policraticus*, I, 6).

[50] *English and Scottish Ballads*, ed. H. C. Sargent and G. L. Kittredge (New York, 1904), pp. 136-39. On the harping of Arion and the centaur Chiron, see *Ars amatoria*, I, 11-18, III, 311-28. Cf. Ovid, *Fasti*, II, 79-118, V, 379-90, and *Metamorphoses*, II, 633-39. According to John of Salisbury, Chiron's harping signifies man's irrational inclinations (*Policraticus*, I, 4). Cf. *Metamorphoses*, XII, 210-12.

[51] For typical moralizations, see *Mythographus Vaticanus III*, pp. 246-47; Giovanni del Virgilio, *Allegorie librorum Ovidii Metamorphoseos*, p. 73. In *Ovide moralisé*, VI, 1,981ff., Marsyas' piping exemplifies *vaine gloire*. Commenting on Dante's allusion to the story (*Par.*, I, 20), Pietro Alighieri (*Commentarium*, p. 549) interprets Marsyas

Vainglory also characterizes the trumpeters, who, like the pipers, stand in "a large space" to themselves. Chaucer's comment,

> For in fight and blod-shedynge
> Ys used gladly clarionynge... (1241-42)

is revealing, since these trumpeters—Misenus ("of whom that speketh Virgilius"), Joab, Thiodamas, and others— are those who participated in warfare, not for the glory of God, but for worldly honor or fame. This vainglorious warfare, fought under the banner of Satan, is called up by the trumpeting of Joab, the famous general of King David's army who was condemned by David for having "shed the blood of war in peace."[52] Joab's pagan counterpart is Thiodamas, the Theban augur who in the *Thebaid* incites the besiegers to attack the city.[53] But these trumpeters of vainglory find an especially apt symbol in Misenus, whom Virgil refers to as the trumpeter of Hector. In the commentaries on the *Aeneid*, Misenus is interpreted etymologically as "praise" or "worldly glory," and he is said to be from Aeolia, the windy country of Aeolus, since worldly praise is nothing more than the windy swelling of speech. Thus his trumpet (*tuba*) images the inflated pride or vainglory which, under the guise of

---

as the unlearned man [*non doctus*] disputing with the man of learning and wisdom [*cum docto et sapiente*].

[52] III Kings 2:5. Joab is connected with trumpeting in II Kings 2:28; 18:16; 20:22. Rabanus identifies Joab with Satan, who daily attempts to destroy the faithful with persuasive lies (*PL*, 109, col. 78, on II Kings 3). Cf. Augustine, *PL*, 36, col. 715. Traditionally, there are two kinds of trumpets, indicative of two kinds of warfare: one fought under the banner of Christ, the other fought under the banner of Satan. The trumpet of Satan signifies pride, vainglory, or worldly prosperity; for, says Bersuire, when he cannot tempt men through tribulation, he tempts them with glory or other temporal goods (*Opera*, III, 242).

[53] *Thebaid*, VIII, 342ff.; X. In the Merchant's Tale, 1,715ff., Chaucer links the trumpeting of Joab and Thiodamas.

praise, urges men on to warfare.[54] The kind of fame signified by Misenus and his trumpet is dramatized in the account of his rivalry with Triton, the sea god who defeats him in a contest. Triton symbolizes "contrition" or "tribulation of the flesh" (*molestia carnis*), and the sound of his trumpet is not of praise but of wailing and lamentation. He is victorious over Misenus because "the tribulation of the flesh extinguishes the appetite for worldly glory."[55] In the ensuing drama of Fame and her fickle judgments, Triton and his wailing trumpet—suggestive of the Apocalyptic trumpet of the fifth angel—appear as an ominous reminder of the Scriptural warning of the Last Judgment. In the meantime, Chaucer expands his catalogue to include some of the more modern trumpeters who, like Joab, shed blood in worldly warfare.

The same mixture of pagan and medieval occurs in the catalogue of jugglers and magicians who make up the last group of minstrels performing in honor of Fame. Despite the diversity of this group—

> . . . jugelours,
> Magiciens, and tregetours,
> And Phitonesses, charmeresses,
> Olde wicches, sorceresses,
> That use exorsisacions,
> And eke these fumygacions;
> And clerkes eke, which konne wel
> Al this magik naturel . . . (1259-66)

all share one trait: the ability to summon up illusions contrary to faith and doctrine.[56] The pattern is established

---

[54] Bernard, *Commentum*, pp. 60, 68.

[55] *Ibid.*, pp. 60-62. Cf. *Mythographus Vaticanus III*, p. 183.

[56] The Christian norm for viewing this group is found in the Parson's Tale, 600ff., and the Franklin's Tale, 1,133ff., where the illusions of magicians, necromancers, and jugglers are said to be contrary to "hooly chirches feith." In Is. 8:19, pythonesses ("Phitonesses") and diviners are condemned for their enchantments. In *Policraticus*, I, 9-12, John of Salisbury classifies the various workers of illusions.

by the three pagan sorceresses, Medea, Circe, and Calypso, each of whom used her magical powers for unnatural purposes. For example, Circe, the siren whose magic cup turned Ulysses' men into beasts, is interpreted as worldly goods or riches and her cup as libidinousness, since it turns men from reason to sensuality. Following a similar interpretation, Bersuire equates Circe with Satan and her drink with worldly prosperity, which leads to evil concupiscence and drunken delight.[57] In Scripture the sorcery of Satan and his followers is contrasted with the miracles of Christ and the Apostles. Among Fame's magicians, this contrast is exemplified by the two Biblical sorcerers, Simon Magus and "Limote," the latter presumably being Elymas (or Bar-Jesus), the Jewish magician and false prophet whose attempt to belittle the miracles of Saul and Barnabus was rewarded with blindness. Similarly, Simon Magus was the famous magician of Samaria who was "seducing the people" with his sorcery and astounding them with powers he claimed to be from God. As a result of Phillip's preaching and miracles, however, Simon himself was baptized and converted to the teachings of Christ.[58]

These false magicians, who complete Chaucer's catalogue of famous but tainted "mynstralles" and "gestiours," should leave little doubt as to the kind of praise accorded to Fame. Together these worldly entertainers are the minstrels of Babylon whose doom is prophesied in the

[57] *Metamorphosis Ovidiana* (Paris, 1515), Lib. XIV. Cf. Bernard, *Commentum*, pp. 21-22; John of Salisbury, *Policraticus*, I, 4; *Mythographus Vaticanus III*, p. 254. For a discussion of Circe in relation to the tradition of grotesques in Romanesque art, see Robertson, *Preface*, pp. 153-54. In the Knight's Tale, Circe is portrayed in the temple of Venus, along with Medea. Both are linked with sorcery in the *Roman de la Rose*, 14,397ff. On Calypso, the nymph who through magic detained Ulysses on her island for seven years, see Ovid, *Ex Ponto*, IV, 10, 13; *Odyssey*, I.

[58] Acts 8:4ff.; 13:4-12. Augustine contrasts the magic and illusions of evil spirits with the miracles inspired by God (*De civitate Dei*, X, 8ff.; XXI, 6).

Apocalypse by the angel of "great authority." Significantly, the order of Chaucer's catalogue parallels the Apocalyptic account: "And the voice of harpers, and of musicians, and of them that play on the pipe, and on the trumpet, shall no more be heard at all in thee, and no craftsman of any art whatsoever shall be found any more at all in thee . . . for all nations have been deceived by thy enchantments."[59] These singers (*canentes*) are said to signify all those, like Orpheus, whose meretricious art delights the senses and incites men to love worldly pleasures. In contrast are those whose art is directed to God's praise and whose reward will be not damnation but eternal bliss.[60] In view of this reminder of the Last Judgment, we should not overlook the subtle allusion in Chaucer's apology for not continuing his catalogue:

> What shuld I make lenger tale
> Of alle the pepil y ther say,
> Fro hennes into domes day? (1282-84)

These Apocalyptic overtones lend a deepening note of irony to the remaining details describing the castle. The deceptive beauty and permanence are again apparent in the castle's gate, which Chaucer finds, after much roaming, on his "ryght hond." Like the other outward features of the castle, the gate is wellnigh indescribable, being "so wel corven" and so richly adorned with "corbetz," "ymageries," and other "florisshinges" that "never such another nas." But the transient, time-ridden quality of the House of Fame is again suggested by Chaucer's observation that the gate, despite its magnificence,

> was be aventure
> Iwrought, as often as be cure.[61]

---

[59] Apoc. 18:22. Cf. Ezech. 26:13; Nah. 3:4.
[60] *PL*, 169, col. 1,157; *PL*, 117, col. 1,165.
[61] This detail foreshadows the description of the House of Tidings (1,980ff.), where the personification of Aventure as the "moder of

As we should expect, a reversal of values is detectable in the gate, whose glittering gold, like the gold in the temple of Venus, shines with a false resplendence that blinds the eyes with temporal prosperity. This connotation is implicit in the location of the gate on the "ryght hond"—a position, ironically, which in Scripture may designate either the eternal bliss of Paradise or the temporal bliss leading to idolatry and damnation.[62] The latter meaning is illustrated by the two gates leading into the castle in the *Amorosa Visione*. Whereas the narrow gate on the left, suggesting the Scriptural narrow gate, leads up a steep stair and requires the abandonment of all earthly joys, the wide gate on the right, suggesting the wide gate "that leads to destruction," is the direction of the luxurious garden where Fame holds her triumph. In the *Roman de la Rose* a path on the "ryght hond" brings one to the "wiket" of Idleness and the garden of Mirth—another false paradise enticing the heart of the unwary pilgrim. This idolatrous reversal of the spiritual Paradise is fully at work as Chaucer passes through the gate into Fame's

tydynges" suggests Philosophy's demonstration of the connection of "aventure" or "hap" with the stability of God's providence. From this viewpoint, Fame's gate is a subtle reminder not only of the transitoriness of her abode but also of the divine disposition behind her unstable decrees, an idea increasingly apparent in the imagery of Book III.

[62] Cf. Bersuire, *Opera*, III, 52: "Commonly in Scripture, by the right hand [*per dexteram*] is understood prosperity, either temporal or eternal. By the left hand [*per sinistram*], however, is understood eternal or temporal adversity. Hence, in a manner of speaking, there are those on the left hand of adversity who will finally be on the right hand of the highest bliss [*in dextera summae foelicitatis*]. Conversely, there are some on the right hand of worldly prosperity who afterwards will be on the left hand of eternal adversity [*in sinistra aeternae adversitatis*]." As an image of cupidity, the "ryght hond" has a Scriptural basis in Zach. 3:1: "And Satan stood on his right hand to be his adversary." In *Glossa ordinaria*, PL, 113, col. 1,057, *dextera* and *sinistra* are equated with Jerusalem and Babylon, the Church and the world. Cf. Augustine, PL, 36, col. 773. Applied to fame in particular, the right hand, in reference to charity, designates heavenly fame. Cf. n. 121, below.

ornate "halle." Reminiscent of Solomon's temple, the entire interior—walls, floor, and roof—is covered with gold "half a foote thikke."[63] The walls, moreover, like the foundation of the walls of the heavenly Jerusalem, are thickly set with

> the fynest stones faire,
> That men rede in the Lapidaire,
> As grasses growen in a mede. (1351-53)

As already noted, in the *Lapidarium* of Marbodus of Rennes, to which Chaucer apparently refers, the gems adorning the Church and holy city are interpreted as the various virtues leading the mind to contemplate the truths of the heavenly Paradise. The same meaning underlies the comparison of the stones to "grasses" growing in a "mede"— a familiar medieval figure for Paradise or the "meadow" of the Church "in which flowers of diverse virtues are found."[64] But the falseness of Fame's gems is easily inferred from her beryl, whose splendor blears men's sight and distorts the truth until it seems more than it is.

Such is the ironic setting for the drama of fame that begins as Chaucer finds himself in the presence of the goddess and hears many voices extolling her and all who seek her "grace":

[63] Cf. III Kings 6:22, 30: "And there was nothing in the temple that was not covered with gold: the whole altar of the oracle he covered also with gold. . . . And the floor of the house he also overlaid with gold within and without."

[64] Rabanus, *De universo, PL*, 111, col. 520. This meadow [*pratum*], Rabanus adds, is a spiritual pasture [*pastus*] prepared for men of faith [*fidelibus hominibus*]. Cf. Bersuire, *Opera*, 11, 424; Robertson, "Amors de terra londhana," p. 571. The spiritual meanings of "meadow" appear in the details of Dante's description of the Earthly Paradise (*Purg.*, XXVII, 97ff.). Cf. Chaucer's *Truth*, 25ff. Gems and gold are features of the abodes of Venus and Fortune, for example, Fortune's palace in the *Roman de la Rose*, 5,921ff., whose walls and roof are wrought of gold and silver and adorned with gems. For other examples in literary allegory, see Patch, *The Other World, passim*, who connects the imagery with the Earthly Paradise.

> But in I wente, and that anoon.
> Ther mette I cryinge many oon,
> "A larges, larges, hold up wel!
> God save the lady of thys pel,
> Our oune gentil lady Fame,
> And hem that wilnen to have name
> Of us!" (1307-13)

These colorfully appareled figures—adorned with ribbons and "frenges," some wearing "corounes wroght ful of losenges"—Chaucer soon recognizes as the heralds and pursuivants who "crien ryche folkes laudes" and whose richly embroidered "vestures" bear the coats-of-arms of "famous folk" of "chevalrie." Like everything else in the castle, this heraldic display of kings and rich men is typical of the gilt of worldly renown. The outward show of "gentilesse" is a far cry from that "gentilesse" which Philosophy says is based on virtue and is expressive of true fame. Such heralds, remarks Prudentius, are employed by the strivers after "windy fame" to make others tremble at their names.[65] In the Apocalypse these rich and mighty of the earth are said to have fornicated with the Whore of Babylon, and their destruction is foretold by the angel of "great authority." Since the Whore, like Fortune, is an inclusive symbol of the worship of worldly goods, we are hardly wrong in associating her with the "femynyne creature" who is the object of the heralds' cries: Fame herself, who sits "perpetually ystalled" on her throne:

> al on hye, above a dees,
> Sitte in a see imperiall,
> That mad was of a rubee all,
> Which that a carbuncle ys ycalled,
> Y saugh, perpetually ystalled,
> A femynyne creature,
> That never formed by Nature
> Nas such another thing yseye. (1360-67)

[65] *Hamartigenia*, 437-44. On Boethius' distinction between true and

This queenly figure, whom we soon observe wielding her willful awards of fame, slander, and oblivion, is the central symbol of Chaucer's ironically conceived contrast between earthly and heavenly fame. Although her affinities with Virgil's "dea foeda" are apparent in the details of her description, she has become more than a personification of rumor, especially of evil tidings. As her resplendent throne and regal authority suggest, she has become, like Fortune and Venus, a deity to be worshiped, and as such she is a symbol of the idolatry of worldly renown. Fame's deification, however, is indicative not only of her importance as an object of idolatry but also of her function as an aspect of God's temporal order. Thus her being "perpetually ystalled" on her throne brings to mind Boethius' distinction between "perpetual" and "eternal": "And forthi yif we wollen putten worthi names to thinges and folwen Plato, lat us seyen thanne sothly that God is 'eterne,' and that the world is 'perpetuel.' "[66] As Philosophy explains, it is the idolatrous worship of things in the "perpetual" order that causes men to forget the "eternal" order of God. This contrast could hardly be depicted more vividly than by Fame's glittering throne—reminiscent of the Apocalyptic throne on which Christ sits in majesty:

And behold, there was a throne set in heaven, and upon the throne one sitting. And he that sat was to the sight like the jasper and the sardine stone; and there was a rainbow round about the throne, in sight like unto an emerald.

Unlike Fame's heralds, "corouned as kynges" and dressed in colorful and rich array, are the elders clothed in white, wearing crowns of salvation, who congregate about Christ's throne and sing his praise. But this Scriptural inversion

---

false "gentilesse," see *De consolatione philosophiae*, III, Pr. 6, and above, chap. I.

[66] *De consolatione philosophiae*, V, Pr. 6. Although Boethius refers to Plato, the distinction is also Christian. Cf. II Cor. 4:18.

centers more conspicuously on the ruby or carbuncle of Fame's throne—the equivalent of the jasper or sardine stone to which Christ on his throne is compared.[67] As in the other references to Fame's gems, the significance of this contrast may be found in the lapidaries, where the carbuncle is singled out as the greatest of the precious stones, combining the virtues of all the others, because its resplendence in the dark signifies the light which Christ brought into the world to illuminate the darkness of sin. For the same reason, it is identified with the Blessed Virgin:

> For she, in hyr vyrgynyte,
> Bar a chyld in thys world here
> Mayde & moder bothe yfere,
> The Charbouncle most cler off lyht,
> Chasynge away dyrknesse off night,
> And al thys world doth enlumyne.[68]

Unlike the spiritual gem of Christ and the Virgin, Fame's carbuncle has its equivalent in the resplendent carbuncle adorning the circlet of Richesse in the *Roman de la Rose*, where its false light is associated with idolatrous love.[69] At the same time, it relates Fame once again to her Scriptural prototype, the Whore of Babylon, whose precious stones and rich apparel typify the specious attraction of

---

[67] Apoc. 4:2-3. In Ezech. 1:26 and 10:1, the throne itself is likened to "the appearance of the sapphire stone."

[68] Lydgate, *Pilgrimage*, 7,102ff.; 8,518ff. Cf. *The Minor Poems*, II, 662: "Charbonclys, rubyes of moost excellence,/ Shewe in dirknesse lyght whereso they be,/ By ther natural hevenly influence." In *De doctrina Christiana*, II, 16, Augustine affirms that a knowledge of beryl and "of the carbuncle which shines in the darkness" illuminates many obscure places in books where they are used as similitudes. On the qualities relating the carbuncle to Christ, see Evans and Serjeantson, *English Mediaeval Lapidaries*, pp. 21-22, 41, 110, 123. In Ezech. 28:13, the carbuncle is connected with the Earthly Paradise. Cf. Patch, *The Other World*, pp. 149, 164.

[69] Lines 1,099ff. (Mid. Eng. trans., 1,119-28). In *The Goddess Fortuna*, pp. 61-63, Patch observes that Fortune is sometimes portrayed with details reminiscent of the Blessed Virgin.

worldly goods.[70] The worship of one of these goods, earthly fame, underlies the particular details describing the goddess.

Although Chaucer's portrait of Fame derives basically from Virgil, the mixture of pagan and Christian imagery is a constant reminder of the contrast between temporal and eternal fame. As in the *Aeneid*, Fame's shifting stature, ranging from "the lengthe of a cubite" to such a height

> That with hir fet she erthe reighte,
> And with hir hed she touched hevene,
> Ther as shynen sterres sevene. . .

is indicative, Boccaccio tells us, of the growth of rumor, which is restrained at first by fear but soon spreads from lowly men to the exalted hearing of the great. But Chaucer's wording also echoes the description of Lady Philosophy, whose head likewise touches heaven, not through worldly exaltation or falsehood but through the contemplation of divine truth. More pertinent to Fame's shifting size is Philosophy's own comment: "But what schal I sey of dignytes and of powers, the whiche ye men, that neither knowen verray dignyte ne verray power, areysen hem as heyghe as the hevene?"[71] In Scripture the same image is applied to the unmerited praise of the wicked, especially of the hypocrite, who, though "his pride mount up even to heaven, and his head touch the clouds," in the end "shall be destroyed."[72] In conjunction with this warning, we should not overlook the Apocalyptic connotations of the "sterres sevene"—another reminder of the kinship of

[70] Apoc. 17:4. Cf. 18:11-12. On the significance of the Whore's gems, see Robertson and Huppé (*Piers Plowman*, pp. 50-52), who connect them with the "riche stones" and "red rubyes" of Lady Meed—another close relative of Fame.

[71] *De consolatione philosophiae*, II, Pr. 6. On Philosophy's shifting stature, see I, Pr. 1.

[72] Job 20:6-7. Cf. the preceding verse: "the praise of the wicked is short, and the joy of the hypocrite but for a moment."

Fame and the Whore of Babylon, whose sins are said to "have reached unto heaven" and to be remembered by the Lord.[73] John's vision is explicitly evoked in the next detail describing Fame:

> For as feele eyen hadde she
> As fetheres upon foules be,
> Or weren on the bestes foure
> That Goddis trone gunne honoure,
> As John writ in th' Apocalips. (1381-85)

In traditional commentary the "four living creatures" before the throne of the Lamb are interpreted as the four Evangelists, and their many eyes "before and behind" signify the knowledge of past, present, and future contained in the Gospels. As such they are indicative of the divinely revealed providence of God, whose eyes symbolize the omniscience with which he observes all earthly thoughts and deeds, open or secret, and records them for future judgment.[74] In contrast, therefore, are Fame's many eyes, which see only in the present and record only the outward words and deeds of men. Together Fame's many eyes and ears denote her endless vigilance, without which, says Boccaccio, rumor would soon disappear into nothing. Equally appropriate are her numerous tongues, whose mixture of truth and falsehood depicts the distorted and erroneous judgments of mankind. But in one important detail Chaucer modifies Virgil's portrait: in lieu of the many feathers on Fame's body, an image of the swiftness

[73] Apoc. 18:5. For the Apocalyptic "sterres sevene," see 1:16 and 2:1. This parallel, along with other Apocalyptic details suggested by Chaucer's imagery, has been noted by L. J. Henkin, "The Apocrypha [sic] and Chaucer's *House of Fame*," *MLN*, LVI (1941), 583-88.

[74] "God is said to have eyes because he sees all things, and nothing is hidden. As the Apostle says, no creature is invisible in his sight, for 'all things are naked and open to his eyes' [Heb. 4:13]" (Eucherius, *Liber formularum*, PL, 50, cols. 750-51). On the eyes of the "bestes foure," see, for example, *PL*, 165, col. 628: "For these four creatures are the four Evangelists. . . . They are full of eyes before and behind because they contemplate past, present, and future."

and irrevocability of rumor once it is started, he substitutes "partriches wynges" on her feet. This striking alteration, however, may be viewed as another instance of Fame's metamorphosis into a Christian symbol; for the partridge, as we learn from medieval writers, has traits especially characteristic of earthly fame. Among its dominant traits is its fearfulness, an attribute it shares with Virgil's goddess and one applied in Christian doctrine to the worship of such unstable gifts as love and fame.[75] Because of its fear, moreover, the partridge is said to fly close to the earth, another attribute suitable to Fame, since the desire for fame is rooted in the love of earthly things.[76] Finally, the partridge in Scripture, as in the bestiaries, is connected with cupidity, and even with Satan, a fact suggesting that the pursuit of fame not infrequently is prompted by the prince of all vanity.[77]

Although Fame retains her basic identity with the pagan personification of rumor, Chaucer's alterations, especially his minimizing her more monstrous features, serve to emphasize her idolatrous nature, which appears also in her "perry" and "richesse"—details again relating her to the

[75] Cf. chap. III, n. 58.

[76] Bersuire connects the fear of the partridge [*perdix*] with the smallness of its wings and its consequent inability to fly far. Since it is a fearful bird, it is often put to flight and caught in the fowler's net (*Opera*, II, 211). As an attribute of fame, the goddess's winged feet may be contrasted with those of Pegasus, whose swift flight is indicative of the good fame accompanying virtuous deeds (*ibid.*, IV, 185). We need not, perhaps, assume that Chaucer mistranslated Virgil's *pernicibus alis*, since he gives the proper rendering in *Troilus*, IV, 661 ("with preste wynges"). The modification of traditional iconographic details is characteristic of Chaucer's art. In this instance, the portrayal of Fame was perhaps influenced by the attributes of Fortune, whose winged feet are an image of her fleeting gifts. See Patch, *The Goddess Fortuna*, p. 45.

[77] In the bestiaries, the partridge is called an evil bird because it steals and hatches the eggs of other birds, just as Satan steals the souls of those who cannot resist his wiles but who later desert him to seek their true home with God. Cf. Jerome, *PL*, 24, col. 820ff. (on Jer. 17:11).

Whore of Babylon—and in the "hevenyssh melodye" sung "eternally" about her throne:

> And, Lord! the hevenyssh melodye
> Of songes, ful of armonye,
> I herde aboute her trone ysonge,
> That al the paleys-walles ronge!
> So song the myghty Muse, she
> That cleped ys Caliope,
> And hir eighte sustren eke,
> That in her face semen meke;
> And ever mo, eternally,
> They songe of Fame, as thoo herd y:
> "Heryed be thou and thy name,
> Goddesse of Renoun or of Fame!" (1395-1406)

In this instance we can safely distinguish the Muses who sing Fame's praise from the Muses who signify *scientia* and are invoked by Chaucer at the beginning of Book II. Like the "comune strompettis" banished by Philosophy from Boethius' chamber, these are the "poetical Muses" whose music denotes the outward, sensuous appeal of art, not its "sentence," and whose sweet "flateries" destroy the "fruytes of resoun" and hold men's hearts "in usage." Their music, therefore, like that of the minstrels outside the castle, is a worldly harmony directed to the praise of men, not the praise of God.[78] This contrast is called up above all by the "hevenyssh melodye" they sing "eternally" before Fame's throne—a reversal of the Apocalyptic songs of praise sung eternally before God and the Lamb: "To him that sitteth on the throne, and to the Lamb, benediction, and honour, and glory, and power, for ever and ever."[79] Chaucer's Scriptural inversion is perhaps reminiscent of the *Paradiso*, where Dante, after rejecting the songs of the Muses as inadequate for his higher theme,

---

[78] On Boethius' contrasting Muses, see Boccaccio, *Genealogia deorum*, XIV, 20, and Petrarch, *Invective contra medicum*, ed. P. Ricci (Rome, 1950), p. 36. Cf. Robertson, *Preface*, pp. 117, 121.

[79] Apoc. 5:13. Cf. 7:10.

describes the heavenly harmony accompanying the crowning of the Blessed Virgin (XXIII, 55-111). But unlike
Dante's Muses, whose song is attuned to divine truth,
although a lower truth than Apollo's, Fame's Muses sing
a song expressing the worldly glory of the two famous
pagans whose "armes" and "names" the goddess sustains
upon her shoulders,

> Alexander and Hercules,
> That with a sherte hys lyf les!

Since Alexander and Hercules exemplified for the Middle
Ages both the worst and the best aspects of the pagan
pursuit of glory, it is appropriate that Fame herself should
bear the burden of their "large fame." Alexander, whose
conquests spread his name over the known world, is the
most notable example of the spirit corrupted by an insati-
able desire for fame.[80] Equally renowned, but for a different reason, is Hercules, whose wisdom and glorious
deeds made his name a medieval synonym of good fame.
But as Chaucer's allusion to his death implies, Hercules'
fame is not without its flaw; for like Orpheus he fits the
pattern of those who through irrational love departed from
the path of virtuous renown.[81]

The tainted pagan glory of Alexander and Hercules
finds symbolic expression in the remaining details describing Fame's ornate abode: the pillars sustaining her

[80] On Alexander's vainglorious pursuit of renown, see I Mach. 1-10;
Augustine, *De civitate Dei*, IV, 4; John of Salisbury, *Policraticus*, VIII,
5. Cf. chap. IV, n. 44, above.
[81] Bernard Silvestris interprets Hercules as *sapientia* and his name,
etymologically, as *gloria* (*Commentum*, p. 71. Cf. pp. 56, 87). Hercules' death, resulting from the poisoned shirt sent by Dejanira, is
moralized by Giovanni del Virgilio as an example of virtue succumb-
ing to lust [*libidinem carnalem*]. Released from the flesh, however,
Hercules' spirit ascends heavenward (*Allegorie librorum Ovidii Metamorphoseos*, p. 83). Cf. Boccaccio, *Genealogia deorum*, II, 637. In
Ovid's account (*Metamorphoses*, IX, 134-40), *Fama loquax* is said to
bear the distorted tidings of Hercules' love of Iole.

airy hall. On either side of her dais—"streight doun to the dores wide"—Chaucer sees "many a peler" made of metal "that shoon not ful cler" and adorned with "folk of digne reverence." Whereas the goddess holds up the heavy renown of Alexander and Hercules, these worthy figures hold up the renown of other illustrious men. Their importance is suggested not only by their pillars, which are "mad for gret noblesse" and for "hy and gret sentence," but also by their position about Fame's throne. Unlike the entertainers in the "habitacles" outside the castle, these "folk of digne reverence" are no mere singers of carnal love and warfare or performers of magic and illusions. Instead, they are some of the greatest writers of former times—including Homer, Virgil, and Chaucer's "owne poet," Ovid—whose writings perpetuate the famous names and deeds of men and nations alike.

Chaucer's imagery again evokes the medieval accounts of the Church, where the pillars sustaining the roof are said to represent the various saints and ecclesiastics who by their wisdom and rectitude raise the whole structure in God's glory.[82] By the usual process of exegesis, the pillars of the Church are related to the pillars of John's vision, symbolic of those who resist temptation and achieve the "new name" of Christ: "He that shall overcome, I will make him a pillar in the temple of my God, and he shall go out no more."[83] On the same basis they are associated with the seven pillars supporting the house of Wisdom: "Wisdom hath built herself a house, she hath hewn her out seven pillars" (Prov. 9:1). Whereas Wisdom's house, like Solomon's, is interpreted as the Church, Wis-

[82] Honorius of Autun, *Gemmae animae*, *PL*, 172, col. 586; Durandus, *Rationale divinorum officiorum*, I, 1, 27. Cf. E. de Bruyne, *Etudes d'esthétique médiévale* (Bruges, 1946), II, 364.

[83] Apoc. 3:12. Bede relates the Apocalyptic pillars to those in the porch of Solomon's temple (III Kings 7:21-22), symbolic of holy men [*sancti viri*] whose strength and aspiration fortify and adorn the Church (*PL*, 93, col. 141).

dom herself is Christ—"Dei virtus et Dei sapientia"—who founded the Church as a dwelling "for the living and the elect." Her pillars signify the seven gifts of the Holy Spirit, for by these gifts, which bring all wisdom and knowledge to perfection, the structure of the Church is raised to heaven.[84] In medieval churches the pillars of Wisdom are imaged in the seven pillars sometimes separating the aisles from the nave. Of particular bearing on Chaucer's columned statues, however, are those pillars depicting the famous heroes of the Old Law who prefigured Christ or foretold his coming, or those depicting the apostles and saints who spread his tidings of charity and future salvation.[85] As Chaucer's predominantly pagan imagery makes clear, the worthy figures sustaining Fame's house are hardly to be identified with the saints who raise the Church in God's glory or those who have received the "new name" of Christ and a pillar in heaven. As we are explicitly told, these are writers of "olde gestes"—either authors like Josephus who perpetuate the famous deeds performed under the Old Law, not the New, or those

[84] Honorius of Autun, *Speculum ecclesiae*, PL, 172, col. 1,101. Tropologically, the house of Wisdom designates the heart governed by wisdom and charity, a meaning dramatized in *Psychomachia*, 804ff., where Wisdom's pillars are combined with details drawn from the descriptions of the New Jerusalem and Solomon's temple. Many of the details— the lofty house, the single gem of which it is made, the gate, the names inscribed in gold, the precious stones (including beryl), the inner chamber, the supporting pillars "cut from a glassy rock of ice-like crystal," Wisdom herself on her throne dispensing laws to safeguard mankind—suggest the rich background of traditional exegetical meanings behind the description of Fame and her abode.

[85] On the imitation of the pillars of Wisdom in churches, see Joan Evans, *Art in Mediaeval France* (London, 1948), p. 144. Wisdom's pillars are depicted in churches, says Durandus, because bishops ought to be filled with the sevenfold influence of the Holy Spirit (*Rationale divinorum officiorum*, 1, 1, 27). Fame's pillars suggest an amalgamation of the concepts behind Wisdom's pillars and the columned statues adorning the exterior of the cathedrals and portraying important personages of the Old and New Testaments. On the doctrinal and artistic traditions reflected in the pillars, see Mâle, *Religious Art in France*, pp. 152ff.; Simson, pp. 150-51; Robertson, *Preface*, p. 184.

like Homer and Virgil or the medieval Geoffrey of Monmouth and Guido delle Colonne who exalt the names of the pagan Greeks, Trojans, and Romans. By the same token, the pillars of these writers are not to be confused with the pillars supporting Wisdom's house and signifying divine wisdom. Fame's seven groups of pillars, Chaucer implies, are indeed pillars of wisdom, since they are made for "hy and gret sentence."[86] But, he carefully remarks, they are made of metals "that shoon not ful cler" and therefore contain no great "rychesse." That this contrast between Fame's and Wisdom's pillars is a deliberate one appears likely when we relate the pillars more closely to Chaucer's metal imagery.

Implicit in Fame's pillars of metal "that shoon not ful cler" is the contrast, already noted, between the "pure" metals, gold and silver, and the "base" metals, such as iron, lead, tin, brass, and copper. As observed of the "table of bras" in the temple of Venus, this contrast has acquired importance in Christian doctrine as a distinction between man's spiritual life before and after the Fall. The base metals, to pursue this doctrine, signify the degradation of nature and of human nature in particular as a consequence of Adam's sin, that is, the life of man in a state of cupidity under the Old Law. Gold and silver, on the other hand, denote aspects of charity, as in Solomon's temple, where the gold of the pillars and other ornaments symbolizes the wisdom of Christ and the New Law.[87] This contrast takes

---

[86] Although Fame's house is supported by "many a peler," only seven —the number in Wisdom's house—are described: those of Josephus, Statius, Homer, Virgil, Ovid, Lucan, and Claudian.

[87] Bede, *De templo Salomonis*, PL, 91, col. 752. In *Psychomachia*, 804-10, the temple of Solomon is the model for the temple of Wisdom, "a house adorned with gold, to be the majestic home of Christ." The concept of nature's degradation since the Fall underlies the medieval accounts of the Golden Age, for example, in Lydgate's *The Fall of Princes*, VII, 1,209-11: "This goldene world long while did endure,/ Was non allay in that metal seene,/ Til Saturn cesid, be record of scripture." See Singleton, *Journey to Beatrice*, pp. 184-203; Robertson, *Preface*, p. 202.

on more specific meaning in relation to the pillars. Thus Bersuire, commenting on the pillars of the Church, explains that they are made of gold and silver—metals "quae summe fulgent et lucent"—because gold designates the inner sense of Scripture and silver denotes the outward, rhetorical clothing in which this wisdom is veiled. The same meanings are applied to the writings of the prelates and other ecclesiastics, for just as the columns of the Church are of gold and silver, so the words and deeds of such men ought to shine with the wisdom of gold and the eloquence of silver.[88] In his allegorical exposition of the Church and its ornaments, Honorius of Autun uses the distinction between pure and base metals to contrast the higher wisdom of Scripture with the wisdom of the pagan and other secular writers. Since gold and silver denote the wisdom and charity necessary to man's salvation, they are the chief ornaments of the Church. But if the lesser metals shine less clearly, they are not without use; for just as the splendor of gold is set off by the dullness of iron, so the wisdom of Scripture is made to shine even more brilliantly by the philosophy and arts of secular writers:

For in a great house not only gold and silver vessels but also iron and earthen vessels are necessary. Such a great house is the Church. The gold and silver vessels are the books of sacred authority. The iron and earthen vessels are the secular writings necessary for the exterior. For just as gold acquires lustre

---

[88] *Opera*, IV, 439ff. Cf. II, 439, and *PL*, 168, col. 853: "Gold [*aurum*] signifies the inner sense of Scripture, whereas silver [*argentum*] signifies the outer sense." Bersuire applies these meanings to the pillars of the Tabernacle (Ex. 36:36): "For gold designates wisdom [*sapientiam*] and the beauty of the good life [*bonae vitae venustatem*]. Silver, however, designates eloquence and the truth of good doctrine [*eloquentiam et bonae doctrinae veritatem*]" (IV, 439). On the basis of Cant. 8:9, where silver relates figuratively to the pillars of the Church, Durandus interprets silver as the majesty and clarity with which ecclesiastics sustain the Church by her doctrine (*Rationale divinorum officiorum*, I, 1, 26). In Ps. 11:7, silver is an image of the words of the Lord.

from iron, so Holy Writ appears more glorious through the secular disciplines. . . . Not only do the sacred writings lead us to eternal life but even the letters of the gentiles instruct us. . . . Those who change secular studies into a spiritual exercise are despoiling the Egyptians. They offer these studies for building the tabernacle when they bring forward philosophical arguments for the edifice of the Church. They donate the gold of the Egyptians when they supply spiritual discipline through secular wisdom. They donate the silver of the Egyptians when they turn secular eloquence to the utility of the Church.[89]

In affirming the utility of pagan ideas and disciplines, Honorius follows Augustine, who also cites the Hebrews' spoliation of Egypt as authority that pagan writings contain "not only simulated and superstitious imaginings" but also "liberal disciplines more suited to the uses of truth," "some most useful precepts concerning morals," and even "some truths concerning the worship of one God."[90] This Christian attitude toward pagan wisdom— the orthodox medieval view from Augustine onward— provides the necessary norm for evaluating the importance of the writers "of digne reverence" who stand upon Fame's pillars. Since these are writers of "hy and gret sentence," Chaucer tells us, their pillars are "mad for gret noblesse." At the same time, because they wrote of "olde gestes" rather than the wisdom and charity of the New Law, these pillars are made not of gold and silver but of metals "that shoon not ful cler." This distinction acquires further meaning from the particular metals assigned to the pillars of these writers.

[89] *Speculum ecclesiae, PL,* 172, cols. 1,056-57. For the Scriptural authority behind this passage, see II Tim. 2:20-21.

[90] *De doctrina Christiana,* II, 40. This attitude explains the high position allowed the righteous heathens in *Inf.,* IV, 31ff. Dante's *nobile castello* with its pagan writers of wisdom—Homer, Virgil, Lucan, Aristotle, Plato, etc.—suggests a model for Fame's castle and its "folk of digne reverence." For a discussion of the medieval Christian attitude toward pagan wisdom, see Robertson, *Preface,* pp. 337ff.

The first group of pillars, made of lead and iron and belonging to Josephus and other writers who hold up the fame of the Jews, sets the pattern for the others:

> Alderfirst, loo, ther I sigh
> Upon a piler stonde on high,
> That was of led and yren fyn,
> Hym of secte saturnyn,
> The Ebrayk Josephus, the olde,
> That of Jewes gestes tolde;
> And he bar on hys shuldres hye
> The fame up of the Jewerye.
> And by hym stoden other sevene,
> Wise and worthy for to nevene,
> To helpen him bere up the charge,
> Hyt was so hevy and so large.
> And for they writen of batayles,
> As wel as other olde mervayles,
> Therfor was, loo, thys piler
> Of which that I yow telle her,
> Of led and yren bothe, ywys,
> For yren Martes metal ys,
> Which that god is of bataylle;
> And the led, withouten faille,
> Ys, loo, the metal of Saturne,
> That hath a ful large whel to turne. (1429-50)

The position of honor given to Josephus is explained by his famous accounts of Jewish history, *The Jewish War* and the *Antiquities of the Jews,* whose "hy and gret sentence" is evident in their use by the medieval Church as a source of moral wisdom.[91] But Josephus's significance as a spokesman for the Old Law, rather than the New, is suggested by the epithet "the olde" and the many "olde mervayles" of which he wrote. His identification with the "secte saturnyn," along with the metal and astrological imagery, is an extension of this concept; for Saturn, as the oldest and the slowest of the planets, is a symbol of

---

[91] See Leclercq, *The Love of Learning and the Desire for God,* p. 144.

time and for this reason is associated with the Old Law.[92]
Since Saturn, like Mars, is a malevolent planet, only
when he is in conjunction with a benevolent planet, such
as the sun or Jupiter, is his harmfulness mollified and
turned to good. Such a conjunction with Jupiter, the lord
of the house of faith and religion, is said to have produced
the Hebraic religion—Josephus's "secte saturnyn"—a
view expressed, among others, by Roger Bacon, who appeals to "learned authors" in affirming that "if Jupiter is
conjoined with Saturn it signifies the divine books and the
Hebraic sect, since it is older than other sects, just as
Saturn . . . is older and more remote in the movement
and order of the planets. And just as all religions ac-
knowledge it and it acknowledges none, so all other planets
are in conjunction with Saturn and it conjoins with none
because of its slow motion."[93] Saturn's connection with the
Jewish religion is further imaged in Josephus's pillar of
lead and iron, since lead, the metal of Saturn, is by its
heaviness and dullness indicative of the weight and im-
purity of sin, the state of man under the Old Law. Thus
Bersuire contrasts gold, symbolic of man's conversion to
Christ, with the baseness of lead; for "the good are turned
into gold, because they are made golden through tribulation and good works, but the evil are made leaden and
dull through avarice and evil habits."[94] If the "olde

[92] Bacon, *Opus majus*, ed. J. H. Bridges (Oxford, 1897), I, 255. Cf.
Neckam, *De naturis rerum*, I, 4. Bersuire identifies Saturn with *diabolus
malitiosus* and with human nature since the Fall. Jupiter, in contrast,
designates Christ, who, through his Incarnation, tempered the malice of
Saturn—that is, of the human race—by his benevolence (*Opera*, II, 111).

[93] *Ibid.* This passage is quoted in the same connection by A. H. Miller, "Chaucer's 'Secte Saturnym,'" *MLN*, XLVII (1932), 99.

[94] *Opera*, II, 452. "Lead [*plumbum*] is a gross, dark, heavy, and vile
metal. . . . Such, truly, is the sinner; for he is gross [*grossus*] because
of pride and vanity; . . . dark [*obscurus*] because of ignorance and
uncouthness; heavy [*ponderosus*] because of evil practice, sloth, and in-
difference; and vile [*foedus*] and foul acting because of lechery and
carnality" (*ibid.*). Neckam (*De naturis rerum*, II, 154) identifies lead
with sin [*peccatum*].

mervayles" of the Jews are aptly symbolized by the lead of Saturn, so their "batayles" have an appropriate symbol in iron, the metal of Mars, since Mars, as Chaucer reminds us, is the god of battle, and his metal denotes the strife and tribulation under the Old Law.[95] The kind of warfare signified by Mars and his metal is illustrated by the battles of Joab, whose vainglorious trumpet of "fight and blod-shedynge" was described earlier. As a symbol of the stern justice under the Old Law, the iron of Mars is contrasted by Lydgate with the "merciful" gold of Phoebus, that is, of Christ:

> Of Martis myneral the metal is so strong,
> Inflexible and nat malliable,
> Be sturdynesse to do the peeple wrong
> With rigerous suerd, fureous & vengable,
> The merciful gold [of] Phebus nat plicable
> To haue compassioun, because attemp(e)raunce
> Was set aside & lost hir gouernaunce.[96]

The same contrast underlies Boccaccio's description of the temple of Mars, whose adamant doors and pillars of iron, we are told, signify the hardness and obstinacy which prevent the light of reason and grace from entering the mind.[97]

Josephus's pillar of iron and lead establishes the symbolic pattern for the other famous authors who stand on pillars of metal "that shoon not ful cler." From the great writers on Greece and Troy—including Statius, Homer

---

[95] Citing Ps. 104:18 ("They humbled his feet in fetters: the iron pierced his soul"), Rabanus interprets iron [*ferrum*] as tribulation and distress [*tribulationem et angustiam*], or the tribulation of harsh necessity [*tribulationem durae necessitatis*], whose power overruns the soul (*De universo*, PL, 111, col. 480). Cf. Neckam, *De naturis rerum*, II, 54; Bersuire, *Opera*, II, 452.

[96] *The Fall of Princes*, VII, 1,216-22. Cf. Honorius of Autun, PL, 172, cols. 391-93: "Before Christ's Advent the tempest of warfare especially raged over the whole world; . . . but after the arrival of Christ, the true peace, the storm-cloud of warfare receded."

[97] *Teseida*, ed. Roncaglia, pp. 413-14 (on VII, 33).

(whose pillar is "ful wonder hy"), Dares, Dictys, the mysterious Lollius, Guido delle Colonne, and the English "Gaufride" (Geoffrey of Monmouth), all of whom wrote on pagan "fight and blod-shedynge" and therefore stand on pillars of iron—Chaucer turns to the Roman writers, beginning with Virgil, who on a pillar of "tynned yren cler" holds up "the fame of Pius Eneas."[98] Virgil's "hy and gret sentence" was illustrated in the story of the *Aeneid* portrayed in the temple of Venus. Here it is again imaged in the virtue of "Pius Eneas," whose piety exemplifies the pagans' closest approximation to Christian *pietas* and charity. Because Virgil wrote of pagan warfare, his pillar also is of iron. But this iron is not the obdurate metal of Mars, for it is mixed with tin, the metal of benevolent Jupiter, and is therefore said to be "cler"— a fit expression of Aeneas' piety.[99] Nevertheless, Virgil's "tynned yren" is a reminder that Aeneas' fame is an empty, pagan glory, as we may infer also from Scripture, where tin is an image of false doctrine.[100] Even more

[98] The "hy and gret sentence" of the writers on Greece and Troy is exemplified by the *Thebaid* of Statius, a work which acquired allegorical accretions in medieval commentaries. See Robertson, *Preface*, pp. 125, 260-61, 357. The "taint" obscuring the pillar of Statius is evident in its "tigres blod"—an allusion to *Thebaid*, VII, where two of these beasts kill three Greek soldiers and thus help to renew the hostilities. Although Guido and Geoffrey are Christian, not pagan, authors, they are properly included because their writings help to perpetuate the "olde gestes" of the Greeks and Trojans.

[99] In *Vergil and the English Poets*, pp. 57ff., Elizabeth Nitchie explains Virgil's "tynned yren" as "Mars controlled and directed by Jupiter." According to Bernard, Aeneas' bearing his father on his back in the flight from Troy exemplifies *pietas*, a virtue implanted in the spirit by God and expressed in compassion for one's fellow beings (*Commentum*, pp. 2, 35). Because of its softness, Bersuire interprets tin [*stannum*] as *pietas* (*Opera*, II, 456). Cf. Neckam, *De naturis rerum*, I, 7: "Piety [*pietas*] puts hardness [*duritiam*] to flight and begets compassion." On the Christian connotations of *pietas*, see Robertson, *Preface*, p. 163, n. 52.

[100] *Allegoriae in sacram scripturam*, col. 1,046 (on Is. 1:25: "I will clean purge away thy dross, and I will take away all thy tin"). On the authority of Ezech. 22:18 and 27:12, Rabanus interprets tin as the

flawed is the metal of Chaucer's "owne poet," Ovid—
"Venus clerk"—who has "ysowen wonder wide" the "grete
god of Loves name" and on a pillar of copper exalts his
fame as high as Chaucer can see. As a poet who condemned
the love of Cupid and Venus beneath the surface of his
ironic fictions, Ovid rightly has a high place among the
writers of "hy and gret sentence." His ironic praise of
Love and his servants is implicit in his pillar of copper,
whose substance, like brass, is the metal of Venus and
depicts the outward beauty concealing the torments and
bitterness of those worshiping in her temple.[101] Whereas
Virgil's pillar of "tynned yren" extols the piety and fame
of Aeneas, Ovid's pillar reminds us of his brief sojourn
in the temple and of Dido's idolatrous love and infamy.

Chaucer concludes his account of Fame's pillars with
two more Roman writers, Lucan and Claudian. Lucan,
author of the *Pharsalia,* is accompanied by many other
"clerkes" who wrote of "Romes myghty werkes." Like the
aforementioned writers on pagan warfare, Lucan is standing on a pillar of iron; but unlike Virgil's pillar of iron,
tempered by Jupiter's tin, this iron is "wroght ful
sternely," because the fame borne by Lucan is not of "Pius
Eneas" but of Julius Caesar and Pompey, followers of
warlike Mars. But if his pillar is not as "cler" as Virgil's,
its "hy and gret sentence" is attested by no less a writer
than Augustine, who does not hesitate to quote from the
Pharsalia to show that pagan wisdom sometimes parallels

---

simulation of holiness [*simulatio sanctitatis*] and the sophistical speech
[*sophisticam locutionem*] and simulation of heretics (*De universo*, cols.
478-79).
[101] Boccaccio, *Teseida*, ed. Roncaglia, pp. 421-22. In *The Fall of
Princes*, VII, 1,240ff., Lydgate attributes copper to Venus because it "wil
ternyssh grene"—a "chaungable colour, contrarye to sadnesse,/ A notabil
figur of worldli brotilnesse,/ Like gery Venus." On Ovid's medieval
reputation as a moralist who condemns carnal love, see Leclercq, pp.
121-22, 124; Robertson, *Preface*, pp. 356ff.

the truths of Christianity.[102] The same honor may be accorded to Claudian, who, on a pillar of sulphur, sustains the "fame of helle,"

> Of Pluto, and of Proserpyne,
> That quene ys of the derke pyne. (1511-12)

Just as in Book I, where Claudian is included with Dante as an authority on the torments in Hell, Chaucer follows the medieval view that this author's *De raptu Proserpinae* contained truths approximating the Christian doctrine of damnation. This "hy and gret sentence" is contained in Pluto and Proserpina, "king" and "queen" of "the derke pyne." Whereas Pluto is a type of Satan himself—"diabolus rex inferni materialis, et etiam rex mundi qui est infernus spiritualis"—Proserpina signifies "iniquitas." She is said to be the queen and wife of Pluto because Satan rules with iniquity in sulphur, that is, in the unclean heart of the sinner.[103] In this moralized context Claudian's pillar of sulphur takes on obvious connotations. Not only is sulphur indicative of the earthly infamy whose stench proceeds from the sinful heart; it is also an image of the infamy of eternal damnation destined for all those who succumb to the temptations of earthly love and glory.[104]

As a reminder of the eternal judgment which will reward the vainglorious pursuit of fame, Claudian's pillar of sulphur is a gathering point for the Apocalyptic implications of the preceding description of Fame's mountain and house as well as the ensuing drama of her fickle

---

[102] *De civitate Dei*, I, 11 (on *Pharsalia*, VII, 819). Cf. Leclercq, pp. 45, 119, 122, 143, 145, 305 (n. 65).

[103] Bersuire, *Ovidius moralizatus*, I, ed. Ghisalberti, p. 99. Augustine, in a different connection, praises Claudian for his approximation to Christian truths (*De civitate Dei*, V, 26).

[104] *PL*, 117, col. 1,110 (on Apoc. 14:9-11); *Allegoriae in sacram scripturam*, col. 1,061. Bersuire applies the Scriptural meanings to Pluto's throne, which is sulphurous and stinking [*fetidum*] inasmuch as his justice [*iurisdictio*] is infamous and blameworthy, for about his throne dwell all kinds of wicked men (*Ovidius moralizatus*, p. 99).

judgments. Whereas the contrast between temporal and eternal fame has been embodied up to this point in a more or less static symbolism, it now takes on dramatic life and vividness with the throngs of suppliants who, in answer to the heralds' cries of "Larges," enter the hall and gather before Fame's throne to ask a "boon" and to receive her decrees. By means of their petitions and the goddess's awards of praise, slander, and oblivion, the action dramatizes the various human attitudes toward earthly fame along with the vain and fickle judgments of mankind which make up such fame. But if the action illustrates the nature of worldly fame, the contrast between temporal and eternal fame becomes increasingly evident in the profusion of Apocalyptic imagery. At the outset the Apocalyptic pattern is completed by the "gret companye" crowding about Fame's throne and awaiting her judgments:

> A ryght gret companye withalle,
> And that of sondry regiouns,
> Of alleskynnes condiciouns
> That dwelle in erthe under the mone,
> Pore and ryche. (1528-32)

As we later observe in the whirling House of Tidings in the valley beneath the castle, Fame's suppliants betray their kinship with the personified tidings crowding the abode of Rumor in the *Metamorphoses*. But as the imagery of speech at the end of Book II suggests, Chaucer's "wynged" words, ascending so "naturally" to the mid-point of Fame's house in the likeness of their earthly speakers, have become more than a personification of rumor: they are images of the soul, the spiritual "words" rising to God's house in the clothing of truth or falsehood, or both combined, to be recorded for future judgment. More particularly, in the inverted Apocalyptic setting of

Fame's abode, these embodied words, of "alleskynnes condiciouns," both "pore and ryche," ascending from "sondry regiouns," recounting their earthly deeds, and receiving the goddess's judgments, are the ironic counterpart of the "great and small" who in John's vision ascend to the mid-point of Christ's tribunal and are awarded eternal fame or infamy "according to their works":

And I saw a great white throne, and one sitting upon it, from whose face the earth and heaven fled away, and there was no place found for them. And I saw the dead, great and small, standing in the presence of the throne, and the books were opened; and another book was opened, which was the book of life, and the dead were judged by those things which were written in the books, according to their works.[105]

In traditional commentary, the books of judgment signify the conscience, whose testimony will make manifest all those earthly words and deeds, open or secret, by which the soul will be judged at the end of the world. Peter Lombard applies this concept to Luke 12:2, the verse alluded to earlier in Dido's soliloquy on "wikke Fame": "For there is nothing covered that shall not be revealed; nor hidden, that shall not be known."[106] The self-spoken

---

[105] Apoc. 20:11-15. Cf. Joel 3:2,14. In Ps. 9:5-9, Christ's sitting "forever" on his throne, dispensing eternal justice, provides an ironic contrast to Fame, sitting "perpetually ystalled" on her throne and dispensing her fickle judgments: "But the Lord remaineth forever. He hath prepared his throne in judgment: and he shall judge the world in equity, he shall judge the people in justice." The "gret companye" before Fame's throne also suggests an inversion of Apoc. 7:9-10: "I saw a great multitude, which no man could number, of all nations and tribes and peoples and tongues, standing before the throne and in sight of the Lamb, clothed with white robes." On the literary influence of Love and Fortune on Chaucer's portrayal of Fame and her suppliants, see Sypherd, pp. 117ff. Robinson (*Works*, p. 786) notes reminiscences of the *Inferno*. Especially striking parallels are Fame's and Minos's roles in dispensing temporal and eternal awards to mankind, the assembled throngs confessing their earthly deeds, and the decrees effected through Fame's trumpets and Minos's girding himself with his tail (*Inf.*, v, 4-15).

[106] *Sententiae*, PL, 192, col. 944: "The books are the consciences of

words before Fame's throne, openly proclaiming the deeds
of their earthly speakers, are a fictive elaboration of these
Scriptural meanings. But in contrast to the eternal and
just decrees of Christ, who "hath power to cast into hell,"
are the fickle decrees of Fame, who, disclaiming any "justice," pronounces judgment on the suppliants' petitions:

> And somme of hem she graunted sone,
> And somme she werned wel and faire,
> And somme she graunted the contraire
> Of her axyng outterly. (1538-41)

In commenting on the "injustice" of Fame's awards,
Chaucer again betrays an attitude paralleling that of
Boethius, who at the beginning of Book IV of the *Consolation* similarly questions the justice of the unequal distribution of fame and other worldly awards to the good
and the wicked. Although both have come a long way in
understanding the vanity of seeking earthly fame, they
have yet to perceive the divine providence behind Fortune's and Fame's temporal decrees, or as Chaucer says of
Fame, "what her cause was":

> But thus I seye yow, trewely,
> What her cause was, y nyste.
> For of this folk ful wel y wiste,

---

individuals which at that time will be made visible to others. And then
it will be fulfilled: 'There is nothing covered that shall not be revealed.' When the final judgment comes, not only will the darkness of
the air be illumined, but the secrets of the heart will be made manifest.
By a divine power, therefore, it will come about that all of one's works,
whether good or evil, will be recalled to the memory, and with mar-
velous swiftness will be perceived by the mind's eye. The conscience
will either accuse or excuse the man, and by that witness he will be
damned or saved." Cf. Hugh of St. Victor, *De sacramentis*, Bk. II, Pt.
17, 22-23. These exegetical meanings are reflected in church art and in
the drama, for example, the York Judgment play, in which the souls
revealing their earthly deeds before God's throne bear resemblances to
the self-spoken words before Fame's throne. On the frequency of the
motif of the Last Judgment in fourteenth century English wall painting, see Tristram, pp. 18ff.

> They hadde good fame ech deserved
> Although they were dyversly served;
> Ryght as her suster, dame Fortune,
> Ys wont to serven in comune. (1542-48)

In comparing Fame to "her suster, dame Fortune," Chaucer ironically implies the answer to his problem. For as Philosophy carefully explains to Boethius, Fortune is nothing more than God's agent in the temporal order, and the awards she so "dyversly" serves are those which God himself dispenses but which sometimes seem unjust because man in his confusion has forgotten the justice of God's ways. Thus the "cause" of Fortune's fickleness lies not in herself but in divine providence, which in the temporal sphere is effected through her decrees. Fame's own providential role, suggested by her admission that she has no "justice," is implicit in her elevation to the rank of "her suster, dame Fortune" and in the description and function of her servant Aeolus, god of the winds, whom she now summons, along with his two trumpets, "Clere Laude" and "Sklaundre," to publish her judgments:

> "In Trace, ther ye shal him fynde,
> And bid him bringe his clarioun,
> That is ful dyvers of his soun,
> And hyt is cleped Clere Laude,
> With which he wont is to heraude
> Hem that me list ypreised be.
> And also bid him how that he
> Brynge his other clarioun,
> That highte Sklaundre in every toun,
> With which he wont is to diffame
> Hem that me liste, and do hem shame." (1572-82)

Aeolus' role as Fame's herald is explained more obviously by his winds and trumpets, both traditional symbols of worldly glory.[107] But behind this role is his less conspicu-

[107] Aeolus appears with two trumpets in *Libellus de deorum imaginibus*, ed. A. van Staveren, *Auctores mythographi latini* (Leyden, 1742),

ous function as an agent of providence, a function derived
from earlier poetry and mythography in which Aeolus is
sometimes depicted as the servant of Fortune and his winds
as symbols of worldly prosperity and adversity or the
various perturbations allowed by God to lead the mind to
devotion.[108] As an image of the empty and swollen rumor
that makes up worldly fame or infamy, his winds typify
the forces of cupidity which can destroy the life of the
spirit. Not inappropriately, therefore, is Aeolus said to
dwell in "a contree that highte Trace"—a windy region
to the north whose ice and snow and other adversities
connect it with evil.[109] Indicative of his providential role,
moreover, Aeolus' holding the winds "in distresse"—

> This Eolus, with harde grace,
> Held the wyndes in distresse,
> And gan hem under him to presse,
> That they gonne as beres rore,
> He bond and pressed hem so sore. . .

---

pp. 920ff. Cf. Liebeschütz, *Fulgentius metaforalis*, p. 121. On the
iconographic tradition of Aeolus and his winds, see Panofsky, *Studies
in Iconology*, pp. 45-46.

[108] In *De civitate Dei*, v, 26, Augustine comments on the providential
role of Aeolus and his winds in one of Claudian's poems. Neckam (*De
naturis rerum*, 1, 18) compares the winds to changes in fortune by
which minds formerly terrified are brought to devotion. Bernard, commenting on the storm brought against Aeneas by Juno, interprets
Aeolus' winds as the two temporal fortunes, prosperity and adversity,
which bring men's minds to the shipwreck of the vices (*Commentum*,
pp. 49-50, 79). On the connection of Aeolus' winds with Fortune, see
Patch, *The Goddess Fortuna*, pp. 101ff.

[109] Moralizing his description of the temple of Mars in *Teseida*, VII,
29-37 (Roncaglia, pp. 412-14), Boccaccio identifies Thrace as a very
cold region, subjected to the north wind, where Mars (*appetito iras-
cibile*) has his dwelling: "The house of Mars is in Thrace, in cold and
misty places filled with rain, winds, ice, savage beasts, and barren trees,
and in shadowy places unfriendly to the sun and full of noise. . . . He
says that it is misty [*nebuloso*] to show that anger obscures the counsel
of the reason, which he means by the rays of the sun, from which he
says the house of Mars hides itself. By the ice he means the coldness of
the angry mind, which, overpowered by increasing wrath, becomes
cruel, inflexible, and lacking in charity." In the Knight's Tale, 1,967ff.,

takes on a function similar to that of the four angels whom John sees "standing on the four corners of the earth, holding fast the four winds." Bersuire, following earlier commentary, identifies the four angels with wicked spirits and their winds with false elation or pride, temptation, and worldly prosperity and adversity.[110] These spirits, through whom God is to effect the final destruction of Babylon, are also identified with the angels who will go forth "with a trumpet and a great voice" to "gather together his elect from the four winds, from the farthest parts of the heavens to the utmost bounds of them."[111] Against this Apocalyptic background, Aeolus' two trumpets, "Clere Laude" and "Sklaundre," display the same ambivalence of other major symbols relating to Fame. As aspects of earthly fame, these gold and black trumpets signify respectively the praise and infamy—deserved or undeserved—proceeding from human judgment and opinion. At the same time, Aeolus' standing with his trumpets before the goddess's throne suggests the seven angels of the Apocalypse who stand with their trumpets before God's throne to carry out his judgments on the wicked.

Especially relevant to Aeolus' black trumpet "Sklaundre" is the trumpet of the fifth angel: "And the fifth angel sounded the trumpet, and I saw a star fall from heaven upon the earth, and there was given to him the key of the bottomless pit. And he opened the bottomless pit, and the smoke of the pit arose as the smoke of a

---

Chaucer similarly describes Thrace as a "colde, frosty regioun" where Mars has his "sovereyn mansioun."

[110] *Opera*, VI, 180. Bersuire relates the Apocalyptic passage (7:1) to Dan. 7:2.

[111] Matt. 24:31. Cf. Matt. 13:49-50; I Cor. 15:52. In the Man of Law's Tale, 491-96, Chaucer refers to the Apocalyptic winds as the "foure spirites of tempest" whose "comandour" is God. On the portrayal of these winds in medieval art, see Joan Evans' chapter on "quaternities" in *Cluniac Art of the Romanesque Period* (Cambridge, 1950), p. 119.

great furnace; and the sun and the air were darkened with the smoke of the pit" (9:1-2). One can hardly miss the echoes of this trumpet as Aeolus publishes Fame's judgment on the second group of suppliants:

> What dide this Eolus, but he
> Tok out hys blake trumpe of bras,
> That fouler than the devel was,
> And gan this trumpe for to blowe,
> As al the world shulde overthrowe,
> That thrughout every regioun
> Wente this foule trumpes soun,
> As swifte as pelet out of gonne,
> Whan fyr is in the poudre ronne.
> And such a smoke gan out wende
> Out of his foule trumpes ende,
> Blak, bloo, grenyssh, swartish red,
> As doth where that men melte led,
> Loo, al on high fro the tuel.
> And therto oo thing saugh I wel,
> That the ferther that hit ran,
> The gretter wexen hit began,
> As dooth the ryver from a welle,
> And hyt stank as the pit of helle. (1636-54)

Aeolus' foul "trumpe of bras" calls up the Apocalyptic trumpet most conspicuously by its sulphurous smoke, whose color and stench are indicative of the infamy and asperity of eternal damnation.[112] This meaning is further imaged in the blackness of the trumpet, the color symbolic of slander and detraction or of the sinfulness in which Satan clothes the spirit and leads it to Hell. A similar ambivalence is observable in the brass, whose connotations of both idolatry and damnation are exemplified by the

---

[112] Bersuire identifies this smoke [*fumus*] with the fire and brimstone [*sulphur*] wih which God will torment the worshipers of the Apocalyptic beast: "There is a certain sorrowful and painful smoke [*fumus tristabilis et dolorosus*], and this is the smoke of Hell fire and everlasting punishment of which the Apocalypse speaks [14:11]: 'And the smoke of their torments shall ascend up for ever and ever'" (*Opera*, IV, 235).

story of Dido portrayed on the "table of bras" in the temple of Venus. Although Fame's fickle decrees connect these details with worldly infamy, the Apocalyptic allusions become explicit in the references to "the pit of helle," the "devel," and the "overthrowe" of the world. Equally suggestive is the sound of Aeolus' trumpet, whose reverberation is "as lowde as beloweth wynd in helle." In John's vision the wailful sound of the fifth trumpet expresses the weeping and desolation of the damned at the Last Judgment.[113] This solemn reminder of doomsday perhaps explains the ominous presence of the sea god Triton, whom Chaucer has borrowed from his maritime surroundings to bear Aeolus' two trumpets and to stand beside him somewhat eerily as he publishes Fame's judgments. As observed earlier, Triton is commonly interpreted as "contrition," or "tribulation of the flesh," and his trumpet is said to sing with a voice of lamentation "because the tribulations of the flesh emit a sound of wailing or tears." Thus his trumpet is contrasted with the vainglorious trumpet of Misenus, who is overcome in his contest with Triton because the voice of contrition or tribulation "extinguishes the appetite for glory."[114]

Apocalyptic details are also detectable in Aeolus' golden trumpet "Clere Laude," whose sweet odor of roses accompanies Fame's judgments on the third and fifth groups of suppliants:

[113] *Ibid.*, IV, 234: "There is a wailing [*ululatus*] of sorrow and torment, and this is the wailing of the damned; for, truly, just as a wolf caught in a snare wails from desperation, so the damned imprisoned in Hell are accustomed to utter a wailing of despair." Bersuire connects this meaning with the smoke "which makes the damned weep through endless desolation but which should make us weep through fear and contrition" (IV, 235).

[114] Bernard, *Commentum*, pp. 11-12, 60-61. In *Mythographus Vaticanus III*, p. 183, Triton is interpreted etymologically as *contritum*. Bersuire associates Triton's trumpet with the Apocalyptic trumpets (*Opera*, II, 289).

And, certes, al the breth that wente
Out of his trumpes mouth it smelde
As men a pot of bawme helde
Among a basket ful of roses. (1684-87)

In contrast to the sulphurous stench of "Sklaundre," the
fragrance of "Clere Laude" designates "good fame," the
worldly renown manifested in human praise. This meaning is conveyed by the odor of roses to which this fragrance
is compared, an image of the praise emanating from
virtuous deeds and redounding to God's glory.[115] But as
Augustine and other Christian writers make clear, this
outward odor of praise is but the "accident" or "shadow"
of good fame, not its "substance." For just as virtue may
be slandered, so may evil be praised, as is apparent in the
deceptive fragrance sometimes accompanying the deeds
of the hypocrite. For this reason, the fragrance of true
fame expresses an inward relationship with God that has
nothing to do with the worldly praise of Aeolus' golden
trumpet. This truth is subtly implied by the Apocalyptic
imagery as the odor of "Clere Laude" spreads over the
world and "atte last" goes "on-lofte." Just as the odor of
the black trumpet suggests the stench of the "pit of helle,"
so this sweet smell of roses going "on-lofte" suggests the
smoke of incense accompanying the prayers presented by
the angel (Christ) upon the altar before God's throne.
Unlike the sulphurous smoke of Hell, this is the smoke,
says Bersuire, which comes from the furnace of the heart
—"where there is a fire of charity and love"—and which
is borne upward to God.[116]

---

[115] Bersuire compares the odor of good fame to the fragrance of the
rose: "Just as a good and lasting odor reveals that the substance [*sub-
stantiam*] of the thing from which it emanates is pure and good, as is
apparent in the rose, so a good fragrance proclaims that the one to
whom it belongs is virtuous and good" (*ibid.*, IV, 185). On the related image of the rose of charity and martyrdom, see Robertson,
Preface, p. 96, n. 82, especially p. 225, n. 138.

[116] *Opera*, IV, 235. The Apocalyptic passage (8:2-4) is evoked by

If these Apocalyptic implications of Aeolus and his trumpets are kept in mind, the drama of Fame and her awards is cast into an intensely ironic light. The irony stems not only from the implied contrast between Christ's eternal judgments and the willful judgments of the goddess, who, as she herself admits, has no "justice" in her, but also from the attitudes of the suppliants, who appeal to her variously on the basis of their "werkes." In each instance the Christian norm behind the irony is the fact that true fame has nothing to do with the goddess's temporal decrees. Or to apply Philosophy's comment on Fortune, Fame has no control over the mind whose thoughts are in harmony with God. This basic irony is underscored by the remarks of Chaucer the pilgrim, who, at this point, is confident that all the suppliants appealing to their good deeds "hadde good fame ech deserved" even though "they were dyversly served" by the goddess. That Chaucer does not yet perceive the "cause" of Fame's apparent willfulness should not be weighed too heavily against him; for even though he should be aware that God alone is the dispenser of both earthly and heavenly fame, only at the end of the world, as Augustine says, will God's ways in temporal affairs be fully understood.[117] Nevertheless, his assurance that the "good werkes" of the first few groups are equally deserving of praise reflects a confusion between the outward appearance of their good deeds and the inner motives prompting them. Since the substance of true fame is virtue, it is the virtue that is rewarded, not the good works. Thus Chaucer's indiscriminate sympathy for the

---

the trumpet itself, whose gold and sweet savor suggest an inversion of the golden censer of the angel before the altar. In the Second Nun's Tale, 218-59, the odor of roses accompanies the conversion of the martyr Valerian.

[117] *De civitate Dei*, XX, 2. As a possible pun on Fame's providential role, cf. her pronouncement on the first group: "Ye gete of me good fame non,/ Be God" (1,560-61).

suppliants is in large part misdirected. For of the nine groups petitioning the goddess, only two, the fourth and the fifth—who want no earthly praise for their good deeds —exemplify the proper Christian attitude toward fame. All the rest exhibit the idolatry of those who have confused the goddess's grace with that of God and have therefore subjected themselves to her fickle decrees.

The pattern for those who appeal to their good works is set by the petition of the first group:

> "Madame," seyde they, "we be
> Folk that here besechen the
> That thou graunte us now good fame,
> And let our werkes han that name;
> In ful recompensacioun
> Of good werkes, yive us good renoun." (1553-58)

Although Chaucer is confident that this group "seyden sooth, and noght a lye," we may detect beneath their outward profession of good works the hidden motive of vainglory which Christ condemns in those who wish to be known for their works: "Take heed that you do not your justice before men to be seen by them; otherwise you shall not have reward of your Father who is in heaven." In asking for praise, these suppliants betray their affinity with those who wish their deeds to be trumpeted before them, as do the hypocrites, who want "fame without virtue" and feign an appearance of charity to "hide the iniquity of their hearts."[118] The oblivion awarded to the first group is not without its "justice." But that Fame's judgments have little to do with merit is illustrated by her disparate awards to the second and third groups— infamy to the one and praise to the other. Both, like the first group, appeal to their good works, the second in "honour of gentilesse":

---

[118] Bersuire, *Opera*, IV, 185. Cf. v, 183. For Christ's warning, see Matt. 6:1-2.

"Lady, graunte us now good fame,
And lat oure werkes han that name
Now in honour of gentilesse,
And also God your soule blesse!
For we han wel deserved hyt,
Therfore is ryght that we ben quyt." (1609-14)

In spite of Fame's avowal that they have well deserved "good loos," this group's appeal to "gentilesse" is somewhat suspect. True "gentilesse," as Philosophy remarks, has nothing to do with "the rumour of the peple" but is based upon "the sothfastnesse of conscience."[119] The "gentilesse" to which these suppliants appeal, however, has been observed already in the heralds who "crien ryche folkes laudes" and bear the famous "armes" of "chevalrie." Since the infamy awarded to this group, like the oblivion of the first, is not undeserved, Aeolus' blast on his black trumpet—the trumpet that "stank as the pit of helle"—has its ironic reverberations. Like the trumpet of the fifth angel, it reminds us that another kind of infamy—the infamy of damnation—will be the reward of all those who cover their falseness in the clothing of piety. Chaucer's pity for these "sory creatures" reveals that he still has much to learn about his "neyghebores":

"Allas!" thoughte I, "what aventures
Han these sory creatures!
For they, amonges al the pres,
Shul thus be shamed gilteles.
But what! hyt moste nedes be." (1631-35)

Whereas Fame's awards to the first and second groups seem to be no more than they deserve, the same can hardly be said of her judgment on the third group, who likewise appeal to their good works. Although their motive would appear to be neither better nor worse than the

---

[119] *De consolatione philosophiae*, III, Pr. 6. Cf. III, Met. 6. On the distinction, see also Chaucer's "Gentilesse" and the Wife of Bath's Prologue, 1,109ff., where Dante is the authority.

motives of the other two, the goddess permits their works
not only to be known but also to have "better loos,"

> "Right in dispit of alle your foos,
> Than worthy is, and that anoon." (1668-69)

The inflated, unmerited praise awarded to the third group
is easily recognized as the empty, swollen rumor—rooted
in erroneous human judgment—which magnifies men's
deeds and, like the beryl of Fame's castle, distorts the
truth until it seems more than it is. Such is the false, temporal prosperity which, Augustine says, is sometimes
granted to the wicked in order to teach the virtuous the
vanity of trusting earthly goods.[120] Like the stench of the
black trumpet, therefore, the sweet odor accompanying
Fame's judgment on this group has its irony. For this
smell of roses is not the fragrance of virtue ascending
to God with the prayers of the faithful; it is the false,
alluring odor with which Satan tempts men to pursue
the praise of the world.

In pronounced contrast to these seekers of praise are
the fourth and fifth groups, who ask for no fame at all,
since their works were performed not for praise but for
virtue's sake and the love of God. Accordingly, the petition of the fourth group—who, revealingly, are "wonder
fewe"—is that their works be "hid":

> "Certes, lady bryght,
> We han don wel with al our myght,
> But we ne kepen have no fame.
> Hyde our werkes and our name,
> For Goddys love, for certes we
> Han certeyn doon hyt for bounte,
> And for no maner other thing." (1693-99)

The virtue ("bounte") to which these suppliants appeal

[120] *De civitate Dei*, I, 8.

has its counterpart in the "contemplacioun" of the fifth group:

> And to hir thoo besoughten alle
> To hide her goode werkes ek,
> And seyden they yeven noght a lek
> For fame ne for such renoun;
> For they for contemplacioun
> And Goddess love hadde ywrought,
> Ne of fame wolde they nought. (1706-12)

Since both of these groups performed their good deeds for "Goddys love" and not for praise, they exemplify those in whom inward motive and outward speech are in accord; or, to apply Chaucer's earlier imagery, their words are "clothed" in the red of truth, not in the black of falsehood. Thus, in asking that their works be hid, they fulfill Christ's precept: "And when thou dost alms, let not thy left hand know what thy right hand doth, that thy alms may be in secret; and thy Father, who seeth in secret, will repay thee."[121] Fame's awards to these two groups—oblivion and praise respectively—are the high point of this ironic drama of earthly fame. For of all those who seek her "grace," these are the only ones over whom her fickle decrees have no real control. Since their praise is heavenly praise, not the unstable praise of men, the goddess's disparate awards are at most a proof of the vanity of trusting her gifts. Also, her judgment on the fourth group—"let your werkes be ded!"—merely reminds us that according to Scripture works based upon faith and "Goddys love" are never dead, even though they may go unpraised on earth. Like those whose names are almost obliterated on the south side of Fame's "roche of yse,"

---

[121] Matt. 6:3-4. Cf. Augustine's and Bede's glosses (chap. 1, n. 18, above). At the beginning of *Perceval*, Chrétien follows the commentaries in identifying the left hand with vainglory, which stems from hypocrisy, and the right hand with charity, which does not boast of its good works but hides them so that no one knows of them except God.

these are the ones whose sins have been melted by the heat of charity or the Holy Spirit and who are now remembered by God: "And there are some of whom there is no memorial: who are perished, as if they had never been. . . . But these were men of mercy, whose godly deeds have not failed."[122] This truth is brought home with even greater irony as Fame pronounces judgment on the fifth group: "Nay, ye shul lyven everychon!" Nor should we overlook the Apocalyptic parallel as the sweet odor of "Clere Laude" spreads throughout the world and at last goes "on-lofte."

In the sixth and seventh groups, Chaucer again dramatizes the attitudes of those who seek earthly praise. But unlike the first three groups, who at least can appeal to their good works, these are the "ydel" or slothful who have performed no works at all but who wish nonetheless to have

> as good a fame,
> And gret renoun and knowen name,
> As they that han doon noble gestes,
> And acheved alle her lestes,
> As wel of love as other thyng. (1735-39)

As Fame herself characterizes the seventh group,

> "These ben they that wolde honour
> Have, and do noskynnes labour,
> Ne doo no good, and yet han lawde." (1793-95)

These suppliants, who have done "neither that ne this," exhibit the attitude of those who are condemned by the angel in the Apocalypse: "I know thy works, that thou art neither cold nor hot."[123] Such laxity in performing good works, says Chaucer's Parson, stems from sloth, because

. . . he that is enclyned to synne, hym thynketh it is so greet an emprise for to undertake to doon werkes of goodnesse,/

[122] Ecclus. 44:9-10.   [123] Apoc. 3:15.

and casteth in his herte that the circumstaunces of goodnesse been so grevouse and so chargeaunt for to suffre, that he dar nat undertake to do werkes of goodnesse.[124]

In wanting fame without works, Fame humorously remarks, these two groups are like the lazy cat that wants fish but "wolde nothing wete his clowes." Their hypocrisy is amusingly illustrated by the sixth group's request to have fame as lovers even though they have received neither "broche ne ryng" from women. Their appeal to "Goddes love" echoes ironically the petition of the fourth and fifth groups:

> "For Goddes love, that sit above,
> Thogh we may not the body have
> Of wymmen, yet, so God yow save,
> Leet men gliwe on us the name! . . ."

Although the seventh group's request is the same, Fame's unequal awards are true to her nature. To one she grants —"withouten slouthe"—the unmerited praise of the golden trumpet; to the other she gives, "justly" enough, the infamy of the black, evil-smelling trumpet that sounds as "lowde as beloweth wynd in helle."

The same apparent willfulness marks Fame's judgments on the last two groups—the eighth and the ninth—who, though prompted by different motives, have one characteristic in common: their deeds of crime and violence. Unlike the two preceding groups, who have done "neither that ne this," both of these have consciously pursued evil acts, such as those of the eighth group,

> That had ydoon the trayterye,
> The harm, the grettest wikkednesse
> That any herte kouthe gesse. (1812-14)

Although the suppliants in this group do not receive the fame with which they wish to conceal their wickedness,

---

[124] Lines 690ff. Cf. Rabanus, *PL*, 112, col. 1,215.

neither do they get the infamy they deserve. Instead, their evil works remain in oblivion; for, Fame explains, in a masterpiece of understatement, "hyt were a vice" to give them praise:

> "Al be ther in me no justice,
> Me lyste not to doo hyt now,
> Ne this nyl I not graunte yow." (1820-22)

With obvious "justice," however, does Fame oblige the ninth group, who not only deserve their infamy but even request it; for these deliberately seek notoriety and, as they explain to the goddess, rejoice in their wickedness and in being known as "shrewes":

> "Lady, leef and dere,
> We ben suche folk as ye mowe here.
> To tellen al the tale aryght,
> We ben shrewes, every wyght,
> And han delyt in wikkednesse,
> As goode folk han in godnesse;
> And joye to be knowen shrewes,
> And ful of vice and wikked thewes;
> Wherefore we praye yow, a-rowe,
> That oure fame such be knowe
> In alle thing ryght as hit ys." (1827-37)

If we classify Fame's suppliants according to the nature or the degree of their guilt (excepting the fourth and fifth groups, who desire only oblivion), we can detect a progression from those seeking fame for their good works and those seeking fame without works to these "shrewes" willfully seeking notoriety for their vicious deeds. For though the craving for fame, says John of Salisbury, is always a fault, no matter what the motive, a much deadlier error is the desire to be known for one's crimes. Such a seeker of notoriety was Pausanias, who slew Philip of Macedon and thereby perpetuated his own infamous name. Another was Herostratus, who set fire to the temple of

Diana at Ephesus "so that his name would be spread over the entire world."[125] Although Chaucer substitutes the temple of Isis at Athens, it is presumably this notorious personage, adorned with "pale" and "belle," who is spokesman for the ninth group and who identifies himself at Fame's behest:

> "Madame," quod he, "soth to telle,
> I am that ylke shrewe, ywis,
> That brende the temple of Ysidis
> In Athenes, loo, that citee." (1842-45)

Just as "other folk," he explains, receive "gret renoun" for "her vertu and for her thewes," so he "wolde fayn han had a fame" even though "hit be for shrewednesse":

> "And sith y may not have that oon,
> That other nyl y noght forgoon.
> And for to gette of Fames hire,
> The temple sette y al afire.
> Now do our loos be blowen swithe,
> As wisly be thou ever blythe!" (1855-60)

Although Fame "gladly" obliges the ninth group with a sound from the black trumpet, we can again catch overtones of the Apocalyptic trumpet as Aeolus "gan to puffen and to blaste" until their infamy spread to "the worldes ende." This punning allusion to the Last Judgment gives even more poignancy to John of Salisbury's warning that a far greater madness than destroying the temple of Diana is that of destroying the temple of the Holy Spirit.

Fame's judgment on the ninth group concludes Chaucer's dynamic and richly connotative allegory of the god-

---

[125] *Policraticus*, VIII, 5. John's examples come from Valerius Maximus, *Factorum et dictorum memorabilium libri novem*, VIII, 14 ("De cupiditate gloriae"). Chaucer's last two groups, who glory in their wickedness, are condemned in Ps. 51: "Why dost thou glory in malice, thou that art mighty in iniquity? All the day long thy tongue hath devised injustice: as a sharp razor, thou hast wrought deceit." On the frequent illustration of this Psalm in manuscript illumination, see Robertson, *Preface*, p. 164.

dess and her awards. Her fickle decrees of praise, slander, and oblivion, irrespective of merit, leave no doubt as to the temporal nature of her judgments. At the same time, the attitude of the fourth and fifth groups of suppliants and the accompanying Apocalyptic symbolism suggest that behind Fame's seemingly willful awards lies an eternal order of justice opposed to the unstable opinion of mankind. Chaucer's confusion as to the "cause" of the goddess's willfulness indicates that his education in the nature of fame is not yet complete. Appropriately, therefore, the focus of the allegory shifts once more to his search for tidings; and the problem of fame, hitherto objectified in Fame and her awards, is again brought into relationship with the motif of the pilgrimage. Although Chaucer has yet to hear tidings which will clarify his confused notions about fame, he has nevertheless learned in Fame's court significant truths preparing him for what he will later see and hear. What he has and has not learned up to this point is made clear in the brief but revealing conversation with the mysterious stranger behind his back who addresses him as "frend," asks him about his business in the House of Fame, and finally directs him to the whirling "hous" in the valley below the castle.

Although an aura of mystery surrounds this unidentified figure who so curiously questions Chaucer, his possible identity is suggested by several details, one of which is his position behind the dreamer's back. Like the position of the castle gate on the "ryght hond," this detail has both a good and an evil significance in Scriptural commentary. Thus in the Prophecy of Isaiah the voice spoken behind the back is the voice of reason or Christ, who warns men to follow the path of virtue: "And thy ears shall hear the word of one admonishing thee behind thy back: This is the way; walk ye in it, and go not aside, neither to the

right hand nor to the left.''[126] Christ is also identified
with the Apocalyptic angel whose voice John hears behind
his back, admonishing him to record all that he sees and
hears: "I was in the spirit on the Lord's day, and heard
behind me a great voice, as of a trumpet.''[127] In view of
Chaucer's inversion of Scriptural details, we may perhaps
safely assume that the voice addressing him behind his
back is neither the voice of reason nor that of any heavenly
messenger. Rather, by his position, the stranger enacts a
role more in keeping with the worldly environment of
Fame. In relation to cupidity, his position behind Chaucer's back is the position of subjection to which Christ
consigned Satan and all his followers who would tempt
men with fame and other temporalia: "Go behind me,
Satan, thou art a scandal unto me, because thou savourest
not the things that are of God, but the things that are of
men.''[128] Not only is the stranger's position the same as
Satan's in the role of the tempter; it is also, with equal
appropriateness to Chaucer's allegory, the position of the
detractor or backbiter, who, as the Parson says, sometimes
"preiseth his neighebor" to his face but slanders him behind his back.[129] Considered in this light, the subtle questioning of Chaucer by this strange personage who calls
him "frend" is suggestive of the Scriptural warning

[126] Is. 30:21. Haymo (*PL*, 116, cols. 867-68) identifies the voice
behind the back [*post tergum*] as the voice of Christ exhorting be-
lievers to follow him, the true way: "I am the way, and the truth, and
the life" (John 14:6). Cf. *Glossa ordinaria, PL*, 113, col. 1,275.

[127] Apoc. 1:10.

[128] Matt. 16:23. Alanus identifies *post* and *retro* with things of this
world (*Distinctiones, PL*, 210, col. 926). Bersuire, citing Jos. 8:14,
associates *post tergum* with the deceitfulness of the wicked (*Opera*, v,
269). The image of devils behind the back is a frequent motif in
medieval art. See Tristram, pp. 103, 108-10.

[129] Lines 493ff. Bersuire identifies *retro* with detractors (*Opera*, II,
401; III, 46-47). In the *Roman de la Rose*, 777ff., the position is assigned to the flatterer who slanders behind the back. Cf. *Piers Plowman*, B, XIII, 321-24. As Tristram illustrates (pp. 108ff.), devils are
portrayed especially behind the backs of janglers and backbiters.

against the friend who offers counsel but who "layeth a snare."[130] Thus Satan himself, in the guise of the hunter or fowler, is the false friend who by crafty speech leads the unwary pilgrim astray and captures him in the snare of sin. In these terms the stranger's greeting Chaucer as "frend" betrays the sophistry which is an inseparable attribute of Satan in this role.[131] Similarly, Chaucer's comment—"me thoughte [he] goodly to me spak"—suggests the insidious manner of the questioning, the subtle probing to see just where the dreamer's heart lies.[132] The question—"Artow come hider to han fame?"—brings the motif of temptation into view. But Chaucer's reply indicates that his "frend" will get nowhere on this score:

> "Nay, for sothe, frend," quod y;
> "I cam noght hyder, graunt mercy,
> For no such cause, by my hed!
> Sufficeth me, as I were dede,
> That no wight have my name in honde.

[130] Ecclus. 37:1-7. Cf. Ecclus. 37:21; 51:3; Prov. 29:5.

[131] On Satan in this role, see Robertson, "Why the Devil Wears Green," *MLN*, LXIX (1954), 470-72, and B. G. Koonce, "Satan the Fowler," *MS*, XXI (1959), 176-84, in which Scriptural and literary examples are discussed. On the appearance of the same figure in manuscript illumination, see Robertson, *Preface*, pp. 94-95. In Scripture, *vox*, in an evil sense, can designate *suggestio diabolis* or *hostis* (*Allegoriae in sacram scripturam*, col. 1,083). In the Friar's Tale, 1,412ff., the sophistry of Satan is depicted in the "softe speche" with which he ensnares the summoner under the pretense of friendship.

[132] The "frend" and his "goodly" voice parallel the earlier description of the eagle (II, 554ff.), who also calls Chaucer "frend" and speaks to him with a "goodly" voice. In traditional commentary, the voice of the true friend [*amicus*]—Christ or his followers, whose friendship stems from reason and charity—is contrasted with the voice of the false friend "who is a Christian in name only" (*Allegoriae in sacram Scripturam*, col. 857). In Matt. 22:12—the basis of the preceding gloss—this contrast appears in the parable of the wedding feast, where the false friend denotes those who are unworthy of participating in the wedding feast of Christ the Bridegroom. The parallel between the question put to the sinning guest ("Friend, how camest thou in hither not having on a wedding garment?") and the question put to Chaucer ("Frend, . . . what doost thou here than?") suggests a further inversion of Apocalyptic meanings in the details of Fame's abode.

246

> I wot myself best how y stonde;
> For what I drye, or what I thynke,
> I wil myselven al hyt drynke,
> Certeyn, for the more part,
> As fer forth as I kan myn art." (1873-82)

The possible pun at the beginning of Chaucer's reply—
"Nay, for sothe"—should not be overlooked. In any
event, it is clear from his attitude that his contemplation
of Fame's "feble fundament," falsely resplendent castle,
and fickle awards has not been without "lore" and profit,
as the eagle promised earlier. Even though he may not
understand the "cause" of Fame's fickleness or the unequal
deserts of those who have performed "good werkes," he
at least has had tangible evidence ("preve") that any
trust in earthly renown is at best a vain and fleeting consolation. As he tells his "frend," although he has always
known that "somme folk han desired fame," "loos," and
"name," not until now has he known "how" and "where"
Fame lived, her "descripcioun" and "condicioun," and
"the ordre of her dom." But Chaucer's knowledge of
fame is still incomplete. He has observed, as it were, the
end product of rumor as crystallized in the goddess's fickle
awards. He has yet to complete the picture by viewing
the origin of these awards in the irrationality of men's
hearts: the confusion of truth and falsehood which makes
up the tidings of his "verray neyghebores." Of greater
importance, he needs to hear "glad" tidings of a "fer
contree" which will remind him that behind the temporal
judgments of mankind lies an eternal order of justice and
rewards. In his own words to his "frend," he must learn
some "newe tydynges,"

> "Somme newe thinges, y not what,
> Tydynges, other this or that,
> Of love, or suche thynges glade." (1886-89)

In these tidings of "newe thinges" or "newe tydynges" of
love "or suche thynges glade" we can again recognize
those glad tidings of the New Law of charity and future
salvation which in Proverbs are identified with the heavenly "far country" and which in Chaucer's allegory are
implied throughout as the opposite of the idolatrous love
symbolized by the worship of Venus and Fame. More
particularly, Chaucer's imagery derives from the Gospels
and Acts 17:16-34 where tidings of "new things" (*nova*)
are defined as Christ's "new doctrine" of the Resurrection
and God's coming judgment on the good and the wicked:
"He hath appointed a day wherein he will judge the world
in equity, by the man whom he hath appointed, giving
faith to all by raising him up from the dead."[133] Chaucer's
quest for these tidings of a "fer contree," along with the
worldly tidings of his "verray neyghebores," controls the
remainder of the allegory. This quest is fulfilled in the
revolving "hous" in the valley beneath the castle to which
his "frend" now directs him and where, he is assured,
he will hear many a tiding.

Whoever this obliging "frend" might be, he has led
Chaucer where Satan the fowler would wish to lead him:
to the snare or cage of the world. This meaning of the
whirling house is implicit in its many details, including
those borrowed from Ovid, whose personified rumors
have been transferred "bodily" to a new abode. The division of the Ovidian house of Rumor into two separate
houses—a House of Fame and a House of Tidings—is
part of Chaucer's attempt in Books II and III to adapt
his pagan imagery to the Christian contrast between earthly
and heavenly fame. Whereas the House of Fame is an
idolatrous reversal of the Scriptural "fer contree," the
heavenly Paradise or house which is the source and end
of true fame, the House of Tidings is an image of its

[133] Cf. Mark 1:27.

opposite, the "house" of the world, the dwelling of those earthly "words" of truth and falsehood which, as images of the soul, ascend to God's house to be recorded for future judgment. Viewed in this broad perspective, the House of Tidings, the valley, and the mountain and castle of Fame compose a larger Scriptural pattern bringing this contrast into vivid focus. All the elements of the pattern appear in the opening description of the "hous":

> Tho saugh y stonde in a valeye,
> Under the castel, faste by,
> An hous, that Domus Dedaly,
> That Laboryntus cleped ys,
> Nas mad so wonderlych, ywis,
> Ne half so queyntelych ywrought.
> And ever mo, as swyft as thought,
> This queynte hous aboute wente,
> That never mo hyt stille stente. (1918-26)

In the Prologue to *Piers Plowman*, where a similar pattern of imagery occurs, the "toure on a toft"—like the house or castle on a mountain—is a symbol of the heavenly Jerusalem, the abode of Truth and her daughter Holy Church. At the other extreme, the "depe dale" or valley beneath the tower signifies Hell, the dark "dongeon" in which the souls of the damned are held in captivity. Between the tower and the valley lies a "faire felde ful of folke," an image of the world, or Babylon, where a few pilgrims follow the road to Truth but most are caught in the maze of cupidity.[134] Although Fame's mountain and house are inversions of the holy mountain and city, their ambivalent Scriptural meanings, along with the symbolism of the valley, suggest a contrast similar to that between the tower and the "depe dale"—the opposing

---

[134] On the exegetical meanings of these images, see Robertson and Huppé, *Piers Plowman*, pp. 35ff. Both the tower and Holy Church appear as symbols in *The Shepherd of Hermas*.

goals of man's pilgrimage.[135] Chaucer's equivalent of the "felde ful of folke" is the revolving house in the valley beneath the castle. The worldly nature of this house is mirrored in its ceaseless whirling "as swyft as thought"— a conventional comparison applied both to Fortune's turning wheel and to the contrast between temporal bliss and "the joy that is eterne":

> For present tyme abidith nought;
> It is more swift than any thought.
> So litel while it doth endure
> That ther nys compte ne mesure.[136]

Chaucer, we should bear in mind, is observing this whirling house from the outside, that is, from the vantage point of reason and contemplation; therefore he sees it for what it really is: a "Domus Dedaly" or "Laboryntus"—the labyrinthine "house of Daedalus" which in Christian mythography has become a symbol of the maze of the world or the mind in which the guidance of reason has been lost. Thus Boethius uses the image to characterize his own confusion when he accuses Philosophy of leading him into a maze of reasoning—a "hous of Dedalus, so entrelaced that it is unable to been unlaced."[137] Bersuire,

---

[135] As Patch copiously illustrates (*The Other World*, pp. 87, 95, 118-19, 133), the castle and valley are closely related images in literary allegory, where the valley is often associated with Hell. Bersuire interprets *vallis* anagogically as *infernus* or *status damnatorum*. Allegorically, it is the world [*mundus*], for "just as the valley is by nature a darker place [*locus obscurior*], more remote from heaven and closer to hell, so the world and the worldly person are darkened by ignorance, vices and sins" (*Opera*, VI, 167).

[136] *Roman de la Rose*, Mid. Eng. trans., 5,023-26. Cf. *HF*, III, 1,257-58. Tristram (pp. 27-28) discusses the image in relation to the Wheels of Fortune and Life portrayed on medieval church walls. Cf. Lydgate, *Reson and Sensuallyte*, 1,901ff.: "thy lyff . . . ys lyk a cercle that goth aboute, round and swyfft as any thouht, wych in hys course ne cesset nouht . . . tyl he kam to hys restyng place wych ys in God."

[137] III, Pr. 12, 154ff. On *domus* as a Scriptural symbol of the mind, see *Allegoriae in sacram scripturam*, col. 911. For the pagan source of

moralizing Ovid's account of Daedalus in the *Metamorphoses*, interprets the labyrinth as the world, or Babylon, and its artificer as God, who guides men through its maze.[138] From such a maze, as we have seen, Chaucer and Boethius are rescued by their intellectual flights with the eagle and Philosophy. For if one is to extricate himself from the house of Daedalus, remarks Bersuire, he must put on wings of contemplation and fly mentally to Paradise.

That the House of Tidings is a "Domus Dedaly," an image of the world or Babylon, is suggested more particularly by its maze-like structure, which is shaped "lyk a cage":

> And al thys hous of which I rede
> Was mad of twigges, falwe, rede,
> And grene eke, and somme weren white,
> Swiche as men to these cages thwite,
> Or maken of these panyers,
> Or elles hottes or dossers;
> That, for the swough and for the twygges,
> This hous was also ful of gygges,
> And also ful eke of chirkynges,
> And of many other werkynges. . . (1935-44)

In the "twygges," "gygges," and bird-like "chirkynges" of this cage we have a familiar guise of Satan the fowler's snare: the cage of the world in which he ensnares unwary souls (the birds) in the "twygges" of sin. Thus St. Jerome,

---

Chaucer's image, see Ovid, *Metamorphoses*, VIII, 158ff., and *Aeneid*, V, 588, VI, 27ff., where it appears as both *labyrinthus* and *domus*.

[138] *Ovidius moralizatus*, IX (pp. 129-30). Cf. *Ovide moralisé*, VIII, 1767-1867. In *Piers Plowman*, B, I, 6, the image of the maze is applied to the "felde ful of folke," a symbol of the world. In medieval cathedrals, the labyrinth was frequently represented on the floor of the nave and used by penitents, who followed the maze on their knees to the center—a figure for the soul's pilgrimage through the maze of Babylon to the heavenly Jerusalem. See Evans, *Art in Mediaeval France*, pp. 87, 112; Robertson, *Preface*, p. 373. An illustration appears in the sketchbook of Villard de Honnecourt.

commenting on the Scriptural fowler and his snare, contrasts those birds who follow their true nature and fly
above the earth with those others who "lose the wings by
which they were once borne heavenward" and fall to
earth where they are caught in the viscous lime of sin.[139]
Along with the birds, the image of the cage echoes the
Apocalypse, where the angel of "great authority" compares Babylon to a stronghold "of every unclean and hateful bird" which will be destroyed at the Last Judgment.[140] This warning of the destruction of the world is
aptly expressed by the material of Chaucer's cage, whose
"tymber"—unlike the "timber" of Solomon's house, a
symbol of the strength of Holy Church—is "of no
strengthe" and "is founded to endure" only as long as

> hyt lyst to Aventure,
> That is the moder of tydynges,
> As the see of welles and of sprynges.[141]

[139] *PL*, 25, col. 1,065 (on Amos 3:5). Haymo, glossing the same
passage, identifies the fowler [*auceps*] with the devil, who captures the
elect, like birds, in the snare of the world (*PL*, 117, col. 111). In
Ecclus. 11:32-33, the cage [*cavea*] is associated specifically with the
partridge as an example of those easily caught in the "snares of the
deceitful." Bersuire applies this passage to the sinner, who, like a bird
lured into the fowler's net, is enticed to sins and vices by the delights of
the world or flesh (*Opera*, IV, 355). In Chaucer's "cage," this context
is called up particularly by the "gygges," an obsolete meaning of which
is "a set of feathers arranged so as to revolve rapidly in the wind, for
the purpose of attracting birds to a net" (*OED*). On the meaning of
"chirkynges" as the sound of birds, see *OED* and the Summoner's Tale,
l. 1804.

[140] Apoc. 18:1ff. The King James Bible translates *custodia* (Vulg.)
in this passage as "cage." In Ezech. 19:8-9, the cage is an image of
Jerusalem's captivity in the chains of Babylon: "And the nations came
together against him on every side out of the provinces, and they
spread their net over him. . . . And they put him into a cage [*caveam*];
they brought him in chains to the king of Babylon, and they cast him
into prison, that his voice should no more be heard upon the mountains
of Israel."

[141] In Zach. 5:4, the destruction of Babylon is foreshadowed in the
house which God will cause to be consumed "with the timber [*ligna*]
thereof." Cf. Ezech. 26:12; Hab. 2:11. For the contrasting timber of
Solomon's house, see III Kings 5:18; 6:9-10.

As in the earlier description of the gate to Fame's castle, the association of this whirling house with Aventure is merely another proof of its transitoriness, for "aventure," like "hap" and Fortune, is a Christian image of God's temporal order, which appears to be confused only because men fail to perceive the providential plan behind it. This meaning is evoked by the comparison of Aventure—"the moder of tydynges"—to the sea, the source of "welles and of sprynges," imagery used by Lady Philosophy to explain the "welle of purveaunce" from which springs the seemingly willful play of "hap" or "aventure" in the world.[142] In this Boethian context, Chaucer's attributing the longevity of his whirling house to Aventure reminds us further of the divine disposition behind the world and its temporality. In short, like the cage of Babylon whose destruction is foretold by the angel of "great authority," this time-ridden cage with its timber "of no strengthe" is destined to endure only as long as God, who created the world, allows it to endure. This Apocalyptic warning perhaps explains the reference to the size of the cage, which is "sixty myle of lengthe," a detail, like the timber, suggesting an inversion of Solomon's house, whose dimension, "sixty cubits in length," says Bede, designates the long-suffering of Holy Church, "which patiently endures various adversities during the exile of its pilgrimage until it arrives at the native country it is awaiting." For "sixty" is formed from "six" (*senarius*), the number signifying the completion of God's work at Creation and the perfection of all good works. Thus "it is necessary, through long-suffering, to bear the adversities of our pilgrimage

---

[142] *De consolatione philosophiae*, v, Pr. 1, 91-99; Met., 1, 1-11. Cf. Eccles. 1:7. Although Boethius explains "aventure" as an aspect of Fortune (for example, 1, Pr. 4), sometimes, like Chaucer's Aventure and Fame, it is personified with the special functions of Fortune. See Patch, *The Goddess Fortuna*, pp. 39-40.

so that we will be worthy of entering the promised land, whenever it appears, by virtue of our good works."[143]

The remaining details describing the House of Tidings evoke other contexts—Scriptural and pagan—which point up the contrast between temporal and eternal. Borrowed from Ovid are the many "entrees" or "holes" that stay open both day and night to emit the tidings which fly up to Fame's abode:

> And eke this hous hath of entrees
> As fele as of leves ben in trees
> In somer, whan they grene been;
> And on the roof men may yet seen
> A thousand holes, and wel moo,
> To leten wel the soun out goo.
> And be day, in every tyde,
> Been al the dores opened wide,
> And by nyght, echon, unshette;
> Ne porter ther is noon to lette
> No maner tydynges in to pace. (1945-55)

In ascribing "dores" to the numerous openings of his cage-like house, Chaucer again modifies Ovid's house of Rumor, whose "thousand apertures," open both day and night, are said to have "no doors to close them." But this departure may be viewed as another adaptation of his pagan source to a Christian contrast between earthly and heavenly fame. Just as Ovid's personified tidings have become an

---

[143] *De templo Salomonis, PL*, 91, col. 749 (on III Kings 6:2). Cf. *PL*, 93, col. 200, where Bede applies similar meanings to the dimensions of the New Jerusalem (Apoc. 21:16-17), and Augustine, *De civitate Dei*, XI, 30, who explains the significance of the Scriptural *senarius*. In "Dante's *DXV* and *Veltro*," *Traditio*, XVII (1961), 196ff., R. E. Kaske discusses the eschatological implications of "six" and "sixty" in relation to Beatrice's prophecy in *Purg.*, XXXIII, 31ff. On the use of these numbers in the symbolic dimensions of medieval churches, see Simson, pp. 37ff., and K. J. Conant, "Mediaeval Academy Excavations at Cluny," *Speculum*, XXXVIII (1963), 1-45. Like other symbolic features of the Church, the Biblical dimensions appear in literary portrayals of the abode of Love, for example, the palace in Andreas's *De amore*, I, 5 (Fifth Dialogue), and the cave in Gottfried's *Tristan*.

inversion of the spiritual "words" ascending to God's house, so these doors, open day and night, suggest an inversion of the Apocalypse and Isaiah, where the perpetually open gates of the heavenly city denote its accessibility to those whose names appear in the Book of Life: "And thy gates shall be open continually: they shall not be shut day nor night."[144] More in keeping with Chaucer's labyrinthine house is Virgil's description of the entrance to the House of Dis—a maze easy to enter but difficult to leave without divine guidance: "Easy is the descent to Avernus: night and day the door of gloomy Dis stands open; but to recall thy steps and pass out to the upper air, this is the task, this the toil! Some few, whom kindly Jupiter has loved, or shining worth uplifted to heaven, sons of the gods, have availed."[145] In the *Inferno* Virgil's imagery appears in the account of the gate to the City of Dis, through whose maze Dante is guided to a higher stage of contemplation. Bersuire alludes to the same passage in describing the gate to Hell, whose exit is obstructed because "whoever enters there never comes out, as was true of the labyrinth of Daedalus, a certain house which a man was able to enter but not leave."[146] In the House of Tidings this anagogical meaning of the "Domus Dedaly" is mirrored in its lack of a "porter," a feature attributed by Ovid to the House of Morpheus, whose associations with Hell have already been noted. Ovid also supplies the image of the many leaves to which Chaucer compares the "dores"—an image applied to the

[144] Is. 60:11. Cf. Apoc. 21:25: "And the gates thereof shall not be shut by day; for there shall be no night there."

[145] *Aeneid*, VI, 126-31. In *Mythographus Vaticanus III*, pp. 200-201, Virgil's imagery is interpreted in the light of the Platonic doctrine of the soul's descent into the prison of the body. Whereas the soul freed from sin easily returns to its heavenly origin, the impure soul remains in the body and thus is always among the shades in Hades [*apud inferos*]. Cf. Lucan, *Pharsalia*, IX, 1; Macrobius, *Commentary*, I, 9-14.

[146] *Opera*, V, 264.

phantom-dreams hovering about the god of sleep and borrowed by Dante to describe the souls of the damned
gathering just inside the gate of Hell to await the awards
of Minos, the infernal judge.[147]

That the House of Tidings is itself an earthly or spiritual Hell, a maze or prison where divine guidance has
been lost, is only too apparent in the confused tidings
issuing from its holes:

> Ne never rest is in that place
> That hit nys fild ful of tydynges,
> Other loude, or of whisprynges;
> And over alle the houses angles
> Ys ful of rounynges and of jangles
> Of werres, of pes, of mariages,
> Of reste, of labour, of viages,
> Of abood, of deeth, of lyf,
> Of love, of hate, acord, of stryf,
> Of loos, of lore, and of wynnynges,
> Of hele, of seknesse, of bildynges,
> Of faire wyndes, and of tempestes,
> Of qwalm of folk, and eke of bestes;
> Of dyvers transmutacions
> Of estats, and eke of regions;
> Of trust, of drede, of jelousye,
> Of wit, of wynnynge, of folye;
> Of plente, and of gret famyne,
> Of chepe, of derthe, and of ruyne;
> Of good or mys governement,
> Of fyr, and of dyvers accident. (1956-76)

Chaucer's catalogue very nearly exhausts the human condition. It is his counterpart of the "felde ful of folke," of
the confusion of Babylon, a concrete allegorization of the
mingled joy and sorrow, truth and falsehood, charity and
cupidity, proceeding from the hearts of men. Although
tidings of charity and truth can be heard, the predominant
note is one of cupidity and discord: the "whispering" and

---

[147] *Inf.*, III, 112-17. Cf. Ovid, *Metamorphoses*, XI, 608ff.

"jangling" of war, death, sickness, hate, strife, fear, jealousy, folly, famine, ruin, misgovernment and other crimes and misfortunes which, says Augustine, spring from the root of error and misdirected love born with every son of Adam. From this "hell on earth," he adds, no escape is possible, except through the grace and guidance of Christ.[148]

Although Chaucer has been led to the labyrinthine cage of the world, he is not to be caught by any cunning fowler. Like Aeneas he is under the divine protection of Jupiter, the "well-willing" planet.[149] Like both Aeneas and Dante, moreover, he has a guide who can bring him into this earthly Hell and direct him through its intricate maze. Not fortuitously, therefore, as he contemplates the whirling house and wonders how he might get inside, he sees the eagle "faste by" perched "hye upon a stoon." In his reply to Chaucer's request that he be taught "for Goddis love" some "good" from the "wondres" of this house, the eagle resumes his role as the intellect or reason which guides the mind through the labyrinth of error to truth and salvation. "Petre! that is myn entente," he replies; "therfore y duelle":

> "But certeyn, oon thyng I the telle,
> That but I bringe the therinne,
> Ne shalt thou never kunne gynne
> To come into hyt, out of doute,
> So faste hit whirleth, lo, aboute." (2002-2006)

In conjunction with the "stoon" or rock on which he is perched, the eagle's appeal to St. Peter is perhaps a subtle hint of his own role as spiritual physician.[150] In any event, recalling that Jove has sent him "of his grace" to relieve

---

[148] *De civitate Dei*, XXII, 22.

[149] In *Mythographus Vaticanus III*, pp. 200-201, Jupiter is identified as the benevolent planet by whose influence Aeneas and other virtuous spirits are guided through the maze of Dis to the stars.

[150] Cf. Matt. 16:18.

Chaucer's "hevynesse" and to "solace" him with "unkouthe syghtes and tydynges," he completes his earlier diagnosis of the poet's malady by portraying him as one who is "disesperat of alle blys" because Fortune has deprived him of his "hertys reste." Since Jove pities his "distresse" and "thrugh hys myghty merite" wishes to bring him consolation, he has commanded that Chaucer be carried where he may "most tidynges here." Therefore, the eagle concludes, he will take him into the whirling house where he will "anoon many oon lere."

Significantly, as soon as Chaucer is led through a "wyndowe" into the House of Tidings, its whirling seems to cease; for he is no longer viewing it from the outside and seeing it for what it really is—the confused maze of the world. Instead, he is back once again, with renewed perspective, among his "verray neyghebores"—such a great "congregacioun of folk," he observes, echoing Dante's description of the lost souls in Hell,

> That, certys, in the world nys left
> So many formed be Nature,
> Ne ded so many a creature. (2038-40)

The eagle's promise of tidings is soon fulfilled. Indeed, among this great "congregacioun" every "wight" is seen either whispering a "newe tydynge prively" to his neighbor or telling it openly:

> "Nost not thou
> That ys betyd, lo, late or now?"
> "No," quod he, "telle me what."
> And than he tolde hym this and that,
> And swor therto that hit was soth—
> "Thus hath he sayd," and "Thus he doth,"
> "Thus shal hit be," "Thus herde y seye,"
> "That shal be founde," "That dar I leye." (2047-54)

Even more remarkable, when one "wight" has heard a tiding he approaches a second person to whom he repeats it, while the second adds to this tiding more "than hit ever was." And as soon as the second leaves he tells it to a third, who, whether the tiding is "soth or fals," repeats it "evermo with more encres" than "yt was erst."

This matchless portrayal of rumor distorting the truth as it grows brings us to the heart of Chaucer's dramatic allegory of earthly fame. Whereas the goddess's judgments illustrate the fickleness of worldly praise, slander, and oblivion, here we may observe the human origin of these awards: the confusion and irrationality of men's minds.[151] Although Chaucer's fiction dramatizes Ovid's description of the growth of rumor, the Scriptural overtones become distinct as each tiding goes "fro mouth to mouth,"

> encresing ever moo,
> As fyr ys wont to quyke and goo
> From a sparke spronge amys,
> Til al a citee brent up ys. (2077-80)

---

[151] Cf. Dante's description of the growth of rumor in *Convivio*, I, 3, where Virgil is cited: "The good report [*fama buona*] of a man is generated in the first place by the favourable process [*buona operazione*] in a friend's mind, and by this it is first brought to the birth; for the mind of an enemy, although it receives the germ, does not quicken it. The mind which first brings it forth, both in order to embellish its own gift, and through affection [*caritade*] for the friend who receives it, does not keep within the bounds of truth but oversteps them. And when the mind in order to embellish what it affirms oversteps the bounds of truth, it speaks against conscience; when affection misleads it to overstep them, it does not speak against conscience. The second mind which receives what is said is not content merely with the exaggeration [*dilatazione*] due to the first, but is careful to embellish its own repetition of it, as being in this case the effect proper to itself; and so, by this action and by the deception which the affection generated in it practises on it, makes the report greater than it was when received, whether in agreement or in disagreement with conscience, as with the first mind. The third mind that receives it does the like, and so the fourth, and thus the report is enlarged to infinity. So when the action of the causes above mentioned is reversed, the reason of ill fame [*infamia*] which is magnified in like manner may also be perceived. Wherefore Virgil says in the fourth book of the *Aeneid* that 'Fame thrives on motion and acquires greatness by going onward'" (trans. W. W. Jackson, Oxford, 1909, pp. 38-39).

In Scripture the spark (*scintilla*) is a recurring image of speech which when fed by cupidity burns like a fire and consumes the soul.[152] The comparison of rumor to a fire that spreads until "al a citee brent up ys" is found in Ecclesiasticus, where the related images of the spark, the fire, and the city are applied to the speech of the "whisperer" and the "double-tongued":

A hasty contention kindleth a fire; and a hasty quarrel sheddeth blood; and a tongue that beareth witness bringeth death. If thou blow the spark, it shall burn as a fire, and if thou spit upon it, it shall be quenched: both come out of the mouth. The whisperer and the double-tongued is accursed, for he hath troubled many that were at peace. The tongue of a third person hath disquieted many, and scattered them from nation to nation. It hath destroyed the strong cities of the rich.[153]

The "third person," whose tongue has destroyed strong cities, is dramatized by Chaucer's third bearer of tidings, who, whether a tiding is true or false, distorts it beyond what it was at first. The "third person," to quote a related Scriptural passage, "bringeth wrath and destruction":

Two sorts of men multiply sins, and the third bringeth wrath and destruction. A hot soul is a burning fire: it will never be quenched, till it devour something. And a man that is wicked

---

[152] For example, Wis. 2:2; Ecclus. 11:34; 28:13-17. Chaucer's Parson applies the image to wrath; for just as the "fir of smale gleedes" is quickened by brimstone, so wrath is quickened by pride, "that ay bloweth and encreesseth the fir by chidynge and wikked wordes." Cf. *Glossa ordinaria*, PL, 113, col. 1,168.

[153] Ecclus. 28:13-17. Cf. Bersuire, *Opera*, II, 141: "A spark [*scintilla*], it is agreed, may be a small thing, but when it is covered by inflammable materials, such as straw or tow, a very great fire is sometimes started by which houses and cities are many times burnt up. In like manner, from a small wrathful word set among straw and stubble—that is, among wrathful persons—an enormous fire of strife and discord begins by which houses and towns are literally destroyed by wars and animosities. For this reason, it is said in Ecclus. 11: 'Of one spark cometh a great fire, and of one deceitful man much blood.' Or a spark signifies a slight temptation, or a small and careless word, from which, certainly, a great fire of powerful concupiscence and temptation sometimes is born, unless it is carefully extinguished at the beginning."

in the mouth of his flesh will not leave off till he hath kindled a fire.[154]

St. James uses the same imagery in describing the abuses of the tongue; for just as a small fire may kindle a large forest, so the tongue is a fire defiling the whole body, being itself "set on fire by hell." Although every kind of beast and bird has been tamed by mankind, the tongue "no man can tame—an unquiet evil, full of deadly poison." With it "we bless God and the Father," and with it "we curse men, who are made after the likeness of God." Out of the same mouth proceed "blessing and cursing."[155] These Scriptural implications of the speech of the "whisperer" and the "double-tongued" are amusingly portrayed as Chaucer describes how each tiding, when it was "ful yspronge" and "woxen" on every tongue more "than ever hit was," flew out a window; or, if there were two tidings—"a lesyng and a sad soth sawe"—how both competed for the same opening and compromised as one tiding:

> "Lat me go first!" "Nay, but let me!
> And here I wol ensuren the
> Wyth the nones that thou wolt do so,
> That I shal never fro the go,
> But be thyn owne sworen brother!
> We wil medle us ech with other,
> That no man, be they never so wrothe,
> Shal han on [of us] two, but bothe
> At ones, al besyde his leve,
> Come we a-morwe or on eve,
> Be we cried or stille yrouned." (2097-2107)

In this manner, Chaucer concludes, he saw "soth" and "fals" or "fals and soth compouned" fly straight up to the abode of Fame, who gave each tiding a "name," according to her "disposicioun," and also a "duracioun"—

154 Ecclus. 23:21-23. Cf. 22:30.
155 Jas. 3:5-10. Cf. Prov. 16:27; Is. 9:17-18.

some to wax and wane "as doth the faire white mone" —and "let hem goon."[156] Here he saw twenty thousand of these "wynged wondres" blown about by Aeolus.

These mingled tidings of truth and falsehood, it should now be clear, are those tidings of his "verray neyghebores" which Chaucer has been promised for his "game" and "lore." This much of his education, therefore, is complete: through Jove's grace and the guidance of reason (the eagle), he has not only viewed the world in perspective and seen the vanity of trusting Fame's judgments; he has also penetrated the maze of human error and observed the source of the distorted tidings which make up her fickle decrees. But these confused tidings would seem to be anything but the glad "love-tydynges" with which Jove has promised to console Chaucer. Indeed, the only tidings of love he has heard up to this point are those of earthly love, such as the "dissymulacions," "jelousies," and other sorrows described by the eagle as the rewards of "Loves folk" and exemplified by Dido in the temple of Venus. In contrast to these worldly tidings, he has yet to hear the tidings of heavenly love which in Proverbs are said to be brought by messengers from a "fer contree" to relieve the soul from the heat of tribulation. Ironically, the messengers who might be expected to bring such tidings—the pilgrims and pardoners—do not do so; for, as Chaucer observes, their tidings are clothed as falsely as those of anyone else:

> And, Lord, this hous in alle tymes,
> Was ful of shipmen and pilgrimes,
> With scrippes bret-ful of lesinges,
> Entremedled with tydynges,
> And eke allone be hemselve.
> O, many a thousand tymes twelve

---

[156] As a conventional symbol of Fortune's inconstancy, the image of the moon further illustrates Chaucer's transference of Fortune's attributes to Fame. Cf. Patch, *The Goddess Fortuna*, p. 50.

> Saugh I eke of these pardoners,
> Currours, and eke messagers,
> With boystes crammed ful of lyes
> As ever vessel was with lyes. (2121-30)

Along with the punning allusion to the vessel filled with lees, a Scriptural image of the wicked, these false pilgrims, pardoners, and other worldly wanderers are a reminder that the House of Tidings is the equivalent of the "felde ful of folke," a "Domus Dedaly" in which the voice of truth and charity has been lost in the maze of cupidity.[157] But that Chaucer's quest for tidings of a "fer contree" has not been forgotten in this Babylonian confusion is confirmed by his own statement that he still hopes

> a tydynge for to here,
> That I had herd of some contre. (2134-35)

The precise nature of this "tydynge," however, is obscured by his comment that it will "not now be told":

> For hit no nede is, redely;
> Folk kan synge hit bet than I;
> For al mot out, other late or rathe,
> Alle the sheves in the lathe. (2137-40)

What, then, is this tiding? Why does Chaucer not feel the "nede" to tell it? Who are these "folk" who can "synge" it better than he can?

We should not be misled by the irony of Chaucer's avowal not to divulge his "tydynge." He has no "nede" to reveal it because both the tiding and the identity of those who can "synge" it are implied throughout the

---

[157] In *Piers Plowman*, B, Prol., 46-52, pilgrims and palmers are associated with "lyes" and false tidings. For the image of the vessel filled with lees, see Jer. 48:11; Is. 51:17,22; Ps. 74:9. If twelve is multiplied by twelve thousand, Chaucer's "many a thousand tymes twelve" suggests an inversion of the Apocalyptic number of the redeemed (7:4-8; 14:3). On the significance of the number twelve as a symbol of the universal Church, see Rabanus, *De universo*, PL, 111, col. 492.

allegory of Book III. That the tiding is to be one of love and consolation is already clear from Chaucer's earlier remark to his mysterious "frend" that he has been promised some "newe thinges," some "newe tydynges" of love "or suche thynges glade." In Scripture, as we have seen, these tidings of love or "newe thinges" (*nova*) are the tidings of the "new doctrine" of charity, the "glad tidings" of future salvation and bliss announced by the prophets, manifested in Christ, the divine Word, and taught and spread by the apostles and all those preachers and earthly vicars of Christ who, Chaucer subtly tells us, can "synge" of them better than he can. This liturgical connotation of "synge" is imaged more broadly in the Apocalyptic "new song" (*canticum novum*) prefigured in David's psalms and sung by the Redeemed before the throne of the Lamb—a song expressing the soul's marriage to Christ through the New Law of love and contrasting with the worldly songs performed by Fame's harpers and by the Muses before her throne.[158] In the liturgy for Advent, the tidings of "newe thinges" are foreshadowed in the prophetic imagery from the Old and the New Testaments, especially the coming of the Sun of Justice, whose appearance at the winter solstice anticipates Christ's advent at the Nativity, his advent into men's souls, and his advent at the end of the world to judge mankind.[159] In this liturgical and

[158] Apoc. 5:9; 14:3. Cf. Pss. 95:1; 97:1. In the lyric "Quis est hic?" the *canticum novum* is connected with the tidings brought by Christ to announce his liberation of the soul from captivity (*The Oxford Book of Medieval Latin Verse*, ed. F. J. E. Raby, Oxford, 1959, p. 158). For an example of similar imagery in English lyrics, see Brown, *Religious Lyrics of the Fourteenth Century*, p. 24. On the closely related meanings of "new song," "new law," "new dance," "new man," etc., and their reflection in medieval art and literature, see Robertson, *Preface*, especially pp. 127ff. A liturgical connotation of "synge" appears in the *OED* under the obsolete meaning "to chant or intone, in the performance of divine services; to say mass." Cf. the same usage in *Piers Plowman*, B, Prol., 86.

[159] Cf. chap. ii, n. 56. For pertinent passages in the medieval lit-

Scriptural context, we may infer, Chaucer has no "nede" to reveal his "tydynge" because it is implicit both in the date of his vision on "the tenth day of the tenth month"— the time of the winter solstice and, in Ezechiel's vision, a figure for Christ's final coming to release mankind from captivity—and in the Apocalyptic imagery of Book III.[160] From the opening description of the castle on its "feble fundament" to the description of the whirling House of Tidings with its "tymber of no strengthe" the symbolism points toward some consoling tiding which will reveal behind the flux and transitoriness of the world a time when the confused tidings of truth and falsehood, Jerusalem and Babylon, will be forever separated and when those who merited good fame on earth will receive it eternally. This promise of the Last Judgment—when Fame's fickle "justice" will yield to the eternal justice of Christ the divine Judge—would seem to be the lesson Chaucer learns and one he would convey to his reader in the obscure ending of his prophetic vision.

That the conclusion of the *House of Fame* fulfills these prophetic implications of the allegory becomes apparent when Chaucer, still in search of his tiding, finds himself in a "corner" where "men of love-tydynges tolde" and observes the confusion caused by the appearance of a mysterious "man of gret auctorite":

---

urgy for Advent, see *The Sarum Missal*, ed. J. W. Legg (Oxford, 1916), pp. 14 ff.

[160] On the eschatological meaning of the date of Ezechiel's vision, see n. 10, above. For the same symbolism of "ten" in the *cinquecento, diece e cinque* of Beatrice's prophecy (*Purg.*, XXXIII, 34-45), see Kaske, "Dante's *DXV* and *Veltro*," pp. 196 ff. The exegetical material in this article suggests a common tradition behind Chaucer's and Dante's eschatological imagery, for example, the connection between Christ's first and second advents with the disposition of the heavens (pp. 214 ff.) and the analogy between the poet as beholder and recorder of an "apocalyptic" vision and John as beholder and recorder of the vision in the Apocalypse (p. 210).

> Atte laste y saugh a man,
> Which that y [nevene] nat ne kan;
> But he semed for to be
> A man of gret auctorite. . . . (2155-58)

Although Chaucer can not "name" this man of great authority,[161] his identity, along with that of the "tydynge" he is presumably to tell, is suggested by several revealing details. Ironically, Chaucer himself provides a clue when he gives his reason for not divulging his tiding:

> For al mot out, other late or rathe,
> Alle the sheves in the lathe. (2139-40)

This subtle allusion to the Last Judgment—when all truth must be manifested and all "wheat" gathered into the "barn"—echoes the Gospels, where Christ, as one bearing divine authority, warns mankind of the coming separation of the good and the wicked:

Suffer both to grow until the harvest, and in the time of the harvest I will say to the reapers: Gather up first the cockle, and bind it into bundles to burn, but the wheat gather ye into my barn.[162]

Christ's warning is prefigured in John the Baptist's prophecy of the coming of one "mightier" (*fortior*) than himself:

[His] fan is in his hand, and he will thoroughly cleanse his floor and gather his wheat into the barn; but the chaff he will burn with unquenchable fire.[163]

---

[161] The emendation of Skeat, Koch, and Robinson, who insert "nevene" in the reading of the manuscripts—"Whiche that y [nevene] nat (naught) ne kan"—fits the preceding irony of Chaucer's refusal to "tell" his tiding.

[162] Matt. 13:30. On the significance of the "lathe" or barn [*horreum*] as a symbol of the earthly or heavenly Church, see Augustine, *Sermo LXXIII, PL*, 38, col. 471. In *Piers Plowman*, B, XIX, 312ff., Grace instructs Piers to build a "barn" in which to gather his harvest and which she names the House of Unity—"holicherche in Englisshe."

[163] Matt. 3:11-12. Cf. Mark 1:6-7; Luke 3:16-17; Apoc. 14:14-20.

Christ's association with "great authority" is recurrent in the New Testament. Thus, as the future judge of mankind, he is identified in traditional commentary with the Apocalyptic angel of "great authority" (*habentem potestatem magnam*) whom God will send to foretell the destruction of Babylon:

And after this I saw another angel coming down from heaven, having great authority, and the earth was lighted up by his glory. And he cried out with a mighty voice, saying, "She has fallen, she has fallen, Babylon the great; and has become a habitation of demons, a stronghold of every unclean spirit, a stronghold of every unclean and hateful bird."

As the angel of "great authority," according to one gloss, Christ performs the role of heavenly messenger who brings tidings of eternal life.[164] In the Gospels the authority by which he preaches his "new doctrine" is questioned by the scribes and priests: "By what authority dost thou these things? And who hath given thee this authority that thou shouldst do these things?"[165] In John 5:26-29 Christ reveals the source of his authority to execute judgment on mankind:

For as the Father hath life in himself, so he hath given to the Son also to have life in himself, and he hath given him power to do judgment, because he is the Son of man. Wonder not at this, for the hour cometh, wherein all that are in the graves shall hear the voice of the Son of God. And they that have done good things shall come forth unto the resurrection of life; but they that have done evil, unto the resurrection of judgment.

[164] *PL*, 117, col. 1,151 (on Apoc. 18:1-2). Cf. *PL*, 169, col. 1,149: "Properly, therefore, he says 'having great authority' [*habentem potestatem magnam*]—the authority of executing judgment or damnation on the harlot." *Potestas* is translated as both "power" and "authority" in the Douay-Rheims Bible. In Mark 11:28-29 and Luke 20:2, the latter rendering is applied to Christ as "man of gret auctorite." For its closeness to Chaucer's phrase, the New Catholic Edition (New York, 1949-1950) is used in this instance to translate the Apocalyptic passage.

[165] Mark 11:27-28. Cf. Matt. 21:23-27; Luke 20:2-8.

At the conclusion of the Sermon on the Mount and in his preaching in the synagogue, Christ is again described as one whose authoritative teaching astonishes the people: "And they were astonished (*stupebant*) at his doctrine. For he was teaching them as one having power, and not as the scribes."[166] The same amazement greets Christ upon his entry into Jerusalem: "And when he was come into Jerusalem, the whole city was moved, saying: Who is this? And the people said: This is Jesus, the prophet from Nazareth of Galilee."[167] Elsewhere the crowd's astonishment at the "authority" of Christ's "new doctrine" is associated with the spread of his fame throughout Galilee: "And they were all amazed, insomuch that they questioned among themselves, saying: What thing is this? What is this new doctrine? For with power he commandeth even the unclean spirits, and they obey him. And the fame of him was spread forthwith into all the country of Galilee."[168] The crowd's commotion and astonished questioning of one another about Christ's "new doctrine"— "What thing is this? What is this new doctrine?"— are closely paralleled in Chaucer's description of the confusion and astonishment in the "corner" where "men of love-tydynges tolde" and everyone questions the other and runs to see and hear the "man of gret auctorite":

[166] Mark 1:22. Cf. Luke 4:32 ("And they were astonished at his doctrine, for his speech was with power") and Matt. 7:28-29, which follows Christ's parable of the two houses.

[167] Matt. 21:10-11. Cf. the Vulgate—*Et cum intrasset Jerosolymam, commota est universa civitas, dicens: Quis est hic?*—and the New Catholic rendering: "all the city was thrown into commotion." In the commentaries, as well as in art and literature, the Entry into Jerusalem is a key episode in allegorizing Christ's power and authority as the future champion and judge of mankind. Cf. n. 170, below.

[168] Mark 1:27-28. Cf. Luke 4:36-37: "And there came fear upon all, and they talked among themselves, saying: What word is this? [*Quod est hoc verbum?*] For with authority and power [*potestate et virtute*] he commandeth the unclean spirits, and they go out. And the fame [*fama*] of him was published into every place of the country."

For I saugh rennynge every wight,
As faste as that they hadden myght;
And everych cried, "What thing is that?"
And somme sayde, "I not never what." (2145-48)

That we are to identify the inquiry of these tellers of tidings with the crowd's similar inquiry in Mark—"What
thing is this?"—seems clear in the Scriptural context. The
"thing" which is the object of their amazed questioning is
the "new doctrine" of love, the "tydynge" of man's salvation and future judgment which is Christ's teaching as
a "man of gret auctorite."[169] Chaucer's inability to "name"
the speaker of this tiding is itself reminiscent of the Apocalypse, where John sees Christ figuratively portrayed as
the mighty judge of mankind who has a name "which no
man knoweth but himself." In traditional commentary,
this personage appareled in a garment sprinkled with

---

[169] Chaucer's phrase—"What thing is that?"—approximates the Vulgate (Mark 1:27): *Quidnam est hoc? quaenam doctrina haec nova?*
Cf. the King James translation: "What thing is this? What new doctrine is this?" The question in Luke 4:36 (*Quod est hoc verbum?*)
points to the same meaning. In *Purg.*, XXIX, 19ff., Dante applies the
identical question in Mark (*Che cosa è questa?*) to his own amazement
at the sight of the triumphant pageant of Christ (figuratively portrayed as the Gryphon), whose approach is accompanied by the *Ho-
sanna* greeting his entry into Jerusalem and is linked, as Professor
Kaske demonstrates, with Beatrice's veiled prophecy of his future advent ("Dante's *DXV* and *Veltro*," p. 214). In Acts 17:18-21, the
question again appears in the philosophers' interrogation of St. Paul
about Christ's "new doctrine," which is identified with the "new
things" of salvation and Christ's authority to execute judgment: "And
certain philosophers of the Epicureans and of the Stoics disputed with
him; and some said: What is it that this word sower would say? But
others: He seemeth to be a setter forth of new gods, because he preached
to them Jesus and the resurrection. And taking him, they brought him
to the Areopagus, saying: May we know what this new doctrine [*nova
doctrina*] is, which thou speakest of? For thou bringest in certain new
things [*nova . . . quaedam*] to our ears. We would know therefore
what these things mean. (Now all the Athenians, and strangers that
were there, employed themselves in nothing else but either in telling
or in hearing some new thing [*aliquid novi*].)" The Vulgate *nova . . .
quaedam*, translated in Douay-Rheims as "certain new things," appears
to be the basis of Chaucer's "somme newe thinges," which he identifies with "glad" love-tidings of a far country.

blood and called "the Word of God" is identified with the mighty stranger from Edom who in Isaiah's prophecy is clothed in red, a symbol of victory over all his enemies.[170] Again in Isaiah, Christ is the unnamed "man of my own will" whom God will send "from a far country" to destroy Babylon and deliver mankind from captivity. Similarly, in the Book of Kings, he is prefigured in the stranger (*alienigena*) from a "far country" who will spread tidings of God's "name" and "mighty hand" over the whole world.[171]

These prophetic implications of Chaucer's conclusion are

[170] Apoc. 19:12-13; Is. 63:1ff. The passage from Isaiah is the inspiration behind the fourteenth century English lyric "What ys he, þys lordling?" in which the stranger's authority and strength are developed into the familiar allegory of Christ, the knight, in "blod-rede wede," championing mankind and fighting the battle of redemption (Brown, *Religious Lyrics of the Fourteenth Century*, p. 28). The same imagery in other lyrics is discussed by R. T. Davies, *Medieval English Lyrics* (Evanston, Illinois, 1964), pp. 318-19. In *Piers Plowman*, B, XVIII-XIX, Christ's red clothing becomes the armor (*humana natura*) in which he jousts with Satan. On red as an iconographic feature of Christ's clothing in medieval art and drama, see M. D. Anderson, *Drama and Imagery in English Medieval Churches* (Cambridge, 1963), pp. 157-58. Another literary parallel to Chaucer's "man of gret auctorite" appears in Lydgate's *Pilgrimage* (1,385ff.), in which a man of "gret auctoryte" is identified with the stranger who in Ezechiel's vision [9:2ff.] is clothed in linen and marks the sign of Thau (the Cross) on the foreheads of the redeemed. Exegetically, this figure is explained as Moses, a prefiguration of Christ and the New Law of love. Aside from more modern connotations, the phrase "man of gret auctorite" has the traditional meaning of one who has authority or influence in matters pertaining to moral or spiritual wisdom (*OED*). In *Inf.*, IV, 113, Dante applies the epithet *di grande autorità* to the pagan men of wisdom—Plato, Aristotle, Virgil, etc.—who inhabit the *nobile castello* in Limbo. In "The Unity of Chaucer's *House of Fame*," pp. 16-29, Paul G. Ruggiers identifies "the man of gret auctorite" as Boethius, a theory consistent with the Boethian ideas and imagery in the poem. But Chaucer's Scriptural imagery points more meaningfully, I believe, to Christ in his role of authority.

[171] Is. 46:10-12; III Kings 8:41-43. Cf. Jer. 46:27. Chaucer's deliberate concealment of the name of the man of great authority is in accord with the traditional practice in medieval allegory of veiling the heavenly mysteries in an enigmatic *cortex*. This practice is followed by Dante, who refers to Christ figuratively throughout the Comedy.

strengthened by the remaining details describing the "leaping," "climbing," and "treading" upon one another's heels as the crowd gathers to glimpse the "man of gret auctorite":

> And whan they were alle on an hepe,
> Tho behynde begunne up lepe,
> And clamben up on other faste,
> And up the nose and yen kaste,
> And troden fast on others heles,
> And stampen, as men doon aftir eles. (2149-54)

In Luke 12:1-3—the passage reflected earlier in Dido's soliloquy on Fame and in the eagle's discourse on speech—the image of the crowd "treading" on one another is applied to the throngs who gather about Christ as he warns them of the coming judgment:

And when great multitudes stood about him, so that they trod one upon another, he began to say to his disciples: Beware ye of the leaven of the Pharisees, which is hypocrisy. For there is nothing covered that shall not be revealed, nor hidden that shall not be known. For whatsoever things you have spoken in darkness shall be published in the light; and that which you have spoken in the ear in the chambers shall be preached on the housetops.[172]

In the Prophecy of Malachias, the imagery of "treading" and "leaping" is applied more particularly to the triumph of the redeemed over the forces of evil at the final judgment:

For behold the day shall come kindled as a furnace; and all the proud and all that do wickedly shall be stubble; and the day that cometh shall set them on fire, saith the Lord of hosts, it shall not leave them root nor branch. But unto you that fear my name, the Sun of Justice shall arise, and health in his

---

[172] Cf. Matt. 10:26-28; Mark 4:22. A related passage is I Cor. 4:1-5, used in the Epistle for the fourth Sunday in Advent: "Therefore judge not before the time, until the Lord come, who both will bring to light the hidden things of darkness and will make manifest the counsels of the hearts; and then shall every man have praise from God."

wings. And you shall go forth, and shall leap like calves of the herd. And you shall tread down the wicked when they shall be ashes under the sole of your feet in the day that I do this, saith the Lord of hosts.[173]

St. Jerome, in his commentary on Malachias, explains the "leaping" of those who "shall tread down the wicked" as the jubilation of the redeemed when Christ, the Sun of Justice, comes to release them from the chains of captivity.[174] The related image of "treading" on the wicked derives ultimately from Gen. 3:14-16, where Christ is to be identified with the "seed" of Eve who will "crush" Satan's head and make him "lie in wait for her heel."[175] In Rom. 16:20 the power to "crush Satan" under the feet is attributed to all those who distinguish between good and evil. Similarly, in Psalm 90:13 this power is delegated to those who put their trust in God: "Thou shalt walk upon the asp and the basilisk, and thou shalt trample under foot the lion and the dragon." Christ himself, in Luke 10:19, uses the same image in reminding the disciples that he has given them the authority to "tread upon serpents and scorpions, and upon all the power of the enemy."[176] According to a standard gloss on the verse from Luke, the serpents and

---

[173] Mal. 4:1-3. On the image of "leaping" [Vulg. *salire*; *exsilire*], see also Joel 2:5, where it is connected with the trumpet blown on Mount Sion to announce the Last Judgment. Cf. Hab. 3:19.

[174] *PL*, 25, cols. 1,652-53. In *De civitate Dei*, XVIII, 35, Augustine relates the same passage to Mal. 3:1-2, in which Christ is prefigured in the angel or messenger who will bring tidings of eternal bliss.

[175] In Is. 63:3-6, which follows the account of the mighty stranger clothed in red, the images of "treading (upon)" and "trampling" [*calcare*; *conculcare*] are symbolic of Christ's power and victory over his enemies: "I have trodden the winepress alone, and of the Gentiles there is not a man with me: I have trampled on them in my indignation, and have trodden them down in my wrath, and their blood is sprinkled upon my garments, and I have stained all my apparel. For the day of vengeance is in my heart, the year of my redemption is come. . . . And I have trodden down the people in my wrath."

[176] Cf. Bersuire, *Opera*, V, 272: "The power of God [*Dei potestas*] appears not only in his own works but also in the power which he communicated to men. . . . Observe, therefore, that God gave to the saints the power of curing the sick, putting devils to flight, and treading upon beasts [*bestias calcandi*]."

scorpions trodden underfoot signify all those evil men or demons who by their false and venomous persuasion attempt to undermine virtue.[177] In medieval iconography this meaning is behind the numerous representations of the vices—serpents and other beasts—trodden beneath the feet of the virtues or the saints.[178] One of these creatures, the eel—a symbol of Satan or other evil beings who attempt to impede man's spiritual journey—appears at the feet of St. Christopher, the patron saint of pilgrims.[179] It is this medieval emblem of evil that supplies Chaucer's imagery as he completes his description of the crowd who rush to hear the "man of gret auctorite" and "stampen" as "men doon aftir eles."[180]

If we view the conclusion of Chaucer's vision as part of a broader symbolic pattern beginning in Book I, we can detect a further parallel with the *Divine Comedy*, where Dante concludes each of his three books with an image relating to man's salvation. In the *House of Fame* such a pattern is introduced at the end of Book I with Chaucer's appeal to Christ and his rescue from the desert by the eagle, whose associations with Christ, St. John, Beatrice, the sun, and the eagle of the *Purgatorio* all strengthen his function as a symbol of the intellect illumined by grace, directing the mind to the path of salvation. At the end of Book II this pattern again emerges in the eagle's remarks on the ascent of speech in the likeness or clothing

---

[177] *Glossa ordinaria*, PL, 114, col. 285 (cf. col. 518, on Rom. 16:20).

[178] See Mâle, pp. 102-105; Tristram, p. 97; Evans, *Cluniac Art of the Romanesque Period*, p. 81.

[179] Tristram, pp. 116, 120; Margaret Rickert, *Painting in Britain: The Middle Ages* (Baltimore, 1954), p. 141. Christopher is sometimes depicted as carrying an eel spear. Bersuire identifies the eel [*anguilla*] with Satan or evil men [*viri mali*], "who are elusive, changeable, and deceitful [*lubricosi sunt, et variabiles, et fallaces*], who are engendered by sin and produced from the slime of carnality [*limo carnalitatis*], who find delight in the shining waters of worldly prosperity, and who devour the seed and spawn—that is, the riches—of others" (*Opera*, II, 253).

[180] For the literal basis of Chaucer's image of "stamping" on eels, see Robinson's note, *Works*, p. 788.

of the "wight" who spoke the word on earth—an inversion of the doctrine of the resurrection of the flesh and perhaps a punning allusion to Christ, the divine Word, clothed in red, in whose image every spirit should ascend to God's house. This doctrine, the basis of Chaucer's inversion of the Last Judgment in Book III, culminates in the appearance of the "man of gret auctorite," the gathering point for all the prophetic meanings of the vision. As the messenger from a "fer contree," he is the announcer and the embodiment of the "new doctrine" of charity, the glad tidings of heavenly love and fame which are foreshadowed in Aeneas' pilgrimage and imaged in the tidings of love or "newe thinges" promised Chaucer by Jupiter through the eagle. In his role of authority, he is the bestower of eternal fame and infamy, the just rewards for good and evil which are the opposite of the fickle human judgments feared by Dido and illustrated so graphically by Fame's unstable decrees. Finally, as in the *Divine Comedy,* Malachias, and the liturgy for Advent evoked by the date of Chaucer's vision, he is the Sun of Justice, whose approach at the winter solstice in December is a promise of the spirit's liberation from the chains of the world, the flesh, and the devil; whose heat of love melts the ice of cupidity, the "feble fundament" of Fame's idolatrous abode; and whose light of wisdom dispels the darkness of sin and ignorance and awakens the mind from slumber:

Love therefore is the fulfilling of the law. And that knowing the season; that it is now the hour for us to rise from sleep. For now our salvation is nearer than when we believed. The night is passed, and the day is at hand. Let us therefore cast off the works of darkness, and put on the armour of light.[181]

[181] Rom. 13:10-12. This passage appears in the Epistle for the first Sunday in Advent in the Sarum Missal and the modern liturgy. In *Glossa ordinaria, PL,* 114, col. 514, night is interpreted as the darkness of sin, and the approach of day as the advent of the Sun of Justice.

If the preceding analysis of the *House of Fame* approximates the meanings which Chaucer wished to convey in his prophetic vision, we become conscious of a poem with an intellectual scope, artistic control, and spiritual depth worthy of its major source of inspiration, the *Divine Comedy*. As we have seen, the unity of the poem is an inner unity, and its fullest implications, in accordance with traditional methods of poetic allegory, appear not on the surface but beneath a fictive veil of symbolism. Viewed in this light, those aspects of the poem which have led to such charges as thematic confusion, disjunctiveness of subject matter and mood, or incompleteness may be seen in a clearer perspective; and what emerges finally is not a poem of unsure artistry or uncertainty of purpose but a complex symbolic structure skillfully designed to explore the deepest implications of the Christian doctrine of fame. But even though we allow an inner unity to the *House of Fame*, the charge of incompleteness demands attention; for on the surface, at least, the ending lacks the sense of finality of Chaucer's other visions, where the vision framework is completed by the dreamer's awakening. Although this structural peculiarity has elicited explanations ranging from Chaucer's failure to complete the poem to his having adapted the ending to an occasion known only to his audience, with one of these theories, which stresses the occasional aspect of the poem, we might conclude, since the foregoing analysis would seem to substantiate this point of view.

In an article entitled "A Legal Reading of Chaucer's *Hous of Fame*," Professor R. J. Schoeck suggests that the poem "had for the occasion of its offering some high ritualistic surrounding that completed its projections of intentions and meanings."[182] This conclusion is based on an allusion to Chaucer in a sixteenth-century heraldry book

[182] *Univ. of Toronto Quarterly*, XXIII (1953), 185-92.

which pictures Pegasus, the emblem of the Inner Temple, on a "scutcheon of renown" and accompanies it with the comment that Chaucer "buylte unto him (after of his owne nature & condition), a house called Fame, a place mete for the horse of honour whose original the Poetes faine was, when valiant Perseus the soldier of the goddess Pallas, in dangerous fight, achieved by help of her glittering shield, the battle against Medusa."[183] Mainly on the strength of this allusion and of evidence in the poem itself, Schoeck conjectures that the *House of Fame* was written for one of the ritualistic observances of the Inner Temple, most likely for the Christmas Revels, a possibility supported by Chaucer's date December 10 and by the apparent connection of the Revels with a ritual associated with the Order of Pegasus.[184]

This theory, which the author reinforces with relevant details from the poem, is a tempting one, providing as it does a plausible occasion not only for the spirit of "grand playfulness" in the *House of Fame*, as Schoeck observes, but also for its more serious "sentence." For Pegasus, the winged horse in whose honor Chaucer is said to have written his poem, is a medieval symbol of fame based upon virtue and is therefore a contrasting symbol for the fickle fame of the goddess.[185] As the emblem of the Inner Temple, moreover, Pegasus signifies the heavenly renown

[183] The allusion appears in Gerard Legh's *Accedence of Armorie*, published 1562, fol. 118.

[184] The Christmas Revels, Professor Schoeck notes, were by the end of the fifteenth century the most elaborate of the festivities at the Inns. He quotes Legh on those at the Inner Temple in 1561 when the constable—marshall, "patron of the honourable order of Pegasus," presided as Palaphilos the Prince of Wisdom, and when twenty-four gentlemen of the Inn were dubbed Knights of the Order (pp. 186-87).

[185] The medieval moralization of Pegasus as a symbol of good fame is traceable to Fulgentius, whose *Mitologiae* is cited by Bersuire (*Opera*, IV, 185): "By Perseus' horse, Pegasus, who had wings on his feet and flew swiftly through the air, was understood "fame" [*fama*], by which the excellent renown of this virtuous soldier was carried

which should motivate an order dedicated to the ideals of Christian law and justice.[186] If Chaucer did indeed write his poem as part of a ritualistic occasion in honor of Pegasus, it is conceivable that he was extolling the Inner Temple itself as a "house" or "temple" of fame embodying these ideals. Although such a theory puts added weight on the serious "sentence" underlying the dominant mood of playfulness which Schoeck stresses in the *House of Fame,* it also calls attention to an aspect of the ritualistic festivities of the Temple which should perhaps be emphasized: their connection with the season celebrating the Advent of Christ. The basically religious nature of the Christmas Revels would not only help to explain the strong infusion of Scriptural imagery in the poem; it also suggests an explanation for its apparent incompleteness. By examining more closely the connection between Chaucer's prophetic symbolism and the ritualism associated with Advent, we can recognize behind the "whole grand playfulness" a "sentence" highly appropriate to a festival celebrating the coming of Christ.

To begin with, as Professor Schoeck observes, "one of Chaucer's principal intentions must have been to prepare his audience for tidings." On the precise nature of these tidings he does not conjecture; but, as we have seen, the season of Advent is preeminently the season announcing

---

everywhere. For fame, according to the letter, is called a winged horse because it spreads very swiftly: 'the report [*fama*] was quickly spread among all' [Ruth 1:19]. Thus it is the joyful tidings of good things."

[186] Schoeck observes that the Pegasus emblem of the Inner Temple may go back to the seal of the Knights Templar, which portrayed the figure of a horse carrying two knights, symbolizing charity and humility, a device later altered to a horse with two wings (p. 188). Quoting Jer. 4:13—"his horses are swifter than eagles"—Bersuire allies Pegasus with the eagle as a symbol of the just borne aloft by wings of virtue (*Opera,* III, 138). If Chaucer wrote his poem for an audience at the Inner Temple, the contrast between Pegasus' winged feet and Fame's feet with "partriches wynges" would have been especially meaningful. Cf. n. 76, above.

tidings of Christ's New Law and his coming judgment on the good and the wicked. In the poem itself the connection between such tidings and Advent is called up not only by the date December 10 and the central quest for tidings of a "fer contree" but also by the prophetic imagery throughout the poem, above all in Book III, where tidings of salvation and future judgment may be linked with the "man of gret auctorite." In this Scriptural context Chaucer's symbolism points toward an identity for the man of authority far different from the Master of Revels with whom Schoeck would identify him. At the same time, the ending is especially adaptable to an earthly speaker who would deliver such tidings—either the Master of Revels himself or some other personage suitable to the occasion, such as a member of the clergy. The latter possibility is particularly supported by Chaucer's avowal not to tell his "tydynge" himself because others can "synge" it better than he can. The liturgical connotations of "synge," along with the accompanying Biblical allusion to the Last Judgment—"al mot out, other late of rathe,/ Alle the sheves in the lathe"—suggest a sermon or, more likely, a reading from Scripture or the liturgy, especially from the Gospels or Epistles for Advent, either one of which would be a fitting conclusion to the festivities observing the coming of Christ.[187] Moreover, Christ in his role of authority would be a subject doubly appropriate to the setting of one of the Inns of Court. For in this role he is the embodiment of the divine source of all temporal authority and of the spirit of charity and *pietas*

---

[187] On the liturgical implications of "synge," see n. 158, above. According to Durandus (*Rationale divinorum officiorum*, IV, 5ff.), the celebrant's reading of the Gospel in the Mass is a figure for the preaching of Christ, whose Advent is symbolized by the entrance of the bishop, the living type of Christ. Similarly, the reading of the Epistle signifies the preaching of John the Baptist, who announces Christ's coming and his authority to execute judgment on mankind.

which should temper earthly law and justice. No better lesson could have been pondered by the group of lawyers and judges whose ideal was a Temple of Fame dedicated to Pegasus.

The theory of an occasional background for the *House of Fame* need not, of course, be pressed. It is, if true, a useful reminder of the intimate contact between Chaucer's art and the lives of his courtly audience. In the last analysis, however, it would provide only the occasion, not the justification, of his art. The poem stands alone on its own strength as an artistically and intellectually integrated design. If the present interpretation has stressed the intellectual implications of the allegory, it has done so only to allow a broader scope to those qualities of art which have always been obvious on the surface. The humor provided by the eagle and his somewhat dull-witted protégé, the dreamer, has a timeless quality which requires no gloss for its appeal. Read for its "sentence," however, such humor is often seen to be a surface manifestation of an underlying irony that gives unity of mood to all three books of the poem. This integral connection between Chaucer's "art" and his "sentence" may be observed also in the rich and colorful pageantry, whose harmony and variety of detail evoke an aesthetic response of their own. But if we view this shifting panorama as the attractive *pictura* leading the reader to the doctrine underneath, it is seen to be a carefully wrought intellectual design into which Chaucer has woven the threads of his complex allegory. Both are here—the "art" and the "sentence." The reader, if he wishes, may choose.

INDEX